THE

KING OF VEGAS'

GUIDE TO

GAMBLING

THE

KING OF
VEGAS'

GUIDE TO

GAMBLING

How to Win Big at POKER, Casino Gambling & Life!
The Zen of Gambling updated

WAYNE ALLYN ROOT
AMERICA'S PREMIER SPORTS GAMBLER

WITH PAUL PEASE

JEREMY P. TARCHER/PENGUIN
a member of Penguin Group (USA) Inc.
New York

JEREMY P. TARCHER/PENGUIN
Published by the Penguin Group
Penguin Group (USA) Inc., 375 Hudson Street, New York, New York 10014, USA •
Penguin Group (Canada), 90 Eglinton Avenue East, Suite 700, Toronto, Ontario M4P 2Y3, Canada
(a division of Pearson Penguin Canada Inc.) • Penguin Books Ltd, 80 Strand, London WC2R 0RL,
England • Penguin Ireland, 25 St Stephen's Green, Dublin 2, Ireland (a division of Penguin
Books Ltd) • Penguin Group (Australia), 250 Camberwell Road, Camberwell, Victoria 3124,
Australia (a division of Pearson Australia Group Pty Ltd) • Penguin Books India Pvt Ltd,
11 Community Centre, Panchsheel Park, New Delhi–110 017, India • Penguin Group (NZ),
Cnr Airborne and Rosedale Roads, Albany, Auckland 1310, New Zealand (a division of Pearson
New Zealand Ltd) • Penguin Books (South Africa) (Pty) Ltd, 24 Sturdee Avenue,
Rosebank, Johannesburg 2196, South Africa

Penguin Books Ltd, Registered Offices:
80 Strand, London WC2R 0RL, England

First trade paperback edition 2006

Most Tarcher/Penguin books are available at special quantity discounts for bulk purchase
for sales promotions, premiums, fund-raising, and educational needs. Special books or book
excerpts also can be created to fit specific needs. For details, write Penguin Group (USA)
Inc. Special Markets, 375 Hudson Street, New York, NY 10014.

ISBN 1-58542-529-X

Printed in the United States of America
1   3   5   7   9   10   8   6   4   2

Book design by Amanda Dewey

While the author has made every effort to provide accurate telephone numbers and Internet
addresses at the time of publication, neither the publisher nor the author assumes any responsibility for errors, or for changes that occur after publication. Further, the publisher does
not have any control over and does not assume any responsibility for author or third-party
websites or their content.

To Benjamin Graham, Wall Street's original "value investor" and the first true Contrarian

To David and Stella Root, my parents in heaven—who always stood by me

To Doug Miller, my best friend, mentor, and loyal business partner

And most of all, to the family I love so much—Debra, Dakota, Hudson, and Remington Reagan Root

Acknowledgments

Let me start with God. Who would believe that a book by the King of Vegas would start by acknowledging God? Now, there's the first bit of Contrarian wisdom in a book dedicated to Contrarian philosophy. God is my foundation, my motivation, my source of inspiration. I am a spiritual being first and foremost. Most gamblers lose. Most gamblers do not build their lives around God. Coincidence? I think not. God is the answer for anyone, anywhere, in any profession—including gambling. *Especially* gambling! I pray to God to start every day. I thank God for the many blessings in my life. I prayed to God for the creativity and wisdom to write this book. I now pray that this book will empower, improve, and enrich the lives of readers all over the world. I hope (and pray) that this book encourages a whole generation of readers (and gamblers) to pray!

Next I must acknowledge my family. Let me start with my wife, Debra Parks Root. Talk about blessings! She is a stunningly beautiful blond goddess. She is college-educated, with a master's and a Ph.D. in homeopathy (the science of healthy living and holistic medicine). She speaks five languages. She's a former Miss Oklahoma. And a former lead singer for music legends like Ginger Baker and Emerson, Lake & Palmer. Too good to be true? I'm just getting warmed up! She's a gourmet cook. A spiritual dynamo (she comes from a family of devoted, selfless Christian ministers and missionaries). Many men say that their wife is the perfect wife and mother. *Debra really is.* She gave up all the beauty contests, stadiums full of music fans, and an acting career to be Mrs. Wayne Root, aka the Queen of Vegas! To be my rock. To be the mother of Dakota, Hudson, and Remington. To serve as CEO of the Root household. I write the books; I host the TV shows; I pick the winners; she does *everything else!* All I have to do is be creative and make money. God has blessed me beyond belief—and Debra is the ultimate blessing.

Then there are the perfect children Debra has created, raised, and educated. Our daughter Dakota is an angel from heaven. She reads as many as five books a week; can outtalk and outdebate her father (a pretty fair debater); she's beautiful like her mother; and she excels at martial arts, tennis, swimming, and fencing. She recently qualified for the Junior Olympics in fencing. My prediction is that a Stanford degree and an Olympic gold medal in fencing are in Dakota's future. But Dakota is not the only special Root. Six-year-old Hudson is smart as a whip, strong as a bull; he's a macho daddy's boy who loves playing football, boxing, car racing, and roughhousing with his daddy and his baby brother, Remington. I bound out of bed just to see the two of them every morning! And finally there's that two-year-old, Remington Reagan Root (named after my hero President Ronald Reagan). If he's anything like Dakota or Hudson, the future holds great promise for Remington Reagan. Debra, Dakota, Hudson, and Remington are the lights of my life.

Speaking of best friends and family: Doug Miller is at the top of any list. Best friend, mentor, loyal business partner. He was the first adult to believe in me and my talents. Without his counsel, advice, and wisdom, I could not and would not be where I am today. There would be no WinningEDGE.com or *King of Vegas*. Doug is now COO and president of my company, GWIN, Inc. He minds the store and runs the day-to-day operations of my business while I'm off writing books, hosting TV shows, giving speeches, handicapping winners, meeting and greeting fans, and being the King of Vegas. I thank God for putting Doug in my life. Another in a series of miracles and blessings. Doug, like Debra, makes it easy for me to be Wayne.

Other family members who must be acknowledged: my in-laws Ralph and Martha Parks, who after the deaths of my parents took over as my mom and dad. They are the reason Debra is a world-class wife and mother. They recently moved to Las Vegas to be in their grandchildren's lives on a daily basis. If my life sounds like a fairy tale, it is, and the Parks family is why. Many people talk about God and spirituality. The Parks family *lives* it. Thanks also to my sister, Lori Brown, and her husband, Doug, and my in-laws Minister Charlie and Darla Finocchiaro. And to my parents, David and Stella Root, and grandparents Simon and Meta Reis. They are all up in heaven, but I feel their wisdom, motivation, and presence in my life every day. They were the original foundation in my life. I think of them often.

Now to a few business acknowledgments. First, my editors at Tarcher/Penguin, Joel Fotinos, Keri English, and Sarah Litt. This book was rushed and released in time for football season only through their herculean efforts and those of all the folks at Penguin. I am forever grateful for their faith, professionalism, work ethic, and teamwork. Tarcher is the finest publisher I have had the honor of working with. Then there's Paul Pease, who worked on the original *Zen of Gambling* hardcover. I owe the success of this book to all of you.

To my team at GWIN, where so many of you run the business, so that I can receive the glory: Jeff Johnson (my CFO), Hollis "Harvard" Barnhart (my VP and general manager), to name just two. Hollis in particular has been by my side in one capacity or another for almost fifteen years. He also has been my teacher and mentor when it comes to the art and psychology of poker. He is like a brother to me. Without friends like him by my side, business would just be work.

Other key players at Team Root who must be acknowledged: My attorney, Lee Sacks, a true spiritual warrior on my behalf. Like Hollis Barnhart and Doug Miller, Lee is a business associate who has grown into beloved friend and virtually family. Michael Yudin, who first believed in my TV talents almost twenty years ago and today serves as cocreator and co-executive producer of *King of Vegas* on Spike TV. Brian Gadinsky, executive producer of *King of Vegas*, who took my dream and created a prime-time TV show. And of course, all the executives at Spike TV who made *King of Vegas* a reality: Doug Herzog, Kevin Kay, Sharon Levy, Tim

Duffy, and the entire Spike TV family. Roger Harrison, one of the nicest and most loyal men I have ever met; today he serves not only as a valued member of the GWIN board of directors, but also as "Uncle Roger" to my children. Doug Fleming, my high school principal back in New Rochelle, New York, twenty-five years ago. Doug and I have a unique relationship—how many students count their high school principal as a close friend a quarter-century later? People often talk about a favorite educator; in my lifetime that one favorite educator who made such a difference in my life was Doug. Petar Lasic, a friend and director of my many TV projects for more than fifteen years now. Arnie Rosenthal, who recognized my talent and had the guts to turn a raw kid into a national TV anchorman back in 1989. Thanks also to all my dear friends who have been invaluable in building my confidence and career over the years.

Finally, I must give thanks and acknowledgment to the critics. No statue has ever been built to honor a critic. They are the people who sit back and achieve, accomplish, and create absolutely *nothing*. They have the easiest job in the world—they just criticize and insult the creativity and work of others. But they do serve a purpose: they have inspired my success every step of the way. To all of you who didn't see the spark, who didn't recognize my potential, who never acknowledged my talents, who criticized me or humiliated me, you are the very ones who made me successful! Thank you. It is you who produced my energy, enthusiasm, passion, commitment, tenacity, fire, drive, and determination. It was your inspiration that led to the publication and success of this book.

CONTENTS

∎

FROM S.O.B. (SON OF A BUTCHER) TO KING OF LAS VEGAS!

This book is not about gambling, any more than one of my all-time favorites, *Zen and the Art of Motorcycle Maintenance*, is about motorcycles. This is a book about successfully navigating the gambles of life. This is a book about successful risk-taking. This is a book about overcoming odds. This is a book about living the life of your dreams. And of course, it also happens to be about winning and profiting at sports gaming, casino gaming, and the hottest game in the gambling world, Texas hold 'em poker.

I am an S.O.B. (son of a butcher). I grew up in a dead-end blue-collar town, Mount Vernon, New York, located just outside the Bronx, a town that could be defined literally as the "wrong side of the tracks." Today I am a nationally recognized TV celebrity, author, self-made millionaire, and high-profile CEO of a publicly traded company. The media have dubbed me "King of Vegas" (the name of the prime-time TV show I created on Spike TV) and "the face of Las Vegas gambling." I'm living my dream—having graduated from misery in Mount Vernon to a mansion overlooking the world-famous Las Vegas Strip.

The lessons I learned from betting on sports have taught me how to become a winner at all forms of gambling (and at life). The principles and strategies that made me a world-class risk-taker and winning gambler have also made me a world-class husband, father, and businessman. They can make you a winner, too, in any field. Risk is what separates winners from losers, survivors from thrivers. Success comes down to a series of gambles: your ability to make positive choices at pivotal moments, to thrive on risk, challenge, and high levels of stress. Sending out a résumé; going on job interviews; asking that stranger on a date; picking up the phone and making the call that could change your life for the better; risking your savings on stocks or real estate; putting your home on the line to start a business—all of life's big decisions and defining moments require a talent, and a willingness, for risk.

Winning at gambling is not about luck. It's about acquired skill. I can teach you that skill. It's about an understanding of history. I can teach you that required understanding. It's about overcoming odds that are almost always against you. I can teach you how to beat the odds and emerge victorious in the biggest wagers of your life. Quite simply, winning at gambling is about choosing the road less traveled. In this book I will show you how to become a Contrarian thinker and a Zen gambler. What you gamble on—career, business, relationships, stocks, casino games, horses, sports—well, that choice is up to you. Gambling has made me a very wealthy man, and if you want to learn about the specifics of sports gambling, Part Two of this book is a great primer on sports gambling. I will also show you how to apply my rules for gambling directly to poker and casino gambling. If you follow the simple guidelines laid out in Part Two, you'll achieve more success as a gambler than you ever thought possible. But more important, in this book, gambling—whether on sports or poker—is a metaphor for life. Zen gambling is a blueprint for being successful in any enterprise—stocks, a new business venture, or anything you choose to tackle. The lessons you learn from this book will be life-changing. Remember to tell your buddies that you learned it all from the King of Vegas!

A NATIONAL PASTIME

Gambling is exploding across America and worldwide. *The New York Times* recently reported that Americans spend more money on gambling than on movies, music, books, videos, and DVDs combined. According to the National Gambling Impact Study Commission, as much as $380 billion is wagered on sports annually in the United States—making sports betting the most widespread form of gambling. That maximum of $380 billion is larger than the annual revenue of the entire U.S. auto industry ($350 billion). It is substantially larger than the annual revenue of the entire women's garment industry ($90 billion). It dwarfs the diet industry ($40 billion). According to *USA Today*, more than fifty percent of all adults in this nation place a bet on sports every year, with the Super Bowl being the largest betting event in the world. When you consider that few women bet on sports, that means that virtually every single living, breathing, red-blooded American male over the age of twenty-one bets on sports!

We are a nation of gamblers. What do I mean by that? Well, for example, my grandparents jumped aboard boats in Russia and Germany to sail to a distant land called America. They didn't have more than a few dollars in their pockets, and they knew no one in the strange new land they were headed for. They were world-class risk-takers. Stepping onto those boats was the risk of a lifetime, the type of risk that few Americans today would consider taking. As a nation, though, we have some of our immigrant ancestors' risk-taking as second nature. This book will help you develop your innate ability to take risks—and win! Can you imagine: In just two generations, my family went from poverty in Russia and Germany to my becoming the King of Vegas. As Don King would say, "Only in America!" This book will empower you with the tools. America will offer you the opportunity. The rest is up to you.

THE LIFE OF YOUR DREAMS!

The whole world—the news media, government authorities, "experts," educators, even NFL officials—all seem to dislike gambling and, more important, to dislike gamblers. Ask any legitimate, educated, "moral" person his opinion of someone involved in gambling, and he will immediately quote scripture and verse on the sins of gambling. The image that society has of gamblers is of low-class, down-and-out losers—outcasts who thumb their noses at society and wind up broke, drunk, and alone in some single-room-occupancy fleabag—or of bookmakers—organized-crime-connected, street-smart con men wearing pinstripe suits, pinkie rings, and gold neck chains, followed closely by bodyguards and blond bimbo girlfriends. It's not a pretty picture. Not exactly "family values" for the twenty-first century.

Mention "Wall Street" to these same morality experts, and the image is quite different: a very stylish, positive picture of Ivy League–educated blue-bloods with framed MBA diplomas hanging on the walls of their wood-paneled offices, and framed photos of smiling families and U.S. senators on their fancy desks. For the homes of these Wall Street investors, the experts picture English-style country manors in Greenwich, Connecticut, or Scarsdale, New York, all filled, of course, with perfectly groomed and well-mannered kids who attend exclusive private schools. Weekends are devoted to horseback riding, yachting, golf, tennis, and polo at the country club. The experts picture our Wall Street geniuses sitting bedside, catching up on their required reading: *Forbes, Fortune,*

Barron's, and *The Wall Street Journal.* Yes, sports "gambling" and Wall Street "investing" would seem to be two extremely different worlds. But are they?

What if those two worlds could meet? What if I told you that I'd spent my life putting those two worlds together? What if I told you I'd managed to live the life of my dreams because of gambling? What if, like Lou Gehrig to that packed crowd at Yankee Stadium, I told you I was the luckiest man on the face of the earth? What if I told you I'd found a way—legally—to earn a wonderful living by picking the winners of football games? And by picking winners in other sports events as well, while living out all my dreams in the sexiest city on earth (Las Vegas), in a mansion overlooking a world-class golf course, in front of seven water-falls and five lakes?

What if I told you that my "career" consists of reading the sports pages, listening to sports talk radio, watching football pregame shows, checking into sports chat rooms on the Internet, spending Saturdays and Sundays passionately watching dozens of thrilling football games on my many satellite dishes and big-screen TVs, all the while rarely leaving my beautiful estate? What if I told you that I conduct all of my business via computer, laptop, BlackBerry, e-mail, fax, cell phone, and pager—all from the comfort of my poolside deck, overlooking the twinkling lights of the world-famous Las Vegas Strip?

Suppose I told you that I spend my time talking to sports bettors and e-mailing with trusted sports-betting experts and professional gamblers to earn my living. And what do I talk about all day long via phone and e-mail? I talk sports, a topic I have a passion for and would gladly talk about for free!

What if I told you that, like those Wall Street heavyweights, I am Ivy League–educated? That, like theirs, my life revolves around nature and family—spending countless hours riding horses, golfing, playing tennis, hiking with my dogs, swimming and body-surfing at our beachfront Hawaii vacation home, and skiing at our mountain vacation home in

Deer Valley, Utah, and enjoying all these blessings with my family by my side: my beautiful wife, Debra; our precious daughter, Dakota, a Junior Olympic fencer; our football-loving son, Hudson; and our youngest, Remington Reagan. What if I told you I owe it all to gambling? Not a bad deal, huh?

I have a confession to make: The life I just described isn't a fantasy; it isn't a dream; it isn't an exaggeration—it's *my* life! And it can be yours, too, because the principles, trends, and strategies that have enabled me to live the life every red-blooded American male dreams of are all explained in this book. What's the catch? There is no catch. Anyone can do what I've done. The problem is, no one ever put it all together: the realization that *investing on Wall Street is virtually the same game as betting on sports*. The same trends, knowledge of history, money management, Contrarian strategy, and value investing that apply to successful stock-picking all apply to successful football (and all sports) betting. The same study of public opinion and relevant periodicals that works for Contrarian and value stock investors works for Contrarian sports bettors. The same strategies and philosophies that allow snot-nosed whiz kids on Wall Street to make millions before their thirtieth birthdays have worked for me for twenty years in the football betting world. And those same strategies and philosophies work in all areas of life—business, entrepreneurship, relationships, on Wall Street or Main Street, at the sportsbook, casino, or poker room. If you're a world-class risk-taker and know how to beat the odds and win at sports, I guarantee that you will be a winner at anything you try in life!

Today, I am a forty-five-year-old self-made millionaire. The only difference between my life and the lives of Wall Street whiz kids is that mine is much better! I've never worked twelve-to-fourteen-hour days in some stuffy office. I'm not trapped on a frenzied, smoke-filled trading floor surrounded by hysterical, screaming, stressed-out madmen! I have no egomaniacal, eccentric, workaholic bosses watching over me for those fourteen unhappy hours per day—deciding when I'm allowed to go home to see my family, and when I've "earned" a day off. I don't have a long, crowded, polluted commute to and from a job I hate.

You see, I've taken sports handicapping public on Wall Street, so I'm the CEO. And everyone from my stockholders to my employees to my clients to my wife *wants* me to watch football and sports all day long! Heck, they beg me to watch football. Honest to God, that's truly my life. I'm paid a fortune to watch sports and gamble all day and night! That's my idea of nirvana. Even Donald Trump, Bill Gates, and Warren Buffett can't match that lifestyle! No billionaire could buy it—it's priceless. And it's all due to the love of my life—gambling.

Does the life I've just described appeal to you? Does it mesh with your vision of what life is all about, or should be? Then read on, because this book is devoted to teaching you how to become a success, step by step, the same way I did!

This book is dedicated to anyone who ever told me that the life I have just described was impossible to achieve—and believe me, that list is long! It's dedicated to you—the reader who has decided to live the dream! If becoming a sports handicapper or professional gambler is not your dream, that's fine.

This book isn't just for gamblers. It's for anyone who has a dream and has heard from critics that this dream is impossible. Yes, I'm one of the best gamblers in the world. True, gambling is the catalyst that has triggered my personal achievements. Gambling will be the most exhilarating journey you've ever taken—if that's your journey. The lessons you'll learn in this book are, even further, aimed at success in any endeavor. What I've learned about successful risk-taking, Contrarian philosophy, and money management from a lifetime of gambling and handicapping will make you a success in whatever you choose to do for the rest of your life. No matter whether you want to be the King of Vegas, the King of Peoria, or the King of Poker. Good luck and welcome to "Wayne's World"!

PART ONE

■

MASTERING
THE ART
OF RISK

ONE

■

BE A RIVERBOAT
GAMBLER!

*"Only those who dare to fail greatly
can ever achieve greatly."*

PRESIDENT JOHN F. KENNEDY

W hat could gambling possibly have to do with success in the
business world? Success as an entrepreneur? Success in relationships? Success in life? The answer is *everything!* You see, I am a professional gambler—and proud of it! But my biggest gambles have all
occurred in the business world, not the betting world. All my life I've
been willing to put my money where my mouth is—to risk everything I
am and everything I own on my ideas, my beliefs, my career, my passions.

As I tell audiences at speaking engagements around the globe, success
comes down to two things: having a *passion* for what you do and having
the guts of a Riverboat Gambler. Without both those qualities, your
odds of success are greatly diminished. Without either, you're finished.

Every single day, business executives and business owners gamble—

they gamble on new ideas, new directions, new employees, new locations for their stores, new product lines, new investments, new lines of capital to better grow their businesses. Almost every move we make in the business world is a gamble, a risk. The fear of risk will destroy a businessperson quicker than any other weakness. In business, he who gets there first (with an idea or product) often wins. He who hesitates is lost. He (or she) who is willing to risk everything and put his business, home, or net worth on the line to support a new venture or the expansion of an old venture is often rewarded. He who is unwilling to put it all on the line often gets left behind.

As a motivational and business speaker, I've studied the histories of hundreds of the most successful people of our times, and the single most important factor I found that separated these winners from the masses, is *a remarkable willingness to risk again and again*. Even in the face of long odds, even after multiple failures, superachievers are not afraid to put it all on the line again. In each case, after many rejections, failures, even humiliating disasters, they were willing to risk again and won! And that one final victory put these superachievers in the history books. All the prior failures were forgotten; they were remembered forever only for their success. The risks had been worth it! "Risk or perish" should be the mantra taught at business schools everywhere.

Let me share a true story with you, a powerful story, a story that changed my life. It is the story of a good man, who was dying of cancer, lying on his deathbed, with his only son by his side. He had been an honest man his whole life; a hard worker, a family man, a devoted husband and father.

He was also a sad man, because somewhere along the way, he had given up on his dreams. When his son was born, he was already thirty-five years old and a broken man. His son never once heard him discussing a goal or a dream—so his son assumed he'd never had any. This good man lacked passion or enthusiasm for life.

He hated his job, but never took a single risk to change his life. He simply went to work every day, earned a living, supported a family, then arrived home at night tired, physically drained and emotionally bankrupt. By the time he reached his deathbed, he had worked for forty years as a butcher. He justified this lifetime of long hours at a job he despised, for mediocre pay, as a necessary sacrifice for his family. Ironically, he rarely ever saw that family. He left for the meat market at 3:30 a.m. and didn't return until 7 p.m., six days a week. Back pains had plagued him most of his adult life—perhaps because he spent his life breaking his back for a family he never saw. What a sad way to live a life.

As his son sat by his side, watching the man dying in agony, thoughts and memories came rushing back—memories he had long ago buried deep in his mind. The son suddenly remembered his father crying at a family gathering twenty-five years earlier. He could clearly see his father's family (seven brothers and sisters, their spouses, his mother) gathered around him at the dining room table, as he sobbed uncontrollably. The boy had blocked this memory out for twenty-five years, yet now it came rushing back, as if it had happened yesterday. He decided to ask his father about that moment before it was too late to get answers.

The father said that he had hated every moment of his job as a butcher; he felt demeaned and humiliated. He felt beneath the customers he served. And he knew they felt his pain too. But it fed his family.

"It fed you," the father said to the son. If he hadn't been married, he explained, "Things would have been far different."

He'd have quit to explore the world—he loved traveling, he admitted to his son.

"He loves traveling?" the son thought to himself. "I've never seen him go *anywhere*."

The father continued to explain his choices—or lack of them. He had felt trapped as a husband and father. He'd had a family to feed. So he'd kept trudging to that same God-forsaken butcher store for forty years. On the day of that emotional breakdown that his son was asking about, he had doubts that he could continue. "I'd been struggling with the idea of leaving your mother," he admitted.

That family gathering had been the crossroads of the father's life. He had called his entire family together that day to discuss and debate his decision. But in the end, he couldn't leave. Because that would have meant abandoning his son and daughter. That he could never do.

So after that breakdown in front of his family, he buried all his dreams for the last time. He never thought about them again. He went back to that butcher store the next morning, and every morning for twenty-five years more. He decided to sacrifice his dreams, his very life, for the sake of his family. In every way that matters, that man died that day. It is said that when a man's dreams die, the man dies too. That boy's father had died that day—over two decades before the cancer. He had died when he had given up any chance at passion, at happiness, at living. He had settled for an existence instead of a life.

As his son sobbed by his father's bedside, he learned many things he'd never known about his dad. It felt like he was learning about a different man. *He was.* The father explained that long before the son was born, he had been a traveler, an explorer. As a teenager during World War II he had left Brooklyn to attend Navy navigator school at Texas A&M. Then he'd traveled halfway around the world to fight the Japanese in the South Pacific. He had won numerous distinguished-service awards at Saipan and Okinawa.

After the war, he had traveled to Europe and Japan. Then he'd found paradise—Hawaii. He spent time at Pearl Harbor before heading back to America. He loved Hawaii; he vowed he'd live there someday. After the war, he became one of the youngest navigators in the air for TWA. At the age of twenty-three, he was flying transatlantic flights from New York to

London to Hamburg, Germany—while most of his friends had never left Brooklyn.

"My dad was flying in a cockpit across the Atlantic?" the son thought. "Impossible. The man I know wears a bloody white apron at a butcher store and is afraid of his own shadow. This can't be true."

The father told how he'd driven a red convertible sports car, and had been quite the dashing ladies' man. He told of being quite a successful gambler, too. He'd played craps on the streets of Brooklyn, then poker in the Navy and after the war. He'd used his winnings to buy the convertible.

Again, the son thought, "Convertible sports car? He's been driving an old four-door Oldsmobile since I've known him. Gambler? I've never seen him take a single risk. This isn't the story of the father I know."

But there the story of the swashbuckling navigator abruptly ended. The man soon married and his wife asked (actually demanded) that he settle down for the sake of marriage and family. She did not want to be married to an airline navigator. She was afraid of the risk of losing him to a plane crash. And she was deathly afraid of the loneliness with him away so often. She wanted a husband who was home every night. She asked him to go to work for her father, in his butcher store. The day he accepted (or settled), the father said, was the day his life had ended. He never traveled again, because his wife was afraid of flying. His son sat stunned at all he was hearing.

The son had by now made it big—he was a TV anchorman in California. He was so proud of the life he'd built and his fancy new beachfront home in Malibu. But his mother and father didn't fly, so they'd never seen his new California life firsthand. The son thought about how much his father would have loved California. He grew even sadder when he realized his father would never leave the hospital and therefore would never come visit him in California.

The son now realized for the first time that his father had not been a passionless man. He had had dreams. He had been a far different person before the son's birth. As a matter of fact, father and son had been very much alike. The son had always thought that he had been dropped down the wrong chimney.

But now he realized he had been a "chip off the old block" all along. More tears came to his eyes. His father had had the life choked out of him before the boy was even born. The boy's mother was afraid of life. She was afraid to risk. To her, risking meant dying. She had stopped her husband from flying because the dangers of a plane crashing made flying an unacceptable risk. She had stopped him from swimming in the ocean (even though he had been a fearless ocean swimmer in the Navy) because the dangers of drowning rendered swimming an unacceptable risk. She had stopped him from working for TWA because the dangers of him having independence, and perhaps leaving her, were a risk she could never accept.

Over the years, she had stopped him from ever leaving that butcher store because cutting meat was now the only way he knew to earn a living. And the danger of trying a new career or opening a new business was a risk too big to take. Everywhere the mother looked, she saw danger. Risk was something she had to avoid, to destroy, to kill. And kill risk she did—choking the very life out of risk, and out of her husband, too. The man had no risk in his life—but no life, either.

The father told the son about his one last hope of all those dreadful years. He had always hoped he'd find a way to take one single around-the-world trip before he died. He'd secretly decided a few years back that he would take this world trip as a retirement gift to himself. He'd give his wife an ultimatum—join him or he'd go alone. He'd spend his life savings if he had to, but he'd make this one last dream a reality.

But then he'd found out that he had terminal lung cancer. He would die without taking that trip. The father and son held hands and cried. He died a few days later, with even his one last dream unrealized.

This story is especially meaningful to me, because it is a personal story. *It is my story.* The man who died without fulfilling his dreams was my father, David Root. But he didn't die in vain. I realized that day why I had become a world-class gambler, as well as a daring risk-taker in business. I had seen the life choked out of my father. I had seen his butcher shop decline to the point where it made no money at all. Yet my father hung on to the shop by his fingernails—after all, anything was better than changing course and risking. Risk was something he had learned to avoid at all costs.

Now I understood why he had no passion, no dreams, and no zest for living. Because without risk, there is no life. There is just existence. Survival. My dad survived for those forty years. But the price he paid was dramatic. He paid with his life. Cancer was just the final curtain closing. For all intents and purposes, the play had closed at intermission.

Subconsciously, I had seen it all happening. I realized that I had vowed, deep down, to never let it happen to me. If I were to lose at business or life, at least I'd go down swinging! I'd not only swing, I'd swing for the fences! I'd decided long ago that my life would be nothing like my father's. I'd embrace risk. I'd be a Riverboat Gambler.

But my lesson in what the fear of risk can do to someone was far from over. The light bulb went off most distinctly when my father got off the topic of himself and started talking about his fears for me and my future. It was only then that I truly understood how deep-rooted his fear was. And it was then that I started to understand why so many individuals settle—for a job they hate, for a mate they don't love with passion, for mediocre pay, and just look to survive, rather than *thrive*. It is all about a fear of risk, and a *fear of failure*.

So many of us are literally petrified by change, by risk, by the prospect of failure, that we'd rather do nothing than risk defeat. We'd rather live in misery than take a chance on our dreams, all because of that fear. On one side is the life of our dreams, on the other side is a fear so strong it chokes the life out of us. We settle—and fear wins.

What did my father say that made this revelation so clear? Just a few words. But they were powerful words, words that made it clear how strong fear can be. Here he was on his deathbed, his life ending in fear and misery—yet he said he feared for *me*.

At that moment, I was a young man living my dreams. Only thirty years old, I was a national TV sportscaster, living on the beach in Malibu. I had just bought Woody Harrelson's home (of *Cheers* fame). My neighbors were TV and movie stars. I was passionately in love with the woman of my dreams, my wife, Debra, (we're still married thirteen years later), a former Miss Oklahoma, an actress and singer, and a gourmet cook, who is fluent in multiple languages—literally a dream girl! Our first baby was on the way. Yet rather than being proud of his son, my father was afraid for me!

"Why?" I asked.

His answer was telling: "Wayne, you've taken such huge risks all your life. You've been disappointed so many times. You've had your heart broken and your head handed to you, so many times. You've always had such big plans—and they always seem to come crashing down. I'm so scared for your future. What's going to happen to you? You can't keep chasing these big dreams! You can't keep risking everything. Or you're headed for a life of pain and disappointment."

At that moment the pieces of the puzzle came together. Now I finally understood why a man so talented, so bright, so special, so loving to his family, had settled for a job he despised and a life of mediocrity. It was a fear of risk—a fear that paralyzed him. He was so afraid of taking a risk that he never did it. He was so afraid of failing he simply never even tried. He was so afraid to reach for the brass ring that he wasted his life away in a butcher shop that he loathed. He had given up his dreams because of this fear, and now I realized he couldn't even bear to watch his own son take the risks he had avoided.

Like so many others in our society, he had been so paralyzed by this fear that he had actually convinced himself that giving up was a better feeling than risking. He was so blinded by this fear that even on his deathbed he could not see that all my risking had been worth it—the reward was the life of my dreams! All he could see with his "tunnel vision" was the risk and failures along the way.

That fear was so powerful, so controlling over him, that the success I reached at the end didn't even matter. It paled by comparison to the pain and disappointment of the rejection and challenges along the way—the same rejection and challenges that he had avoided. That he had hidden from. That my mother had convinced him were deadly beyond reason.

I had risked so many times, and failed so many times, but not one of my failures had ever frightened me, slowed me, or stopped me. "Who cares?" I'd thought. "Look at the end result!" I had learned from each failure and rejection, then moved forward. Onward and upward. My father saw me experience these same risks, and he was horrified. He was shaken. He thought he could not have survived that kind of rejection—and he displaced his fears onto me. To him, no dream, no matter how wonderful, was worth the pain to get there.

My father had missed the point of life. Life is meant to be lived— warts and all—not feared. Risk and failure aren't bad, they are learning experiences. You either learn from them and use those lessons to go on and conquer the world, or you curl up in a fetal position and die. My father had chosen death.

I chose life. I chose to see risk—gambling—as a natural part of life. I understood that to accomplish anything worth accomplishing, you've got to take chances and get messy (as my four-year-old son Hudson's cartoons say). You've got to face challenges. You've got to experience pain. That's how you get stronger. Fire is required to turn steel into iron. To succeed, to *thrive*, you must risk failure and rejection. You must keep fighting and moving.

I suddenly realized, there at my father's bedside, why so many individuals never get to experience the sweet smell of success—because first you must be brave. You must have the fire in your belly. You must be willing to risk, to fight, to die. Without pain, there is no gain. Without risk, there is no reward.

I have lived such an opposite life to my father the butcher. I risked, I continually changed and reinvented myself. I gambled. He just survived without taking a risk—in a continually numb state. But he had missed the ultimate irony of life: that without risk, without going after your dreams with gusto, without facing your fears—your whole life is ruled by fear. By not daring to risk greatly or to fail greatly (as President Kennedy dared us to do), your whole life is one big failure.

Without risk, you can accomplish nothing, create nothing, invent nothing, change nothing, employ no one—you can exist, but you can never really live. A fear of risk and of gambling creates a life not worth living. The lessons I learned from watching my dad live his life in fear of risk were priceless to me. The lessons I learned from becoming a professional gambler led to my success as an entrepreneur.

Now let me give you my favorite example of someone who *wasn't* afraid to take risks: Helen Andreeff. Helen is the mother of my wife's best friend, Starr Andreeff. Helen lived in the same town for over half a century—blue-collar Hamilton, Ontario, Canada. She found herself divorced, overweight, and living the life of a couch potato when she made the bold decision to change her life. As Helen herself put it, "I wasn't just the couch potato—my butt *was* the couch!"

I counseled Helen on the virtues of taking risks. I counseled her to stop complaining and do something to change her life. "Take risks and get *messy*," as my four-year-old son's favorite cartoon recommends. The rest, as they say, was history.

Helen proved that taking calculated risks is far better than accepting defeat or spending your life complaining. Helen started with a *radical* risk. In three short weeks, she sold all her possessions and moved thousands of miles from Hamilton, Ontario, to Los Angeles, California. That took a lot of guts. But risk leads to *reward*. Not necessarily right away, but eventually—as long as you keep risking courageously. In Helen's case, that first big risk was only the beginning. She was 3,000 miles away from her old problems—yet not much had changed. She was still lonely, depressed, and dissatisfied with her life. Just like most people, she had taken her problems on the journey along with her. She was still overweight and still working at a job she despised to pay the rent.

So Helen changed even *more* of her life. She started exercising and eating healthy—to create the positive attitude and self-esteem I'll talk about later in this book. The result, as the pounds melted off, was that she looked *absolutely gorgeous!* Next she took up golf. And finally, she designed a personals ad. That's right—I said a *personals ad*. Talk about Contrarian!

Millions of single American women bemoan the fact that the odds of getting struck by lightning are higher than of finding a good man after age fifty. But instead of complaining, Helen took a chance, something most women would call "crazy" and "risky." Here was a woman willing to be Contrarian (take an ad looking to meet a total stranger), willing to risk (she understood that without risk, there is no reward), and who would not be denied the life of her dreams. No one was going to stop Helen Andreeff.

In her personals ad, Helen described herself as "attractive, over fifty, avid golfer." She received over 100 responses from eligible men all over Los Angeles. That's right—I said *over 100 men!* And not just *any* men. Most were true catches—educated, successful professionals: doctors, lawyers, accountants, retired CEOs. Helen had hit the jackpot. Why? Because golfers are an upscale bunch. And it's rare to find a *female* golfer. Successful single men are dying to find an attractive female that can golf with them into the sunset.

Helen was suddenly a hot property. She dated dozens of men over the next few weeks. The same woman who didn't have a date in Canada was an overnight hot property in Los Angeles. Amazing what a little daring risk-taking can do for your life. And what a Hollywood ending—Helen *married* the best of the bunch.

Helen and Mike have been happily married for over a dozen years now! Mike is one heck of a find—a doctor, lawyer, accountant, and screenwriter all rolled into one! And a heck of a nice guy—a real catch. Instead of living alone in a cramped studio apartment, lonely, working at a job she despises to pay the bills, Helen today commutes between her beautiful home in Beverly Hills and her ranch in Bozeman, Montana. She spends her life golfing, skiing, hiking, and enjoying life with Mike, the love of her life.

Taking a calculated risk changed Helen's life *dramatically*. It can change yours too. But you'll have to think out of the box (Contrarian), take chances (risk), stop listening to experts and critics, and stop complaining. What awaits on the other side of all that toxic negativity is the life of your dreams. Risk, dream, take chances, get messy—and *live*.

Through the years, this great democracy we call America has been reinvigorated and reinforced again and again by the ultimate risk-takers: immigrants, people willing to leave their homes and families behind to journey to a mysterious new land; people willing to risk life and limb, just to taste freedom and opportunity. And we wonder why America is the greatest country in the world? Because it is filled with the bravest risk-takers in the world.

We are a nation descended from people willing to die for opportunity and adventure; willing to start over with no money, no friends, no family, in a strange land. Those who were too timid for these kinds of radical risks stayed home, in Europe and China and Mexico and India. But those bold risk-takers who had the guts and were willing to risk all for glory became Americans. Many of them paid the ultimate price for their risks, but those who survived were the best of the best. And those survivors created a country called America.

No wonder America is the country that invented entrepreneurship. The single largest growth sector in American business for both new jobs and revenues is small business. In other countries, the word "entrepreneurship" is nonexistent. People are born, they take a job with the government or a big corporation, they collect a paycheck for forty years, and then they die. Going it on your own, risking everything on a business idea—that is literally an American concept.

More businesses are created in the United States than in every other nation in the world *combined!* No wonder so many of the world's best ideas, innovations, and trends start in the United States. No wonder the fantasy known as Hollywood was born in America. Only in America would a bunch of European immigrants dare to invent the movie business! Many of the wealthiest businesspersons in the world come from America. It's because risk is something honored, cherished, and encouraged here. Risk is the American credo. From the American Revolution to the Civil War to the taming of the Wild West to World War II to the Internet Revolution, Americans have always been willing to risk and die for freedom, for independence, for innovation. We are a nation of daring risk-takers. A nation of Riverboat Gamblers!

This book is dedicated to David Root. I soar like an eagle because he couldn't. I climb mountains because he wouldn't. I travel the world because he refused to dare. I am willing to risk everything on my passions because he didn't. I'm a world-class risk-taker and professional gambler because he wouldn't be. I am today a self-made millionaire and CEO of a public company that I founded, all because of my love for risk, my willingness to gamble. I dedicate this book to my father. And to all of you reading this story who have never risked, never put it all on the line, never tried to beat the odds, all those who have never really lived. This book is not for sports gamblers, it is for bringing out the Riverboat Gambler in all of us.

"Life is either a daring adventure or nothing."

HELEN KELLER

TWO

■

VIVA LAS VEGAS!

Navigating the Highs and Lows of the
Ultimate Contrarian Dreamland

What enabled a dusty barren desert outpost to become the capital of everything Americana? What exactly is in the air in Las Vegas that created all this opportunity? And what about all of its desperation? Las Vegas is a study in life—the highs and the lows. In this chapter I will show you how to ride the high that is Las Vegas while avoiding the lows—be it the stress of risking it all or, worst of all, an inability to bounce back once you have risked and lost.

I *love* Las Vegas. In my opinion Vegas is the greatest town in the world. Actually it *is* the world: If you want Paris, we have Paris—the hotel (and the Eiffel Tower). If you want Venice, we have The Venetian (complete with canals). If you want the South Seas, we have Mandalay Bay (complete with an amazing wave pool and lazy river). If you want volcanos, we have The Mirage (complete with rain forests, dolphins, and white tigers). If you want Lake Como, we have Bellagio (complete with the greatest fountains you've ever seen). If you want Manhattan, we have New York, New York (complete with the Empire State Building and the Manhattan skyline). If you want Egypt, we have Luxor (complete with pyramids). If you want pirates, we have T.I., formerly known as Treasure Island (complete with pirate ships and blazing gun battles). If you want Rome, we have Caesars Palace (complete with The Colosseum and the bonus of Celine Dion). If you want Rio de Janeiro, we have The Rio (complete with Carnival every hour). If you want Rodeo Drive in Beverly Hills, we have The Forum Shops (the most exclusive and expensive shopping mall in the world), followed closely by the Fashion Show Mall. The entire world is *here* in Las Vegas!

The result is that the whole world is literally coming to Las Vegas—the top entertainers, the best heavyweight fights, "the whales" (the biggest high-roller gamblers from around the globe); almost 40 million tourists—making Vegas *the* leading tourist destination in all of America; and the *people*—that's a whole other story! The people just keep *coming*: 5,000 to 8,000 new residents per month, every month! That makes Las Vegas both the tourist capital of America *and* the fastest-growing *city* in America. That means that many of the tourists that visit, *never* leave.

Las Vegas leads in even more categories: The fastest-growing city, Clark County (where Vegas and Henderson are located) is the fastest-growing county in America; and Nevada is the fastest-growing state for seventeen consecutive years. Nevada is ranked year after year as one of the best places in America to do business. We lead the country in numerous business-growth categories, but none more important than new businesses created, new jobs created, and new homes built. Real estate appreciation leads the country. The numbers are just *staggering*.

What do all these facts mean? They mean I'm not the only one who loves Las Vegas—most *everyone* that experiences this town, *loves* this town. It's the low-tax capital of America (our version of Monte Carlo); the gambling capital; the sex capital (more strip clubs than anywhere else in the world—and legal prostitution just outside town); the entertainment capital (and the entertainment is twenty-four hours a day); the restaurant capital (the best restaurants from all over the world line the Vegas Strip); the economic capital (everywhere you look there are new homes, new office buildings, new schools, new roads, new casinos, and as a result new *jobs*); the convention capital; the sunshine capital (almost 300 days a year of sunshine); and I believe the *spirit* capital of the world.

That's the reason we lead the country, and in many cases the *world*, in so many categories: our frontier, "can-do" spirit; our Contrarian and libertarian streaks; our freedoms—financial, sexual, and business; the *Triple Crown* of freedom and rugged individualism all in one place. This town was *invented* for entrepreneurs and dreamers.

New York is a great town: I grew up in New York, attended college at Columbia, and lived in Manhattan. I'll always love the Big Apple. But why are so many New Yorkers moving to Vegas? Los Angeles is a great town: I lived in Hollywood and Malibu (on the beach) for many years. I'll always love L.A. But why are so many people from Los Angeles moving to Vegas? They leave for the same reason that I *left* those towns—high taxes, too much red tape, a lousy business climate, and too little freedom and opportunity. Las Vegas is the Wild West of the twenty-first century. It's the American Frontier all over again. Political correctness has *not* taken root here. A man can be a man (and women do just fine too). Anything goes, *anything* can happen here, and as the saying goes, "What happens here, *stays* here." Well, it's true. I'm staying. I would *never* go back to New York, L.A., or any other place. Vegas will be my home for life. Because what happens here in Vegas is simple: *opportunity and freedom*. It's in the air.

Two Jewish mobsters—Benjamin "Bugsy" Siegel and Meyer Lansky—saw it fifty years ago. They were visionaries who saw the potential for wealth, opportunity, and freedom. And after fifty years, *none* of that has changed! This town has *opportunity* in the air. Anyone can come here and strike it rich *tomorrow*—or if not rich, certainly live a nice life without being taxed to death or strangled by government red tape. Certainly a nicer life than *wherever* they came from.

The way I look at it, the money that I save in state income taxes and business taxes pays the mortgage on my mansion on the most beautiful golf course you've ever laid eyes on. Because so many other people (and businesses) want to move here, my house (that the government is literally paying the mortgage on) goes up in value every day. And by the way, I get to live in a home twice as big (at least) as the home I'd get for the same dollars in New York or Los Angeles, with *half* the property taxes.

The sun is out almost every day, *all* day. I have a choice of dining out every single night at a world-class restaurant, and *never* go to the same one twice! Instead of commuting two hours a day in bumper-to-bumper traffic, I save at least an hour and a half (because traffic is nonexistent compared to New York, Los Angeles, or any big city on the East Coast), which I use to exercise and take care of my body. So, because of Vegas, I'm going to *live longer*, too!

Instead of working twelve hours a day to pay my taxes, I work only ten hours a day, thereby saving another two hours that I can use to pray, meditate, practice yoga, walk with my dog in a beautiful park filled with lakes, streams, fountains, and ducks, play in the pool with my wife and kids, or watch sports on my bank of big screen TVs (also paid for by the low taxes).

Are you now understanding why everyone in America is moving to Las Vegas? Keep in mind that after I die, there is *zero* inheritance tax, which means my kids will gain more money, peace of mind, and extra time to enjoy life (hours that they'd be forced to work in any other state to earn the extra dollars to pay those inheritance taxes). Sunshine, legal sports gambling, the best restaurants and spas in the world, natural beauty, freedom, opportunity, and no taxes—*Las Vegas is my definition of heaven!*

What exactly is in the air in Las Vegas that created all this opportunity? What enabled a dusty barren desert outpost to become the capital of everything Americana? Why here?

The answer is simple: we are an entire city of Contrarian thinkers and Riverboat Gamblers! *Everyone* is a gambler here in Vegas—whether we gamble in casinos or not. That's why we all came here. To take a risk and get away from someplace or someone. We pulled up roots (excuse the pun) and escaped from New York, L.A., Chicago, Philly, Pittsburgh, or Cleveland. We literally ran away for the hope of a better life. The people with no hope, the less adventurous, those scared of change, stayed behind.

Las Vegans are the dreamers, the risk-takers, the ultimate *Contrarians*. Who but a Contrarian dreamer would even think of risking billions of dollars to recreate Rome, Rio de Janeiro, Venice, Egypt, the South Seas, the pyramids and volcanoes, all in the middle of the God-forsaken desert? Who but a Contrarian dreamer would see opportunity where others before them saw only desolate, unbearably hot sand dunes and sagebrush? Who but a Contrarian risk-taker would think to combine dolphins, white tigers, and Siegfried & Roy with gambling?

It is Contrarians and dreamers and Riverboat Gamblers that built Las Vegas, and who every day change our world. Men and women with spirit and optimism and American chutzpah! The gamblers. They are the people of Las Vegas, often descendant from the original daring dreamers and courageous risk-takers who poured through Ellis Island, and who tamed the Wild West. They have combined to build the greatest city on earth—the adult fantasyland known as Las Vegas.

THE ZEN OF VEGAS

Okay, this all sounds great, you might say, but what about that other Vegas—that capital of the down and out? Nicholas Cage in *Leaving Las Vegas*. Well, yes, absolute power corrupts absolutely. But learn how to navigate the ultimate Contrarian land of dreams that is Las Vegas and you will be able to take risks in life without the negative repercussions. You will be a Zen Gambler. In order to illustrate what I'm talking about, let's take a close look at the casino. Follow my rules for the casino— which are really just rules for life—and you will spend your days not at Motel 6 but at the Bellagio.

> **Author's Note:** Before I get to my critique of some casino gamblers, let me present a disclaimer: Nothing I say below about casinos or their strategies to beat you, confuse you or distract you is an attack on those casinos. I've met many of the executives and CEOs who run the most successful casinos in Las Vegas. They have never failed to impress me as being among the sharpest, brightest business leaders in America. They run billion-dollar empires, and they do it well. These are men and women who, if they were not heading up MGM, Mirage, Bellagio, Caesars, Mandalay Bay, or Wynn Las Vegas, would be heading up Goldman Sachs or Bear Stearns or IBM or Microsoft.

You can gamble anywhere in the world. You can gamble on riverboats, Indian reservations, Atlantic City, Monte Carlo, the Caribbean, and many, many other places. Businesses can host conventions and meetings anywhere. But given a choice, people choose Las Vegas. Why? Because the people of Las Vegas have figured out that tourist is not a dirty word.

Even if your room isn't comped, from the minute you arrive in Las Vegas until you leave, you are treated like a VIP. From the person who takes your room reservation to the doorman who greets you to the cab driver who takes you around town, everyone welcomes you. The customer-service and cordiality training employees go through at many Las Vegas restaurants, hotels, and casinos is the best in the world. Where else can you get that kind of service from an entire city? The executives that run the casinos in this city figured it out.

Even if you don't go to Las Vegas to gamble, you can be entertained by great stars like Wayne Newton, Celine Dion, and Elton John, or you might take in the Cirque du Soleil. The hotels bring you New York, Paris, and the Pyramids of Egypt in one block. It's the entertainment glitz of Los Angeles, combined with the energy of New York City, in the middle of the Nevada desert. Kudos to the many casino executives who have figured out that in Vegas the customer is *king!* They have made Las Vegas the tourist capital of America.

Having said all that, gambling is still the reason most visitors come to Las Vegas. And if you're going to gamble, whether it's here in my hometown or anywhere in the world where there's a casino, you should know "the rules." I want you, the gambler, to have a fighting chance. The job of any casino is to beat you. Their goal is to figure out ways to distract you, confuse you, outsmart you. Their mandate is to create shareholder value— to make profits. If they don't, they won't keep their jobs.

You have a job description, too. The gambler's job is to beat the casino. It's a cat-and-mouse game. Neither party is at fault for wanting to win or profit. Those are their respective roles! The problem is that often, only one participant in this game actually knows it's role—the casino. The gamblers are often so naïve or ignorant that they don't even realize they are in a game. They don't realize they are being played. Here in this chapter, I'm attempting to enlighten the gambler as to the game going on around you, and what your role and reaction should be if you intend to win.

I am not condemning the casino for being better at the game. To the contrary, I shake my head in awe at the job they've done, the palaces in the desert they have created. They are so damn good at the game, they are the Picassos or Monets or da Vincis of their art. Most gamblers are so outclassed in this battle that they have lost *before* they walk in the door of the casino. My goal here is to teach you the rules and the psychology of casinos.

Never mistake my comments for attacks on the strategy or psychology employed by the casinos to win this cat-and-mouse game. It's a free world. Anyone can choose to gamble or not. No one puts a gun to your head. Anyone can choose to not accept comps. No one is forcing those free rooms and food on you. Anyone can choose to play only high-percentage bets, where the house advantage is close to nil. And guess what? The casinos will let you!

You are welcome in their house to gamble as smartly or as dumbly as you want. Knowing that, I give the casinos all the credit in the world for trying as hard as they can to make you choose "dumb." What's amazing is how many of you say, "Sure, I'm dumb. Bring me more dumb! I love dumb."

And do you know why so many gamblers choose "dumb"? Greed. They have stars in their eyes. They want to hit the jackpot; they want to get *everything* for free—booze, food, lavish high-roller suites, shows, massages, gifts, the whole nine yards. And they want to win a fortune, too. They want to break the bank while enjoying all the lavish hospitality of the casino for free. The gamblers want to have their cake and eat it too. They are just too greedy to see that it's tough to have both; that they are putting themselves at a huge disadvantage by choosing both; that they would be better off choosing one or the other.

If the gambler chooses all the freebies and gifts, he or she has to play by the house rules. And those rules are slanted against you. If the gambler chooses to play that way, I say more power to the brilliant executives and marketers who run the casino. It's a battle between casino and gambler—and the casino has won.

Casino execs earn my respect and admiration as the greatest field generals (and salesmen) in the world, bar none! I just want to even the odds by drawing a picture of the battlefield for the typical gambler, and explaining in detail "the rules of engagement." My guess is that 99 percent of you will ignore common sense and my Contrarian strategy, and continue to play dumb. And that, my friends, is how they are able to build those amazing palaces of gold in the desert that we call casinos!

Casinos

This section will not attempt to pinpoint the specific strategies you need to succeed (and profit) at individual casino table games like black-jack, roulette, baccarrat, craps, slots, etc. There are literally hundreds of quality gambling books that describe play strategy. Instead, my goal here is to dispense commonsense advice that alone can change you from a casino loser to a winner.

The single biggest problem for most intelligent and successful people who want to gamble in a casino is that the moment they walk into the casino, they *lose* their intelligence. They throw away everything that has ever made them successful in the first place! I have seen men and women who treat their jobs and careers seriously, and do everything in their power to acquire knowledge and control in their professional lives, literally transform into undisciplined *idiots* (if not raving lunatics) once they step foot inside a casino.

Picture this: The craps table in a casino in Las Vegas is surrounded by wealthy men and women—investment bankers, stockbrokers, doctors, corporate executives, business owners, and CEOs. Regardless of their level of wealth and status, or their fancy titles, they have all come to the casino for "action and excitement." They slouch over the craps table while smoking, drinking, ogling, and eventually become exhausted after hours of nonstop gambling.

Yet they don't call it a night. Perhaps they don't know when to say "when." Perhaps they are getting "comped" a free penthouse suite, but to keep it they must gamble eight hours a day. Perhaps they are too numb (from drinking, smoking, eating to excess, and no sleep) to know it's time to quit. Or perhaps they are so drunk that losing thousands of dollars just seems (at the moment) like fun. They are dazed and confused, yet they're still tossing chips around like they've forgotten that those bits of round plastic represent real money. Winning no longer seems to be the point of the evening.

For the men, much of the action is centered on *breasts*. The male gamblers are watching the busty cocktail waitresses walk by. They are focused on the open cleavage like a laser-guided missile. When the breasts pass out of view, it's time to focus on the waist, hips, thighs, calves, and finally the high heels. How the gamblers love those thin, tall, spike heels! Those moments of fantasy can be costly, since they have diverted the gambler from his goal and totally shattered any attempt at concentration on the game at hand.

Isn't gambling the reason we're all here in the casino? These gamblers have wasted thirty seconds minimum, perhaps one minute, lost in their adolescent fantasies. Doesn't sound like much time, but it could make all the difference to their bank account. The gambler may very well have cost himself momentum (ruining a nice winning streak), or made a losing streak much worse, or missed a roll of the dice (or two), therefore totally losing track of what's happening in the game (or where their money should be placed). And don't forget this "dancing with breasts" routine goes on not once but repeatedly all night long (every time a pretty woman walks by).

So does anyone wonder why casinos hire only beautiful, sexy, young gals with ample cleavage, then put them in skimpy, skin-tight outfits, and parade them back and forth in front of the gamblers with free drinks? Sounds like pretty smart business strategy to me. If it happened at the office in the daytime, sharp executives would catch on in seconds. But in the dark, at night, with no clocks and lots of booze, and exciting sounds piped in (the sound of ringing slot machines and people screaming, "I won!"), and after hours of gambling, the senses are numbed. So the gamblers play on and lose. And lose. And lose some more.

After five or six hours of this sexual ogling and other similar (and sinful) diversions, not to mention the consumption of five to ten drinks and a pack or two of cigarettes, a fatigued and disoriented banker or salesman or entrepreneur will stagger to his room and collapse on the bed. He will not, however, be quite certain what time it is, why he lost, or where his money went. For that moment, he is too tired to answer questions thoughtfully or honestly. Tomorrow he'll shower, shave, get a bite to eat, and try to forget his bad luck of the night before (rationalization is the key to happiness). Then he'll start the process all over again.

Talk about Bill Murray's *Groundhog Day*—that movie should have been filmed in a Las Vegas casino. For most gamblers, this is the ritual known as a "gambling trip." The trip and the losing are repeated year after year (often several times a year). Where's the fun? Where's the greatness in plummeting toward poverty after spending a lifetime struggling to get away from it, or at least avoiding it?

What is wrong with this scenario? Start with . . . *everything*. If these same gamblers were to apply this surprising lack of common sense to their careers, businesses, and marriages, they would soon be bankrupt, divorced, and living on government assistance, finding it difficult to earn respect, either at the office or at home.

This disastrous approach to gambling starts *before* these gamblers ever leave for the casino. In business, every move they make is all about succeeding or winning, beating the competition, gaining the competitive edge. Yet when these same sharp businessmen head for a casino, they aim for fun, not profit. Most casino gamblers assume they will lose, even referring to their cash as "fun money."

But why is gambling treated differently than any other form of investing? Can you even imagine stockbrokers suggesting to their clients that they should play the market just for fun and expect to lose whatever they invest? Can you imagine buying a new home with the following advice from a real estate agent: "Whatever you invest in this house, expect to lose it all." Can you imagine opening a new business expecting to fail miserably and lose everything? My philosophy is certainly a revolutionary one, but I believe that casino gambling is an *investment*, just like sports betting, stocks, bonds, art, and real estate. You should be playing to win at all times. And you really can win, if you put the odds in your favor. Here are some vital factors for casino success:

• Your attitude must be positive.

From the start, you must aim and plan to win. This isn't just about fun. Winners treat gambling like a serious business. So do all the casino employees. (If you don't, that puts you at a significant disadvantage, don't you think?)

• Speaking of planning to win, what is your plan?

What is your goal? How are you going to get there? Without a plan in any business venture, you are *dead*. What games will you play at the casino? Do you know anything about those games? Do you have a strategy? If you don't, you have no right to play them. Do you have a monetary goal (how much do you want to win)? Nothing kills more gamblers (or their bankrolls) than simply not knowing when to stop.

When I gamble, I know everything about the winning strategy for the game I'm playing. I know exactly how long I'm going to play. I know exactly how much I expect to win. And I know at all times exactly how many chips (how much money) I have in front of me. When I hit my goal, I *leave*. Simple as that!

Most gamblers at some time during the night (or day) are up a good amount of money. They've *won*. If they leave now, they've beaten the odds. But there are no clocks, there are lots of scantily clad women, and there is lots of free-flowing booze, all for a reason: to *distract* you from treating gambling like a professional business. To keep you from focusing on your goals. To keep you gambling way past the point where you should have left.

Once again, everything I'm teaching you is *Contrarian*. It goes against the way most gamblers have treated gambling their whole lives. It goes against the way casinos (and casino hosts) want you to think. Yet it's pure common sense. When you really analyze it, Contrarian thinking is always simple common sense. Yet it's often hard to see the simplicity of it all under layers of complicated, confusing, intense, high-pressure, stressed-out modern living.

- **If you expect to come out ahead, you must grind out a profit. (You'll see this theme reoccur later, when we talk about sports gambling and Wall Street.)**

Like in sports gambling or stocks, those who go for broke *go broke*. It goes back to the idea that at some point during the evening, most gamblers are up a substantial amount of money. Forget the distractions, the booze, the breasts, or the disorientation. Let's assume the gambler in question is focused and completely "in the zone." But he, too, has a problem: *greed*. Most gamblers want to break the bank. They gamble at all times looking for "the score of a lifetime." They want to retire wealthy, *tonight!* Just like sports bettors, their goals are absurd. A $40,000-per-year secretary or a $60,000-per-year middle manager wants to double his or her annual salary in a night or a one-week vacation. Or hit a $1,000,000 jackpot. That's just unrealistic.

For every one lucky bastard that stumbles onto the run of a lifetime and does win $50,000 in one night, there are thousands of other gamblers who were up $1,000 and kept gambling, then lost the profit plus the original $1,000 they brought along to the casino. It is that fantasy of breaking the bank that ruined it for the thousands. *Greed*. The image of that one winning gambler fueled the greed of thousands of others. And it cost all the rest of the gamblers big-time.

Interestingly, after a lifetime of observing gambling, I can tell you without any doubt that the one lucky bastard who won big (and ruined it for everyone else) will lose back the entire $50,000 (and then some) in his next few casino visits. So *everyone* has come out a net loser because of this recurring (and foolish) fantasy. My advice is to forget it; erase the fantasy from your mind. You might give up one lucky, once-in-a-lifetime winning streak by playing it my way, but in the long run you'll come out ahead—far ahead.

Educate yourself on the game you choose to play. Play only high-percentage gambles (where the house edge is limited). Set a goal. Stay focused. Know your chip count. Aim to grind the casino out. When you reach your goal, *walk away*. You are done for the night.

▪ Understand that the casino is set up to beat you 100 percent of the time.

The house always (yes, I said *always*) has an edge over the gambler. When I talk about high-percentage plays, I'm talking about cutting the house edge to a tiny percentage. But think about that for a minute. What I'm telling you is that even under the best of circumstances, the house still has a slight edge. So if you played a set amount of time, all things being equal, you'd lose. That house edge (over time) automatically grinds you down. Every single time, over time.

That's the whole point of my strategy: set a goal and *walk away* when you hit it. Over time you'll automatically lose at gambling. The odds demand it. But luck takes over in the short run. Most gamblers will experience good luck and good runs (streaks of winning) at some time during the night. If you can freeze that moment in time, stop and walk away while you're ahead—you win!

As soon as you decide to keep going, to try for the streak of a lifetime, you are dead. The odds will beat you. Any winning streak 99 out of 100 times will turn the other way and you'll lose back everything you won—and then some. By the time that happens, you've been playing for hours. You're tired and worn out, which only makes it worse. Your judgment is poor and you're sure to make bad decisions at the end of the night, like increasing your bets at just the wrong time; playing long-shot exotic bets to gain back your losses; or going double or nothing on one roll or hand because you're tired and you've lost patience. At the very moment you shouldn't be gambling at all, that is the precise moment when most gamblers are risking their *largest* bets of the day. Sound familiar?

This is exactly what sports bettors do when they bet double or nothing on Monday Night Football. An entire weekend of discipline and patience and winning strategy is out the window for one bet, because the game is on TV and it's the last bet of the weekend. Great strategy, huh? What I'm saying is that perhaps 80 percent of all the money lost at gambling (on anything) is lost in the final few reckless, exhausted, disoriented moments. Long after that gambler should have stopped gambling. Almost everything gamblers do is wrong, stupid, reckless, and guaranteed to burn them. Almost everything they do is contrary to logic and common sense. Your job as a devoted Contrarian is to do the *opposite* of what any typical gambler would do in any typical casino.

▪ More Contrarian common sense: Casinos do not give anything away for free!

Most gamblers want to be comped. They *live* for being comped. Do you know what that makes them? Greedy. Winning gamblers are not comped. I've never in my entire life been comped by a casino. Never. You know why? I only wager on high-percentage bets where the casino has very little advantage. Now keep in mind that this is fine with casinos. They'll welcome my money, too. But they certainly see no reason to motivate or encourage me to come play in their casino. They don't see a need to ply me with free suites and fine food to beg me to bring my style of high-percentage play to their casinos. They'd much rather beg the gamblers who play dumb, who play the way that offers the biggest advantage to the casino. Smart. Nothing wrong with that strategy. I'd do the same thing.

But think about it. If the casinos are eager to attract you, shouldn't that set off bells in your head? I am not seduced by the the free hotel suite and food. That very comp is what promotes the losing attitudes I've described above. It's not easy to "quit while you're ahead" if you're comped—the casino expects a certain amount of "play" (guaranteed gambling time).

If you leave too soon they'll take your comp away, or never give you another one. Why? Because they know that if you play a certain amount of hours, the law of averages will catch up, and you will lose. They know that with *certainty*. That's why they are so eager to give away free suites and food (and even gifts, if you're a "high roller"). They are paying you to accept their bad terms.

So if you're tired and losing focus at the tables, too bad, you have to keep gambling. Getting confused and disoriented? Too bad, you have to keep playing. On a bad losing streak and need a break to clear your head? Sorry, you're comped, that's just not in the cards! Want to change tables to change your luck? Sorry, you're out of luck.

When I gamble at a casino, I change tables often. I take constant breaks. I leave as soon as I start to feel the momentum changing. All things I'm free to do because I'm not comped—I'm a free man. I owe the casino nothing. I can play five minutes or five hours. I can wager $25 a roll for the first hour until I see a pattern, then shift to $500 a roll when I get on a hot streak, then lower my risk back down to $25 when things start to cool off. Or leave while I'm ahead.

Not so for the comped gambler. He has a debt, an *obligation*. He has a big account he has to protect. And a big ego. He wants (perhaps needs) to look like a big shot. It's just not *macho* to change tables. It looks cowardly. He has to stand there gambling at the same table for his guaranteed eight hours. To leave might offend his gracious hosts. To change tables several times a night might offend them even more, as will quitting while he's ahead. And to reduce the size of his bets once he's far ahead, so as to protect his profit—that *absolutely* will offend his gracious hosts. As will playing only high-percentage bets where the house has little advantage. Doing those smart, high-percentage things certainly won't get you comped ever again.

Comps go to *reckless* gamblers. Guys (and a few gals, too) who are willing to play for long hours, with big dollars (also stipulated by the gracious host—play less than the amount you promised on every roll and there's no more comps for you), and often at games with lousy odds. They don't give free money away at casinos, or anywhere else for that matter. There's always a price to pay.

You get comped precisely because you are willing to play the way a casino *wants* you to play. Why? Because casinos know that that kind of play will automatically make you a loser over time. So they can afford to comp you—they already know the outcome! You're dead before you walk in the door, if you agree to play by their rules.

Do you get the message now? Contrarian thinking to the tenth power at work here. Virtually every gambler in the world lives to get comped. They see it as an honor. A goal. A reward. In reality, the very *result* of getting comped is to put yourself at a huge disadvantage. When a gambler signs for that comp (with glee), they are signing their own death warrant. The very thing they want will kill them. How Contrarian!

But wait, I've saved the best part about comps for last. Those who get lavished with gifts are even dumber (or more naïve) than those merely getting a free room and food. Some high rollers (or "whales," as the biggest of the big gamblers are called) get presented with Ferraris and $100,000 diamond rings for their spouses upon arrival at the casino. Yes, casinos give them $250,000 cars and $100,000 trinkets of jewelry! Why? Because the casino execs have done the math. They only give away a $250,000 gift if they think it will entice a gambler to lose *$5,000,000.* So all they've done is given away 5 percent of his loss beforehand. They know that nine times out of ten this gambler will lose back that 5 percent, plus the other 95 percent. The casino that gives him the most lavish gifts will get his business.

In other words, comping a big player is just a business transaction. The thought by casino execs is, "The more we give him for free, the more indebted he'll feel psychologically." That's the game played by casinos. They want you to feel guilty and indebted. So you'll gamble only at their casino, and gamble *much* longer than you intended, and for *higher* stakes than you intended. Guilt causes people to do strange things. Without the Ferrari, a high roller might leave after one day of gambling, while up $1,000,000. But because he now feels indebted (or his wife feels indebted), he'll keep gambling three days longer. That's three days too long. He loses back the $1,000,000 profit, plus another $5,000,000. So that $250,000 gift cost him $6,000,000.

My advice: Don't accept the gift. I never have. I don't owe the casino anything. I'm not indebted to anyone. I play how I want, when I want, and leave when I want. But then again, I'm a Contrarian.

▪ **Speaking of casinos giving things away for free, let's examine breasts and drinks.**

Those are both technically free in a casino, but they are much more expensive than you realize. Why do you think casinos are only too happy to hire young, sexy, busty cocktail waitresses, then parade them in front of gamblers 24/7? The answer, of course, is to distract you. To create a "fun" party atmosphere. To keep you from treating gambling as serious business. The more you stare at those breasts, the more you lose your concentration, and the more you lose money. All those hot, sexy babes make your visit to a casino feel more like a frat party than a business transaction.

So are those breasts really free? Hell, no! One peek could cost you thousands in losses. They are perhaps the most expensive thing in the whole casino! No wonder the casino is only too happy to encourage you to view them absolutely free. Are you getting the idea that *nothing* in life is really free?

Remember my Author's Note at the start of this chapter? Please understand I'm not faulting casinos for featuring young sexy gals with large breasts. It's just smart business. Fashion designers do the exact same thing and never get criticized. Or have you seen any fat women with large moles and lots of leg hair modeling the latest designs from Giorgio Armani lately? Armani's goal is to get you to spend thousands on each dress by convincing you that you'll look as good in that dress as the eighteen-year-old sex goddess with the eating disorder and the incredible fake boobs.

The fact is that most women will never look as hot and sexy in that dress as the eighteen-year-old supermodel. But they buy the dress because they were sold a fantasy. They *want* to believe they'll look as good in that dress as the model. Sex sells. And it works—in *every* business. I just want to be sure you understand it's happening. I want you to understand the rules of the game at a casino.

And in a casino, free booze goes hand in hand with breasts. First, it's the pretty young sexpots that serve you the drinks. Big problem. Second, the drinks are free in a casino to encourage you to order booze with abandon. Another big problem. If drinks cost money, you'd order two or three. Perhaps three or four drinks in a night. But because they're free, the party never ends!

"Hey, order all you want—the booze is on the house." But is it? Just like the "free" breasts, those are the most expensive drinks you've ever had. Those free drinks cause the gambler to lose focus, concentration, intensity, and common sense. If a large portion of all the money lost by gamblers is indeed lost in the very last few minutes of their gambling binge, then alcohol certainly plays a central role in the mistakes of those last few minutes. By the end of the night gamblers are tired, careless, punch-drunk, and in many cases drunk. At the very time you are the most full of alcohol, you tend to make the most careless mistakes, and lose the most money.

Coincidence? I think not. So next time you decide to drink as many "free" drinks as the casino will offer, think again. A few $5 drinks "on the house" could cost you hundreds or even thousands of dollars.

But wait, there's one more psychological trick you should know about. Once a gambler orders those drinks, they seem to take *forever* to arrive. Guess what happens while the gambler waits for that free drink? He loses thousands of dollars. After all, he can't leave, can he? He's ordered a drink. Now he has to stay and wait for it. It would be rude to leave without giving that cocktail waitress a tip. Besides, she's got *great* breasts!

So gamblers wait. And what do they do while waiting? *Gamble!* Those "free" drinks take just long enough to arrive that you lose $1,000 while waiting. So that one "free" drink actually cost you $1,000. Think about that one. That was the most expensive drink of your life. Gambling is all about psychology. The casinos understand it. The gamblers don't. Now hopefully you do.

• While you're gambling for "fun," the casino employees are dead serious!

Watch the pit bosses sometime. Study their eyes and you will see the seriousness of a jeweler appraising a diamond necklace. This is not fun to them, it isn't a big game—it's their *livelihood*. They are able to focus on the game at hand (even if you cannot); they know the odds of every bet on the table (even if you don't); they are assessing your every move (even if you don't understand your own decisions); they know the chip count of every player at the table, how much he is up or down, how long he has been playing (even if you don't even know your own chip count).

The employees of the casino are not ogling the cocktail waitresses; they are not drinking alcohol while on the job or throwing money around just for the fun of it (even while *you* are). They are professionals; this is all business for them. Do you now understand the house edge? Do you think you can beat these professionals with an amateur attitude? Do you know the odds on each bet you are risking your money on? If not, you are at a serious disadvantage.

My advice: Gambling is *not* about fun. Treat it like a serious investment. Understand the game and the odds, or don't play. Otherwise you are just flushing your money down the toilet.

• Another lesson in Contrarian thinking: Know the odds!

The odds on a craps table vary greatly. The odds on the "pass line" and "don't pass line" are high-percentage plays—they offer a minuscule advantage to the house. So guess what? None of the casino employees ever remind you to play those bets. But they constantly remind gamblers to play the prop bets like "No Craps," "No Seven," "Centerfield," etc. Why? These are *terrible* bets for the gambler—they come with horrific odds, *dramatically* in favor of the house.

You'd have to be a brain-dead moron to play these bets. They are "sucker bets," and the casino employees obviously think *you're* the sucker! Yet gamblers respond to the casino's begging them, and they play them! *What are gamblers thinking?* Just because a carnival barker encourages you to play the worst bet in the house, you'd bet it? Why not just hand him your money? That's quicker, simpler, and gets right to the point.

Think of your options: You could place your money on a fifty-fifty bet, or a bet with a little larger house edge, or the third choice—a bet that offers odds so bad that the house pays an employee to *beg* you to play them. Result: Strange as it sounds, many gamblers choose the bets with the absolute worst odds.

Let me paint a picture that helps describe this choice: The house (casino) has laid four bills on the table, $100, $50, $20, and $1. You can choose any one of them. There's action going on all around you. You are drinking. Smoke is blowing in your face. People are yelling. Lights are blaring. Sexy women wearing very little clothing are walking by every minute (or second). You see breasts. You have been up for hours. Casino employees are loudly urging you to pick up the $1 bill. You can choose to keep any bill. You stare right at the $50 and $100 bills. You choose the $1 bill. Great selection, brain surgeon!

This unfortunately is pretty typical of gamblers. A Contrarian lesson again, just like the comps given to high rollers: If the casino offers it to you, if they *want* you to take it, if they're *begging* you to take it, the odds must be stacked against you. Just remember for the rest of your life—anything the casino wants to give you puts you at a natural disadvantage.

▪ **Speaking of purposely choosing the worst odds possible, now we come to a topic worthy of a book all by itself: Slots!**

There is no more popular form of gambling in the world that pays worse odds than slots. Yet this is the favorite game of most gamblers around the world! Why? I guess because most gamblers are *dummies*. There is no other logical explanation.

The payout on a slot machine is horrible. You know in advance that you will lose 7 to 8 percent (or more) of the time. The odds are set so strongly against you that over time you just cannot overcome them. You know that the longer you play, the more you'll lose. Hypothetically, if you were to play slots for twenty years, you know with certainty that you'll lose about 7 or 8 cents of every dollar you put into that machine for the next twenty years.

There is no skill of any kind. It is actually the only casino game that requires no skill or knowledge. It used to be as simple (and stupid) as sitting in a chair and pulling a lever. These days it's even worse—now many slots have eliminated the lever. Now gamblers sit mesmerized by the screen, pushing a button (like a pet monkey might learn to do). It is gambling for *idiots*.

Yet this is the game most amateurs *choose* to play. Again, don't get me wrong. The casinos aren't at fault here. You are. You the gambler have chosen to play the dumbest game on the floor. The one with *Wheel of Fortune* or *I Dream of Jeannie* or Jethro from *The Beverly Hillbillies* screaming at you to pull that lever (or perhaps now it's "push that button"). The casino merely puts all the choices out on the floor. You're the ones choosing the worst car on the lot.

How big is slot gambling? It is the number-one form of adult entertainment in America! According to *The New York Times*, slots take in $30 billion per year. The entire pornography industry (the second most successful adult entertainment business in America) grosses only $10 billion annually. Slots now account for $7 out of every $10 in gambling revenues.

How could people really be this stupid? You cannot win on slots. You have no control when playing slots. You don't need any skills. You cannot possibly understand the odds or you would never play them. Yet almost every gambler chooses to play them. In that same article in *The New York Times*, even Frank Fahrenkopf, head of the AGA (American Gaming Association)—the man paid by the AGA to defend gambling—says the popularity of slots represents the dumbing down of America.

Fahrenkopf says, and I quote, "I don't know if it's the education system, or maybe it's that we as a society have gotten intellectually lazy. But people would rather just sit there and push a button."

Wow! What a statement. I'm a big fan of Frank Fahrenkopf's. He is brilliant and mega-successful. He is the former head of the Republican National Committee and now is the single most important man in the gambling world. Yet even he admits that he thinks playing slots is for complete idiots. Can you even imagine how damning that statement is? He is the voice of gaming, and he can't imagine why gamblers play slots! The only reasoning he can come up with is that they are intellectually lazy (the politically correct way of saying "stupid").

Yet most people that walk into a casino choose to play slots. I guess they didn't get Frank's memo. You know why they never read Mr. Fahrenkopf's words? Because the crowd that plays slots *doesn't* read! How sad. How pathetic. If they knew what the most savvy gambling execs in the world thought of them, they couldn't or wouldn't even think of pulling that lever (or pushing that button).

But these gamblers are just on the lowest level of the evolutionary scale—sitting right alongside the Lotto players in their ignorance or lack of understanding of the odds of gambling. Talk about pathetic—casinos across the United States actually now offer *free oxygen* (for the oxygen tanks of senior citizens) to entice slots players. So, earlier in this chapter I was criticizing the richest, smartest gamblers in the world for accepting Ferraris and diamond rings to lure them to gamble to excess; but the poorest gamblers (the ones who cannot afford to gamble in the first place) accept free *oxygen*. If you are a slots player, you must choose one of two things: either agree to never play slots again, or immediately stop reading this book. It's *not* for you.

▪ And then there's my old favorite: money management.

Money management can be the difference between walking away up or down, despite being dealt the *exact* same cards! The key to winning in a casino is not winning but rather *limiting* losses and keeping losing streaks to a minimum.

The winning professional gambler bets relatively small amounts until the exact moment when he sees an opening and senses a winning streak developing. This requires tremendous patience, confidence, discipline, and killer instinct to hold back until just the last possible moment, then to quickly and dramatically increase your bets in the face of an opportunity. During a winning streak, professional gamblers bet big, but the instant it starts to fade, they retreat, slowing down the bets, stopping for a break, or changing tables.

This is the strategy of a Zen Gambler! Some find this strategy slow and boring, just as they find betting on pathetic underdogs frustrating and boring in sports gambling. But it works. It produces consistent long-term profits. What more can you ask? Do you want action or profits? Personally I get high off of leaving a casino with more money than I came there with. That's *my* definition of fun!

▪ **Finally, a Zen Gambler practices visualization.**

This kind of gambler relaxes and visualizes every move he'll make *before* he ever walks into the casino. He visualizes the pit bosses and cocktail waitresses. He visualizes the tables and games of chance. He clearly sees the faces of those playing alongside him. He sees "the hand he'll be dealt" and visualizes his reaction to each possible situation. Finally, he sees himself winning *big*.

Remember, unlike sports gambling, in a casino *you* are the quarterback! You control the dice. You decide whether to hit or hold. You are the captain of your team. So having a good mental attitude comes in handy when you are making crucial decisions that will affect whether you walk away up or down big money today.

By visualizing, you are taking advantage of the same strategies used by world-class athletes. Golfers and tennis professionals practice the entire match in their minds before playing. Then they go out and actually play their game. It's easy to hit a great shot when you've been there before! Often the Tiger Woods and Andre Agassis of the world have hit that same winner thousands of times in their minds, *before* actually doing it. So have smart professional gamblers—Zen Gamblers.

In the fantasy world of the casino, where every subconscious deck is stacked against you and where you are seldom as knowledgeable as the house you are playing against, the law of averages can and will wear you down. But losing does not have to be a foregone conclusion. Some gamblers do win consistently over long periods of time. All of the successful gamblers I have studied possess many of the same skills as chess masters, Indian trackers, and samurai warriors combined. They are Zen Gamblers.

They do not win by chance or error. Rather, they are patient, disciplined, educated in the nuances of the games they play, and they understand the odds of every possible bet they will make. They also understand the psychological battle they are playing with the casino. They do not feel pressure to gamble on every roll, or to keep playing when their luck has turned bad. They are not in the casino for fun or action, but rather to *profit*. They only bet heavily when the circumstances, luck, and odds are all in their favor. They understand that the law of averages is always in the casino's favor, that the longer you play, the better the odds that you'll lose. They understand that this is why casinos encourage action (and long periods of play), even going to the extreme of rewarding the most active players (read: dummies) with bonuses, freebies, comps, gifts, and point cards.

The winning Zen Gambler knows his job and understands his goal. He attains his goal (profitability) by learning the rules of how to play the game at least as well as his adversary (the pit bosses and other casino employees). He has memorized the odds and probabilities of each and every betting situation. He sticks to a predetermined monetary goal, and once he has reached that goal, he quickly demonstrates what may be his greatest talent of all—the ability to walk away from the game and *leave the casino*. He's not greedy, but he is willing to grind out the profits. He has done his homework. And to top it off, he practices visualization—clearly seeing every successful move before he ever starts gambling.

By taking these steps, some of which are time consuming and complex, the Zen Gambler is guaranteed to wind up far ahead of 99 percent of all the other gamblers. He has reduced the house advantage to almost nil (still not quite nil, but almost). The moral of the story is simple: As Branch Rickey (one of the great baseball managers and executives) once said, "Luck is the residue of design." Winning at gambling (just like winning at life) is *not* a mistake or coincidence. It is planned. It is within your control. It is Contrarian. Now let's go on and learn Contrarian betting strategy.

THREE

■

CONTRARIAN
BETTING STRATEGY

The Road Less Traveled

Time to state a few credentials: I am the only Ivy League–educated sports handicapper in America (Columbia University, pre-law). I am the only former national TV anchor and host (for Financial News Network, now known as CNBC) turned sports handicapper. Today I am the only handicapper in the world who is also chairman and CEO of a publicly traded company, GWIN, Inc. (the only handicapping firm traded on Wall Street).

I don't tell you all this to brag (okay, maybe I am bragging a little). Rather, I report these unique qualifications because they point out why I'm the ultimate Contrarian sports handicapper. As a man with a background immersed in the fields of elite education, media, and Wall Street, I of all people should respect authority. I of all people should report to you that those "in the know" are life's winners. That taking the advice of experts is the key to picking point-spread winners. But these things are not true.

The answer, I'm afraid to say, is quite the opposite. You see, all those so-called experts in the fields of education, news media, and finance are usually wrong about everything they predict. Whether the topic is presidential elections, stocks on Wall Street, the direction of the economy, or picking point-spread winners in the handicapping world, in almost all cases, experts are wrong (and often badly wrong) most of the time! Actually, so is everyone else. The fact is that when given a choice, people make bad choices. That's why bookmakers and stockbrokers (the people who take your bets) drive brand-spanking-new Mercedes and the bettors (or "investors" as they are called on Wall Street) drive used Chevrolets.

I have learned in the seventeen or so years I've spent as a winning professional sports handicapper and NFL analyst on national TV that the more you know, the *less* you win against the point spread! Facts don't work. Stats don't work. Trends are useless. The majority of "betting systems" are futile. Experts are hapless. A keen understanding of player personnel won't make you a dime. Common sense will produce no dollars and cents.

Nothing that seems obvious in sports betting ever is. So if you plan on making money betting on sports, throw all your reams of stats and detailed information out the window, and leave your common sense and gut instinct behind. Most of all, disregard everything you hear, read, or watch the "experts" spout in the media—they'll drive you to the poorhouse.

Winning money—gobs of it—betting on sports is very possible. It happens for a chosen few every day. But in virtually every case, the winners in sports betting are "taking the road less traveled." What do I mean by that? I mean that they are Contrarians—they look for a public consensus (overwhelming agreement) on any one game, and they go the opposite way. They have a keen understanding that the "masses are asses," and that the so-called "experts" are even worse! When it comes to making betting decisions, the winners assume that Murphy's Law is in effect to the tenth power: anything they read, hear, see, or choose is dead wrong most of the time.

If your habit is to follow the advice of friends, fans, relatives, commentators, NFL TV analysts, sportscasters, professional handicappers, expert newsletters, odds-makers—anyone at all—please know that the majority is wrong a majority of the time. Period. Just like on Wall Street. At the exact moment most experts and the masses of investors think the stock market is going to crash and that stocks are an awful investment, the stock market is always headed for a historic rally!

This Contrarian strategy has worked throughout history, and the opposite has held true as well. At moments in Wall Street history when a large majority of experts and the masses of investors believed stocks could only go up higher and higher, that the future looked limitless, at that very moment the stock market was headed for a crash of epic proportions! This last occurred in the spring of 2000, when the Internet Revolution crashed at the very peak of its popularity, crushing millions of small investors and wiping out trillions of dollars in equity.

Sports wagering is a mirror image of stock investing. When things look the worst, when bettors can't even stomach the idea of betting on a team, that's precisely the moment to bet on that team! Because that is the moment when the bookmaker is giving you the most value. When the masses of amateur bettors are all betting on one side, the other side is a fabulous investment. In sports betting (or in life in general), nothing is ever as it seems. Whatever appears obvious is not.

Whatever looks like a bad bet is actually a solid investment. Whatever looks so easy it's like taking candy from a baby is actually a sucker's bet (and a guaranteed loser). The value, and therefore the profits, always lie with taking the road less traveled: betting on teams no one else wants to bet on, betting against teams that everyone else loves, and going the opposite way of friends, fans, sports columnists, TV experts, handicapping experts, and talk-radio know-it-alls. This is how you win!

So my sports-betting advice is simple. You'll be hearing about it throughout all of the next few chapters, but in the end it comes down to being the ultimate Contrarian. Throw all the stats and trends out the window—they are misleading. Understand that there is no value in favorites. Focus primarily on underdogs. But I'm not talking about just any underdogs—your hard-earned money should only be risked on *painful* underdogs! Pathetic, hopeless dogs that no other bettor is willing to risk his money on. Underdogs that experts give *zero* chance of winning.

Ask your friends what they think; read all the sports columnists you can get your hands on; listen to sports talk radio; surf on over to sports handicapping and betting web sites; log onto Internet chat rooms; subscribe to handicapping newsletters; listen to TV experts; and then, when you find a consensus from all those sources on one game, whatever they tell you, *go the opposite way!* That strategy has made me a huge point-spread winner for almost twenty years. It has made me famous. It has made me wealthy. It has given me the life others only dream of. I *do* love this country, but most of all, I love the masses of asses!

Now that we've established that the key to success in sports betting is to think contrarian and to invest in value, the question is, how do you determine value? The very definition of value is to travel the road less traveled. Don't follow crowds, friends, family, or the news media. Don't put your faith in "experts" or authority figures. Don't assume that the information you just read is valuable, one of a kind "inside info," and that you now have an edge over other bettors. If you read it, the rest of the world has read it also. If it's public knowledge, you can bet it's misleading, worthless, and/or simply dead wrong 99 percent of the time! Start thinking critically and cynically. Start assuming that most everything you read and hear is either worthless or misleading. Start thinking and living like the ultimate Contrarian.

Now don't get me wrong. Being Contrarian doesn't mean being anti-everything. It means questioning trends to create critical thinking so you can make valued investments. *It's setting your own trend.*

Look at the founding of the United States of America. An incredible cast of people willing to journey the road less traveled, thinkers who were all Contrarian to the masses, the experts, and the critics: Alexander Hamilton, Benjamin Franklin, George Washington, John Adams, Thomas Jefferson, Thomas Payne, John Hancock . . . and the list goes on and on. All different in their styles, their roles, and their effectiveness, but all united to a great cause that not only freed themselves but set their nation's government on the right path for future centuries.

Another Contrarian fact to note about our Founding Fathers: They were all successful and stinking rich—flat-out wealthy. They were the group with the most to lose by far. They would have been better off, at least in the eyes of the average observer, to stay with the status quo. Why risk everything over ideals? Why risk your wealth and reputation when you're already at the top? Yet these ultimate Contrarians did risk everything they'd ever earned and achieved. They all knew that if the revolution failed they'd be stripped of all worldly goods and hanged as traitors. Their families would be left penniless and tortured. Yet they not only fought, they led the American Revolution. Now that's Contrarian thinking! That's the definition of taking the road less traveled.

One thing is for certain: You will never be able to duplicate any great legendary leader's path. You must find your own. You can, however, master a few fundamental principals that successful people have in common. This book will show you the fundamentals that have worked for many successful people, as they have for me, and as they can for you.

While some people think Contrarian thinking means failing, being a nonconformist, being confrontational, or just trying to gain attention, let me tell you what contrarian means to me: independence, freedom, the thrill of the hunt, and ultimately, winning! (By the way, what city in America signifies Contrarian thinking, freedom, and independence all at once? Las Vegas!)

Who are the natural sports gamblers? Entrepreneurs: restaurant owners, car dealers, business owners, professionals who own their own practices (lawyers, doctors), commission-based brokers of all kinds (including stockbrokers, real estate brokers, and insurance brokers)—all people who have their homes and assets on the line every time they open a new store, dealership, or restaurant. They're not afraid to take a chance. They're also not stupid about the chances they take. That's what separates them from the rest of the masses. They put up with all the experts who tell them they'll fail, and ignore the critics who tell them what they do wrong. They're Contrarian. They're winners!

Who is *not* cut out to be a gambler? The type of person who is happy collecting a paycheck signed by someone else every week. The lawyer who owns his own legal firm is often a gambler. The sky is the limit for his earnings. He can make zero one week and $100,000 the next. The corporate attorney that works for a large law firm and collects a weekly paycheck is not. A corporate human resources officer for Merrill Lynch is rarely a gambler. They're all living in the "safe" world of the butcher— and many hating it just as much!

A stockbroker who lives on commission for the same firm is almost always a big-time gambler. That's because business owners and stockbrokers earn performance-based pay—if they don't succeed, they don't eat. Most employees on the other hand—those who live on a set paycheck each week—get paid whether they win or lose, whether the business is profitable or not.

When the savvy entrepreneurs gamble, they typically wager $1,000 per bet. Enough to have an impact on how much they win, but not so much that they could lose their restaurant over it. But they don't plan on losing their restaurant. They study their bet like they're opening a restaurant, and they never open a restaurant without a plan: they open it with the goal in mind to be profitable from day one, to be a winner. These successful superachievers always expect the best, yet are smart enough to plan for the worst (the unexpected, the worst-case scenario). Most amateur gamblers (read: "losing gamblers") expect the worst (to lose), and worse yet, plan for nothing. They have no goal, no strategy.

What sets my better clients, the entrepreneurs, and me apart from everyone else? We don't quit after losing eight straight bets. The typical Joe will either quit or stay in the rut (not figure out how to fix his problem). My fellow winners and I don't do that. We stay the course, learn from our mistakes, figure out a new and better way to put the odds in our favor, and then make that ninth bet. That is the difference between winning and losing: the willingness to stay through the down times, to study what went wrong, come up with a solution or strategy, and then and only then to make it to the top of the mountain.

Contrarian thinking isn't limited just to overcoming failure and adversity. It includes mastering the right things to do—the ability to see and obtain opportunity where others fail to see it. Look at a great baseball pitcher, Greg Maddux (a Las Vegas native, no less). This three-time Cy Young Award winner (the most prestigious honor for a pitcher in baseball) is one of the greatest pitchers to ever play. For the past nineteen years, he has mastered the major leagues with his Contrarian thinking and risk-taking. Has he done it with an overpowering 100 mph fastball? No, his fastball is around 90 mph. Has he done it with a killer split-finger pitch like Roger "the Rocket" Clemens? No, his split-finger doesn't move quite as much. Maddux uses changing speeds, location, and slight movement action on his pitches to keep hitters off-balance. Ultimately, he's a Contrarian thinker becaue he always throws something the masses of expert hitters would never expect.

But what makes Greg Maddux a complete winner is how he masters all aspects of his game: his hitting (one of the best hitting pitchers in the game), fielding (thirteen Golden Gloves—the best fielder in the National League at his position for those years), preparation (on days he doesn't pitch, he charts pitches to study opponents' tendencies), and health habits (healthy diet; never overweight; stays conditioned to move off the mound as a fielder and on the bases as a runner).

He's so smart that he doesn't set a goal to throw a no-hitter! Do you know why? Because he wants to win the game, and that might include setting up a tough batter early in the game by letting the batter get a hit so that later in game, in a clutch situation, Maddux can throw a pitch the batter would never expect and get the tough hitter out. How Contrarian is that?

What I advocate in this book is that we should be like Greg Maddux: not overpowering, not trying to throw a no-hitter every time you go out there, but to be smart, be prepared, and most of all, *be Contrarian!* With this mind-set, the odds will always be in your favor. You'll have a mental edge—and that's all you need.

FOUR

■

THE CATTLE ARE HEADED TO THE SLAUGHTERHOUSE!

Stop Following the Masses

People love to be popular. They love to be accepted by others. They follow the crowd no matter where it's heading. They live in a nice pasture, eat all the grass and grain they want, and when they are sufficiently fatted, off to the slaughterhouse they go! Misery loves company, doesn't it?

Typically, here's what happens, even with my own masses of clients: I'm a guest on the Dennis Miller show and he asks me how I'm doing. I tell Dennis, "Last week I picked thirteen of seventeen winners!" I feel great that I picked that many winners. It's a wonderful feeling. And I'm not puffing the numbers—I tell Dennis like it is.

So what happens next? I get fourteen bazillion phone calls the next day from people wanting to become my clients because I'm hot! That's their first mistake. They confuse their English verb tenses. They all think I *am* hot and assume next week I *will be* hot. The problem is, Dennis asked me how I did *last* week, and I said I *picked* (past tense) thirteen of seventeen winners. What I *picked* does not project from one week to the next, good or bad. It only reflects what I did last week.

At the very moment when I'm hot is when everyone should be avoiding me, running the other way. But no, the masses call. What's fascinating about this is that if Dennis asked me how my week was and I said, "Terrible. I only picked two out of ten," the phones would go dead. This is the time when people *should be* calling me because the odds are turning to my favor that I'll win.

I'm a professional sports gambler. A national handicapping champion. When I'm suffering through a losing streak, you can bet your last dollar that a huge winning streak is just about to start. But the masses don't get it! They are always a day late, a step behind, a dollar short. They are guaranteed to always have the wrong reasoning, the wrong judgment, the worst gut instincts.

It's only human nature. It's Murphy's Law: Whatever can go wrong, will. And the masses, the average Joe or Jane, is guaranteed to find it, step in it, date it, marry it, bet it, buy it, and of course spend the rest of their lives complaining about it.

So many people miss this small but incredibly significant point about gambling: From one week to the next I can't guarantee that each week I'll pick thirteen of seventeen winners. In fact, the odds are tremendously against that happening. What I can guarantee is that over time, using my methods and strategies will help you succeed (as they have me and others) much more than following the masses. Why don't they get it? Let me explain.

WHO ARE THESE MASSES?

There are three very basic categories of losing bettors that make up the masses heading to the slaughterhouse.

Loser Scenario #1

This group of bettors is uneducated, living on a treadmill (i.e., going nowhere in particular in life), in short, the average "Joe Nobody." Have you met any Joe Nobodys in your life? Are you one? Do these guys seem lucky? Do they seem to have all the answers in life? Do they seem in control of their lives? Of course not!

Remember Murphy's Law? The average Joe Nobody in America goes through life being tossed about by his or her bosses, landlord, union, government officials, spouse, even fate. They are in no more control over their lives than a ship lost at sea without a captain. Most of us go through life lost at sea. We are born, we spend our lives working too many hours at jobs we dislike, we strain to keep our heads above water, enduring a sea of red ink. Then comes the really bad part—we die! Life is rarely "fair" for the average Joe Nobody.

Yet Joe gets a bright idea one day. He (or she) decides to "get rich quick" betting on football. Joe has no connections, no special knowledge or expertise, and does not have any spare money to risk. Yet he decides that betting the rent money will net him ten times his annual income in a few months' time. Good luck and God's blessings to Joe—he'll certainly need them!

The brightest minds on Wall Street invest millions (presumably money they can actually afford to risk) in return for 20 to 30 percent annual returns. Keep in mind that these figures represent extraordinary returns available only in the most bullish of markets . . . or to wealthy "hedge-fund" investors (those with $1,000,000 minimum investments). Yet our friend Joe the butcher, baker, or candlestick maker, expects to earn 300 percent returns *weekly* on a $500 investment! A little unrealistic, wouldn't you say?

Joe knows little about what or whom he is investing in. He has no professional guidance (investment adviser or professional money manager), and knows nothing about money management. Joe doesn't have the time (as a working stiff he already has a forty- to fifty-hour-per-week full-time job) to spend more than a few minutes per week analyzing and selecting his "investments." If Joe starts to lose, he doesn't have the necessary "bankroll" (back-up money) to stay solvent through the dry spells (and believe me, there will be losing streaks). Joe may not know it, but he was a dead man walking from the first moment he decided to wager his first dollar. The poor guy never stood a chance!

Loser Scenario #2

This group of bettors is smart. Highly educated, with college and advanced degrees up the yin-yang. Nice job. Nice house in the suburbs. He or she has a career most of us would envy. Family, kids, the whole shebang. We'll call this guy "Picket," short for "White Picket Fence."

Picket lived and breathed work ethic 24/7 in college and graduate school. He hit the books ten hours per day at the law library. Later, as a junior associate, he worked fourteen-hour days to move up the corporate ladder. Today he's made it. As a partner in the firm, he works twelve hours a day to stay on top of the ladder. His life is devoted to family, career, and professional achievement. His success has always been the result of dedication, commitment, and hard work.

Yet when Picket decides to bet on football, he throws all that out the window. Gambling is different, he decides: "It's fun." Besides, Picket watches one or two games every Sunday and another on Monday Night. He believes he understands football—he's a self-described "expert." All the lessons he has learned his entire life about success are thrown to the wind when he gambles.

Picket bets his hard-earned money on teams he knows nothing about, coaches he knows nothing about, point spreads he does not understand, set by professional oddsmakers who work fifty to sixty hours per week studying nothing but football and whose job it is to know literally everything about the odds. They are true experts at what they do, and their only goal is to set a "perfect" point spread—the definition of "perfect" being a point spread that beats amateurs like Joe and Picket most every time.

Picket's decision to enter the betting world is tantamount to a successful brain surgeon deciding he wants to skydive out of airplanes without a parachute. Not a great decision, and certainly not a very good long-term prognosis! But look on the bright side—the pain and panic will only last until our surgeon friend loses consciousness! After that, death will actually be painless and instantaneous.

For our friend Picket the results are no less certain, and are sure to involve long-term suffering. Picket, like our friend Joe Nobody, never stood a chance. He didn't realize it, but he too was dead from the moment he first decided to wager dollar one. This poor bastard, although he started out with more education, wealth, and advantage than Joe, never stood a chance either!

Loser Scenario #3

This group of bettors encompasses many socioeconomic groups. They might be rich, poor, or anywhere in between. But they all share one common belief system: a respect for authority. The members of this group have been raised since childhood to believe in the power of the written word and the authority of "experts." They believe what they read in the newspapers or books, or what they see on the news, to be the gospel truth. After all, they think, "If it wasn't the truth, how could it be reported on TV by people I depend on for factual and unbiased information?" Or subconsciously, they believe, "If the anchorperson or host or columnist says it, it must be true!" or "If an 'expert' smarter than me tells me it's true, it has to be—after all, that's their job, to dispense the truth."

The masses are a bit naïve. They actually believe in "experts." Stockbrokers certainly know the truth about Wall Street. Right? Doctors know the truth about my body. Right? Lawyers know the truth about the law. Right? The news media will only dispense unbiased facts about the news. Right? These professionals all have my best interests at heart. Right? This group of naïve individuals has been around since the beginning of mankind. Unfortunately, "they" are "us": you and me and most of the rest of the world. We'll call this group of individuals the "masses of asses," or "Ass" for short.

Our typical Ass gets a call from a stockbroker who tells him he has the greatest stock tip since the dawn of civilization. "Would you be interested in the tip?" Ass is asked. "If not, could I at least send you out a recommendation the next time the greatest tip since the dawn of civilization pops into my lap?"

"Of course!" says our friend.

Ass, not wanting to miss out on something usually unavailable to someone like him, will jump at this "once in a lifetime" opportunity! And the next one too. After all, those "once in a lifetime opportunities" don't come around every day, do they? (Actually, on Wall Street they come around on an hourly basis, and on particularly good days, on a minute-by-minute basis.)

Now think about this scenario for a moment. Think of Warren Buffett or Bill Gates (the richest man in America), or Magic Johnson or Leona Helmsley (no explanation needed), or Lee Iacocca or George Steinbrenner, or even O. J. Simpson (even high-profile "alleged" murderers need investment advice!). These just happen to be a few of the wealthiest and most high-profile individuals on the planet. How do you think they got so rich? How do you think they stay rich? Do you honestly believe they took advice from a stranger who called them at random on the phone offering free advice? On the other hand, our naïve friend Ass is sending $10,000 via wire transfer to an anonymous broker sitting in a boiler room in Brooklyn, six months out of college and two days out of broker training school.

Donald Trump and Warren Buffett have teams of Harvard MBAs at their beck and call: investment advisers, hedge-fund managers, pin-striped bankers, money managers, attorneys specializing in mergers and acquisitions, etc. Donald and Bill and Magic and Warren know what's going to happen long before it reaches the newspaper, or the investment newsletters, and certainly before the news gets to the twenty-six-year-old college drop-out turned stockbroker whom Ass is currently on the phone with.

More importantly, these business icons know the real truth, not the hyped-up sales pitch being stuffed down Ass's throat. They also know the right price at which to buy the stock they like, simply because they know about the stock *before* it hits the newspaper or newsletter or boiler room. So they buy at the bottom and ride the stock to the top (which is called "value investing"). Just as they're getting off the train and saying "thanks for the ride," Ass and his mass of friends is getting on! Except now the stock is selling for 2,000 times its price-to-earnings!

At this point all the insiders have already made their money or are selling our stock short (betting it will drop fast). The brokers, brokerage houses, lawyers, investment advisers, takeover specialists, traders, under-writers, and insiders have already made their score! Everyone but Ass has already feasted off the carcass. And guess what's left for the masses of Asses? They're going on a train ride too, just like Donald Trump and his friends who just got off, only Ass and his friends are going back the other way—theirs is the train ride to hell, last stop bankruptcy court!

What does all this have to do with betting on football, you may be asking yourself at this point? Everything! Masses of asses who bet sports act exactly the same as the masses of asses who wager on Wall Street. They too bet on whatever they see on TV or hear from friends or read in the newspaper or hear on talk radio or even hear on the phone from a stranger selling sports-betting advice (just like stockbrokers, legal sports-betting services sell their advice to bettors—I know this because I run one). They bet on this information, thinking it is valuable, exclusive, or "inside" information.

What they fail to realize is that if it were valuable, it wouldn't be in a newspaper, newsletter, or TV news report that anyone could watch! And twenty-six-year-olds wouldn't be peddling it to strangers on the phone! Rarely is anything that is available for the average Ass to see ever valuable, exclusive, or insider knowledge. Valuable information will never appear in a sports journalist's column, or emanate from the mouth of your average television sportscaster.

When in doubt about this theory, refer back to Loser Scenario #1: Do butchers, bakers, truck-drivers, toll-takers, carpenters, or middle managers ever get lucky in life? Is valuable information ever available to the average Joe Nobody? Does great fortune ever pour down on the average newspaper reader for the 50 cents it costs to buy that paper? Of course the answer to all these questions is once again a resounding *no*.

So if you're basing your betting strategy on information available to the masses, like Joe and Picket you're dead from the first moment you decide to wager dollar one. If you read it in the newspaper, saw it on TV, got the tip from a newsletter, listened to it on sports talk radio, or heard about it in a sports-gambling Internet chat room, you are unfortunately, an Ass. You also never had a chance in the first place!

The question becomes, why is this true? Is there some huge, secret conspiracy in the media or among experts against Joe, Picket, and Ass? Are bookmakers or the mob in cahoots with the media? Are the experts purposely trying to mislead you? The answer is a resounding no to all of the questions above. But there are several valid reasons for this phenomenon. In the next chapter, I'll explain why information from "experts" is actually more deadly than from any other source.

FIVE

■

The Experts

Are *NOT*

So after reading the last chapter, you're probably asking, "Why is this true?" Why is the advice and information I get from experts and authority figures not valid or valuable? How could a so-called "expert" possibly be so often dead wrong? The answer is no. But there are several valid reasons for this phenomenon.

MURPHY'S LAW

Life isn't fair. Nothing in life is easy. Rarely do things of importance go smoothly. Successful people work hard to overcome challenges and become winners—real hard! Those who possess that elusive "winning edge" are unique. They question why things go wrong and challenge themselves to come to their own conclusions as to what is the right thing to do or correct way to do it. "The winning edge" comes from accepting the fact that things sometimes go wrong when circumstances are beyond our control (Murphy again). Other times they realize that they have made an error in judgment, but they learn from the mistake. One thing that successful people *never* do is to follow the crowd, or the experts, or the people chasing the experts.

Winners stand *apart* from the crowd. They don't run to follow the masses, who are following the experts. If anyone could pick up a newspaper for 50 cents, read a column, and place a winning bet based on that advice, we'd all be as rich as Donald Trump or Warren Buffett. Look around. Are you or your friends as rich as Donald or Warren or Bill Gates? My conclusion is that the advice you get in most newspapers is only worth the 50 cents you paid for it. And of course, the advice you get on television costs even less, nothing, and that too is generally what it's worth. Hint: Few on Wall Street have ever gotten truly wealthy from reading *The Wall Street Journal* or watching *Wall Street Week*. My experience as an anchorman at Financial News Network taught me that.

WHAT CREDENTIALS QUALIFY SOMEONE AS AN "EXPERT" IN ANYTHING?

We in America put our faith in "experts" and authority figures like no other society in the history of civilization. Maybe that's why we are such a screwed-up society. No casual coincidence there, I'd guess. I mean, let's face it—where else in the world can we have a trial where the defense's "expert" on DNA analysis can refute the testimony of the prosecution's "expert" on DNA analysis?

Let me give you a personal example of this expert phenomenon. Television has credibility. People believe whatever they hear on TV. I was a big-time TV anchorman. I hosted several shows and served as network oddsmaker and NFL prognosticator for Financial News Network (now called CNBC), one of America's most-watched networks. I worked at the network for two full NFL seasons (1989 and 1990), with a team of highly regarded professionals that included five anchorpersons, a general manager and his various assistants, an executive producer, and several producers, directors, and managerial personnel. All had spent their entire adult lives in the sports-television business. All loved sports, most were what you'd call sports trivia nuts, and knew everything down to the jersey number of every player, at every position, on every major college and professional football team. Many of these big-shot execs actually knew the players personally. They interviewed them, dined with them, had their home phone numbers for Pete's sake. They went into the sacred locker rooms. I was intimidated by the vast reservoir of knowledge and contacts that each of these big shots had at his fingertips.

I was also shocked to find that most of these savvy sports big shots and experts (there's that darn word again) were degenerate losing gamblers! They would bet on anything that moved—that was why they loved sports so much. They enjoyed the thrill of being close to the action. They fancied themselves experts and thought they were the privileged few blessed by God himself with the ability to get close to the players, managers, and games themselves, so they quite naturally assumed they'd be able to translate their insider knowledge into betting profits. They assumed their knowledge and access gave them that "winning edge." Boy were they wrong!

This group of media insiders were *by far* the biggest group of betting losers I've ever met in my entire life—and I've spent over twenty-five years around bettors of all kinds. These intelligent, professional, educated insiders—sports executives, directors, producers, and anchormen— would call their bookmakers direct from the newsroom, the dressing room, or the anchor desk, any time they had a sixty-second break.

They'd bet on ten games in the morning, then ten more at night. Then they'd start in all over again the next day.

If a new piece of news information came across the newswire or sports ticker, or if one of our reporters fresh from an interview at a big game mentioned a "hot tip" regarding a last-second injury, twenty TV professionals would drop everything they were doing to all rush to a phone and call their bookies, while simultaneously running a major television network reaching all of America! And did they lose? *They lost and lost and lost some more!* And did I mention they lost? From dawn to dusk, these guys phoned in a nonstop stream of losers.

Even I was shocked at the sheer volume of losers that professional, educated sports-television executives and experts—the very people the viewing public relied on for valuable insights and insider information—were capable of betting! If any of my colleagues had anything left of their paychecks each week after paying their bookies, it certainly wasn't much. By the sheer volume of losing bets that I personally witnessed, my guess is that on numerous occasions, these "experts" were dipping into savings *plus* paychecks to pay off their debts. And what I witnessed is the norm, not the exception.

Remember Chet Forte? Like me an Ivy League graduate, Chet had one of the most impressive resumes in all of sports television. Chet was the director of Monday Night Football on ABC for a couple of decades. It turns out he was also a degenerate gambler—and a pathetic loser. Because of his now-public gambling problem, Chet eventually lost virtually everything, from his personal fortune to his job. Just like my fellow big shots at FNN Sports, he was supposed to be "the ultimate insider." He knew the players, the coaches, the game. He knew more than any Joe or Picket or Ass could ever hope to know in a lifetime. All up close and personal on ABC. And he lost everything he had betting on those insights and expert opinions. *Everything!*

Yet these are the people whose insights and information the common

Joe trusts, values, and relies on to make his betting decisions! In reality these experts are nothing more than Asses themselves, pathetic losing gamblers in real life, just like the masses they are hired to educate and enlighten. Ironically, it turns out that these highly paid experts don't have anything but *bad* information to offer the masses. These experts trade in losing information! Ironically, when the cameras and stage lights are turned off, most of these "experts" and professionals are just as desperate for a winner or valuable inside information as the viewers they were just moments ago busy "educating" and "enlightening."

Get it? The "experts" you watch on TV are the same as you, only with nicer suits, better resumes, and a more confident speaking style. The TV experts always sound so sure of themselves, and the truth is they are. They are buying into their own fame and press clippings. They aren't deceiving you. They are betting their money on the same advice they are giving you. They are confident—but they're also dead wrong.

Trust me when I tell you that Wall Street is no different. The "experts" you see on TV, the columnists you read in *Forbes* and *Fortune* and *The Wall Street Journal*, rarely report anything of value. If it were valuable, they would not be giving it to you on TV for free . . . or for the cost of a newspaper or magazine.

Journalists save the real valuable news, if they have any, for themselves. Brokers, analysts, and mutual-fund managers save their valuable information—if they have any—for private clients that pay them millions of dollars. The stuff you read in the paper or watch on TV is the leftover scraps that have little or no value.

From the example I experienced first-hand at FNN Sports, you can now see what a travesty it is that millions of American sports bettors risk their hard-earned money daily after reading newspapers, newsletters, and magazines, or listening to talk radio, or watching ESPN or FOX Sports. My educated guess (although my friends in the news media tell me it is fact) is that the FNN Sports newsroom was no different than the newsrooms of CNN, ESPN, FOX Sports Net, *Sports Illustrated*, *The Sporting News*, *Pro Football Weekly*, or the FOX and CBS NFL pre-game shows. Millions of bettors look to the professionals at these organizations for betting advice, when in reality those same professionals or "experts" are desperately and pathetically searching themselves for a winner or a valuable "insider" tip—and rarely finding one!

GUT INSTINCT

People bet on what they think is a gut instinct. What they don't realize is that this subconscious voice is based on an entire week of brainwashing—reading dozens of newspaper and magazine articles, watching TV news reports, reading sports newsletters, surfing the Net, listening to sports talk radio, watching pre-game shows, and perhaps worst of all, speaking to friends who've read or watched the same misleading information! So in fact, what you think is "gut instinct" is just the same bogus information that's been force-fed to your subconscious all week by "experts" who are themselves clueless (and often repeating what they've heard from sources and friends who also lose money betting on sports). It's a vicious cycle of loss and misleading information.

True gut instinct—the kind that stands a chance of being correct—is unpolluted and uncorrupted by outside influences. Therefore your sports-betting selections based on gut instinct should be made each week on Sunday Night based on the original, hot-off-the-presses opening line that is set in Las Vegas. The opening Vegas line is posted by halftime of the ESPN Sunday Night Football game for the following weekend's action. Your picks made this early in the week are thereby produced *before* you've been exposed to hundreds of "experts" who seem to have been placed on this earth solely to mislead and confuse millions of gullible readers, viewers, listeners, and fans.

WATERCOOLER EXPERTS: WORK ASSOCIATES, FRIENDS, AND RELATIVES

Many bettors bet not based on gut instinct or what they hear on TV, but from what they hear "on the street" or at the office watercooler. They simply get convinced that a bet is infallible based on what a work associate or someone they respect tells them.

Are you a bettor? How many times in your life have you been talked into a bet you weren't sure about or out of a bet you loved because a friend or group of friends made a convincing argument? Were the results satisfactory?

Is your local neighborhood or office know-it-all usually right? Of course not. If he were so brilliant, why would he be working in the same neighborhood or office as you? He doesn't know any more than you, he's just better at arguing, debating, or getting his point across. He might showcase more confidence than you, but that doesn't mean he's any more right than you!

Beware of listening to friends, neighbors, or family—if they had the secret to either life or football betting they'd live in a guarded-gate mansion by a world-class golf course—like me! If they don't live in a beautiful mansion or drive a $100,000 Mercedes or Ferrari, they probably haven't fared any better at life or football betting than you. So why do you need their advice? Where's the value?

CONTRARIAN POINT

Finally, the most important reason you should not bet based on the advice of "experts" or friends is because *that is precisely what everyone else is doing.* And you don't, under *any* circumstances, want to follow the crowd! Why do people listen to friends, relatives, and experts? *Because there is safety in numbers.* Most bettors are afraid to think for themselves, or don't have enough time to do their own research, or are simply not secure enough to stand alone. They feel safe betting on the same team as everyone in their office, bar, club, or classroom. Their logic is, "If everyone loves the same team (or stock), they can't all be wrong, can they? It must be a good bet." Wouldn't you have loved to book that bet in 1929 (with the Great Crash on Wall Street and the nice added touch of stockbrokers jumping out of windows) or 2000 (with the Internet dot-com meltdown and the nice added touch of twenty-five-year-old dot-com "paper millionaires" ripping up their worthless stock options)?

Obviously everyone *can* all be wrong. As a matter of fact, they usually are. Keep in mind that all these friends or coworkers are all just normal people looking for the easy way to win (read: blind luck). They don't have any more knowledge about sports betting than you. As a matter of fact, their common lack of knowledge may lead them all to make the same wrong decision! They are also all watching the same NFL pregame shows and news reports as you, and reading the same sports magazines. They are in the same Internet sports chat rooms. They are in their cars driving home at 5 p.m., listening to the same sports talk radio. They are all absorbing the same misleading information and drawing the same erroneous conclusions!

But now let's deal with the largest problem of all: Betting on a football game is not like owning a business and selling a product. In the latter case, the more you sell, the richer you become. A businessperson's objective is therefore to sell to as many customers as possible. The higher the number of sales, the higher the revenues, and theoretically the higher the net profit. That's good! But when you place a bet, popularity is a negative. The more bettors that agree with you, the higher the price goes. In other words, the more popular that bet becomes, the more overpriced it becomes.

What was once a great value or a solid investment (at that low price) is now "dead meat"—a sure loser! Popular investments are too popular for their own good—there are too many buyers and too few sellers. The result is exactly the same on Wall Street as it is in sports betting. What everyone wants is *not* a good buy—it's overrated and overpriced. Why? Because everyone wants it! Once again, an offshoot of Murphy's Law, nothing is ever as easy or simple or profitable as it seems. The truth is usually contrary to conventional logic, and of course, automatically the opposite of whatever the masses are doing.

The result on Wall Street is that price is adjusted upward until it gets so ridiculously overpriced that there is a correction—more people finally want to sell than buy! Now comes a panic. As all the investors who bought on the way up realize the scale of their mistake, they can't sell fast enough. But now there are no buyers! As a result, the stock "crashes." It's a wild roller-coaster ride with a severe migraine.

This kind of panic or correction happens every day of the week on Wall Street. Sometimes it happens to a few stocks, sometimes a whole industry, sometimes the whole market. On Wall Street it's common knowledge that people who constantly buy "what's in" or hot, what's popular, what's featured in the newspaper or in *Forbes* or on TV, are consistent *losers*. They are called "suckers." People who buy out-of-favor stocks that no one seems to want are, over the long haul, consistent winners. They are called Contrarians or *"value investors."*

There are even newsletters based on this theory that follow "experts" and chart trends. What have they found? Both "experts" and investors are losers almost all the time! When 60 percent or more of the Wall Street "experts" think the market is headed down, the market invariably goes up! When 60 percent or more think the market will keep rising, it invariably sinks fast! If more than 70 percent think the market is headed up, what follows is a downward spiral of epic proportions (often referred to as a "crash").

Investors' opinions are just as inaccurate. If your objective is to profit, your best choice is to do the *opposite* of whatever popular opinion says!

Why do investors on Wall Street always bet the same way as the experts? Because just like sports bettors, they get their advice from "experts." Just like in the sports-betting world, stock investors feel safer investing in the same stocks as large numbers of friends. Just like cattle, they follow the advice of people of authority. In reality these experts rarely know more than the public, often less. It's a case of the deaf leading the blind. And they all rush straight off the cliff together!

Here's a fact about the Wall Street experts that will blow you away: Every December, *BusinessWeek* polls fifty-four expert economists on what the next year will look like economically in the United States. These fifty-four experts are literally a Who's Who of economists, many earning incomes well into the six- and seven-figure range. Many have degrees and resumes that make them the astronauts of the economy—the best of the best. They come from banks, big investment houses, large insurance companies, big investment-banking companies, the government, and re-spected private enterprise.

In December 2000, these fifty-four experts predicted the average U.S. gross domestic product (GDP) growth for 2001 would be 3.1 percent. They predicted unemployment would be 4.3 percent. The number for GDP growth in 2001 came out to be less than 1 percent—a greater than 3 to 1 miss by the average of the experts! Furthermore, unemployment hit 5.7 percent—off by a full 37 percent of the predicted number! But wait—there's more! The lowest prediction out of the fifty-four experts was that the 2001 economy would grow by 1.7%. So the closest of the fifty-four experts was off by a factor of almost 2 to 1! What does that tell you about "experts"? Perhaps there is no such thing—just people with fancier credentials making the same guesses as you and me. (Incidentally, because the predictions were based on October 1 to the following Sep-tember 30—from the fourth quarter of one year to the next—the pre-diction was based on the year ending September 30, 2001, so the events of 9/11, as devastating to the economy as they were, had little significant impact on the total numbers—just nineteen calendar days out of 365.)

I've heard people tell me, "Well, 2001 was in a down economy—you can't predict that." To which I say, that's exactly the time you have to get it right! That's why these experts make the big bucks. Besides, when things are going well and everybody's making money, nobody cares if the economy is predicted accurately or not. They're all following the crowd, and during upswings the crowd is winning. And if they're wrong in a down market, that makes me think that whoever does get the numbers right in an upswing does it by pure luck, not logical reasoning.

If the experts can't predict things well, what about their hindsight? It's equally bad! Check this quote from *BusinessWeek*, in an article titled "Where Did All the Profits Go?"

On July 27, the government's statisticians lowered their estimates of corporate profits for the past three years: for 2000 alone they sliced a full $70 billion off their 2000 number. Non-financial corporations got the biggest haircut, with estimated profits in 2000 reduced by $81 billion, or 13%. The new data now show virtually no growth in non-financial profits from 1995 to the first quarter of 2001.

This article was dated August 27, 2001. So in August 2001, the experts whom we all rely on to predict the economy finally admitted that the frenzied growth we all thought we had experienced in the late nineties *never happened*. It appears that the Arthur Anderson/Enron debacle wasn't just limited to a few executives playing with numbers. The economists were just as wrong before 9/11 as after it. So, what does that tell you about the experts' ability to even measure things accurately, let alone predict them?

The bottom line is that experts often can't predict the future because they rarely learn from their mistakes, but rather simply "restate" them. In Part II, I'll show you trends you can monitor and actually rely on that are accurate, do repeat, and are therefore much more successful at forecasting the future—and helping you win.

Football betting (and all sports betting for that matter) works exactly the same way as Wall Street investing. The more people who bet one side of a game, the higher the point spread is raised by bookmakers and oddsmakers. Each time it moves higher (or lower), it becomes more overvalued and therefore more dangerous. Investors who jump in at the top are weighing down the ship. They are rushing to catch that train to bankruptcy court. They are overbuying, overvaluing. They are paying too much, at the wrong time, in the wrong place. They are just like the millions of Asses who couldn't wait to put their money into the stock market in 1929 or 1999! When all your friends, family, and coworkers fall in love with one investment or one particular sports bet, don't walk, *run* as fast as you can the other way.

Remember, these are common people in the crowd we have been talking about. They've been losers their whole lives. They have no reliable gut instinct. They've never had any luck except, of course, bad luck (which they use as a clever excuse to justify their mistakes). The masses of asses are good at excuses and don't have the courage to stand alone. When they stampede toward any investment—but especially a sports bet—you can be sure it is a loser! Never lose sight of the fact that these are people who get "brilliant" ideas only after reading about the "hottest" or "greatest" or "newest" or "best-ever" in the newspaper or on TV. At that point, it's always too late!

I've talked about avoiding the masses and the so-called "experts." Is there any other group that can kill our ability to win? You bet! Read on. . . .

■

SIX

THE CRITICS
ARE IDIOTS!

Those Who Can, Do;
Those Who Can't, Criticize

Later in this book, I'll share with you the story of my success. The key to that success, to my achieving the American Dream, was a willingness to dream big, to risk big, and even to fail big. If you are afraid to risk everything, afraid you might fail, you will never succeed in a big way.

The great achievers of our time were all big risk-takers too. Every step along the way, they heard from the critics—not just media critics, not just enemies, not just jealous competitors. Critics can be (and often are) your friends, family, spouse, even your own mother and father. Whether they despise you (enemies, competitors) or love you and mean well (your family), critics all have the same effect: they kill your dreams, destroy your spirit, instill doubts and fears, impede your progress, and many times they even manage to stop you dead in your tracks.

They get you feeling so fearful, so negative, so self-doubting ("that will never work"; "that idea is stupid") or self-loathing ("you're not good enough") that you actually quit. You let your dreams die to pursue "something more realistic or practical." But it is the dreamers and risk-takers who change the world for the better—our world and their own. It was dreamers and risk-takers who discovered the New World, who blazed new trails in America, who tamed the Wild West, who fought Hitler and won, who put a man on the moon, who brought down the Berlin Wall, who created a luxurious adult fantasyland called Las Vegas in the middle of a barren desert, who built Microsoft and Yahoo! and America Online, who invented the Internet, who discovered vaccines for smallpox and polio.

It will be dreamers and risk-takers who, in the future, discover cures for AIDS and cancer and Alzheimer's, who create future modes of transportation that take us from Los Angeles to Tokyo in a short hour, who allow us to explore other universes and perhaps meet other civilizations. If those goals are to be achieved in the future, I can assure you that none of them will be achieved by critics.

Critics do not produce anything—not goods, not ideas, not jobs. Nothing. They just waste a lot of hot air criticizing others. They just sit back on the couch, wait for others to take action, then analyze what the results are from that action and find something to complain about. Those who criticize *never* create anything, *never* invent or discover anything, *never* change anything, *never* save anyone, *never* cure any disease, *never* employ anyone, *never* go where no man has gone before, *never* improve our lives (or their own), *never* make this world a better place.

Risk is at the center of all that is creative, positive, significant. The same willingness to risk that defines a successful gambler defines a successful world leader, scientist, businessperson, or entrepreneur. They are in all cases doers, achievers, explorers, and gamblers. And a successful gambler is by definition a dedicated Contrarian. Risk-takers are willing to do, create, explore, discover, invent, or achieve what critics say cannot be done, created, explored, discovered, invented, or achieved. Risk is essential to success, even more essential to *mega*-success. And ignoring the (negative) advice of "experts" and critics is equal to being willing to risk!

Over the years, I've read hundreds if not thousands of books, newspapers, magazines, newsletters, and online articles on successful people who have proved the critics wrong—usually *dead wrong*. I've compiled many examples of so-called "experts" who were wrong, and the remarkable, often magical results achieved by those who ignored them. Here are a few of my favorites. Please forgive me if I've lost or forgotten the sources of these great quotes. Suffice to say I appreciate and thank all those whose research and tenacity uncovered such priceless sources of motivation. May I present some of the greatest quotes (by so-called "experts") of all time, quotes that prove beyond a shadow of a doubt that critics are *idiots*.

1929: "Stocks have reached what looks like a permanently high plateau."

Who said it? Irving Fisher, America's leading economist, only days before the great stock-market crash of 1929. Fisher was the first in a long line of economists whose predictions never fail to make us laugh (while simultaneously making us broke).

1911: "Airplanes are interesting toys but of no military value."

Who said it? Marshal Ferdinand Foch, commander of the French military forces during World War I. Unfortunately, through the years it has been French military forces that have proven to be of no military value!

1876: "The 'telephone' has too many shortcomings to be seriously considered as a means of communication. This device is inherently of no value to us."

Who said it? Unnamed executives at Western Union! No wonder their names have long since been forgotten. But we all know the name of the risk-taker who invented the telephone: Alexander Graham Bell! Throughout history, critics have *always* been forgotten.

1977: "There is no reason anyone would want a computer in their home."
Who said it? Ken Olsen, founder of the Digital Equipment Corporation, at a meeting of the World Future Society. See what I mean about "experts"? The World Future Society? I'll bet gypsy palm readers have a higher accuracy rate than these pompous "experts." I wonder if Mr. Olsen also missed the value of indoor plumbing.

1967: "Man will never reach the moon . . . regardless of all future scientific advances."
Who said it? Dr. Lee De Forest, a famous and respected scientist and the father of radio. Note the date. Not only are experts often pompous fools, they usually make their absurd predictions only a short time before being proven wrong (and stupid).

1957: "The Edsel is here to stay."
Who said it? Henry Ford, founder of Ford Motor Company. Do you see any Edsels on the road? Enough said. Soon after that brilliant quote, the Edsel went the way of . . . the Edsel!

1915: "The wireless music box has no imaginable commercial value. Who would pay for a message to be sent to no one in particular?"
Who said it? A communications expert talking to David Sarnoff about the radio. Well at least this genius was partially right. Listeners don't pay for radio. Fortunately, advertisers *do*.

1972: "The current craze for bottled water is 'lunatic asylum thinking.' It will fade away as quickly as it came."

Who said it? Dr. Abel Wolman, professor at Johns Hopkins University, known as America's leading authority on water! After selling the stocks of Evian and Perrier short, my guess is poor Professor Wolman didn't have enough money left to buy any bottled water!

1955: "TV can never become truly popular. Who would stare at that 'boob tube' for hours on end?"

Who said it? A radio executive dismissing any chance for TV to overtake radio. First, we read above of telegraph "experts" panning the telephone. Then communication "experts" panning the radio. Now radio "experts" dismissing TV. See a pattern emerging here? Experts are *idiots!*

1966: "The concept is interesting and well-formed, but in order to earn better than a C, the idea must be feasible."

Who said it? A Yale economics professor commenting on college student Fred Smith's idea for an overnight delivery service to compete with the U.S. Postal Service. Fred went on to found Federal Express. FedEx today employs over 200,000 people, serves 211 countries and has annual revenues of over $20 billion! Today many wonder whether the U.S. Postal Service can possibly continue to compete with FedEx.

1988: "Vitamins are a waste of money."

Who said it? Dr. Art Ulene, doctor, TV medical "expert," and a noted medical author. Last time I saw Dr. Ulene he looked old and tired. Perhaps he should have taken his vitamins! By the way, if you listened to this noted authority figure and as a result stopped taking your vitamins, you'll be thrilled to hear his more recent quote in *People* magazine: "I dismissed vitamins as a waste of money. I was wrong."

1989: "Test audiences hate this pilot. They call it weak. They report that both the main characters and the supporting cast are unlikeable. The humor is far 'too New York and Jewish.' The show rated as only mildly amusing. No segment of the audience was eager to ever watch the show again."

Who said it? The television "experts" for NBC, reporting on the reaction by focus groups to *Seinfeld*, which went on to become one of the most popular shows in TV history. Over 50 million viewers watched the last episode of Seinfeld in 1999, where a thirty-second commercial cost $2 million! Lucky NBC didn't listen to the "experts"!

1940: "The United States will not be a threat to us for decades, at the earliest 1970 or 1980."

Who said it in 1940? Adolf Hitler. Luckily for the human race, this madman was off by over a quarter century!

1899: "Everything that can be invented, has been invented."

Who said it? The United States Commissioner of Patents *in 1899*. (I saved the best for last.) This has to be the single dumbest thing ever said by anyone, ever. Like I've always said, governments are stocked full of idiots who couldn't get a job in the private sector!

So what does all this prove? Why are critics so wrong?

• Sometimes things go wrong no matter how well you plan. That's Murphy's Law. A critic can't help here. Besides, you are taking action, which is doing something a critic never does.

• You need to have the confidence, as I do, to get back up from a loss and get back in the game again. Critics only destroy confidence and increase self-doubt. Critics try to convince you to quit.

• If you do what I suggest in this book, you're going to have a *lot* of critics because you will be a philosophical Contrarian. Since you'll always be in the minority, going *against* the crowd, you'll attract more critics than you can count. Who will be the most vocal critics? The masses in the majority who are threatened by your Contrarian stance.

"They don't boo nobodies."

BASEBALL LEGEND REGGIE "MR. OCTOBER" JACKSON

ARMCHAIR QUARTERBACKS TO IGNORE

Have you ever decided not to go to a movie because a critic gave it a bad review, but when it came out in the video stores, you rented it, and loved it? Right then you wished you had seen it on the big screen in the theater with that great sound system. Why do you think C-SPAN is gaining popularity? Because they don't have a critic telling you what you are seeing—C-SPAN has figured out that you can judge for yourself.

What about when the critics are reviewing and judging *you*? The fact is, despite the harshest criticism you could possibly receive, you are ultimately your own toughest critic. So critics are pointless. If something goes wrong, what's the point in someone telling you what you should have done? You saw the same thing they did (*after* the fact)—that it didn't go right. What they don't know is all the things you did—the homework, the planning and preparation, the decision to do something based on your homework and "reading the current status"—prior to executing the action (or the bet). Then something didn't go exactly according to plan, and you lost. How can someone possibly give you any constructive criticism when they weren't inside your head for the planning, preparation, or the "situation read" just as you made your decision to take action?

Critics are the same people who point out that the quarterback is a genius for calling an audible at the line of scrimmage and throwing a touchdown pass on a play, but on the very next play say the quarterback is an idiot for calling an audible at the line of scrimmage and then throwing an interception. Put these same critics in the heat of a battle, making split-second decisions on the field, and they'd throw an interception every time. Or they'd curl up into a fetal position and start crying in the face of a blistering pass rush of angry 300-pound men!

The only criticism worth listening to is that from your best friends—not your chummy go-out-for-dinner-and-have-a-few-laughs friends, but *real* friends who have supported you in tough times, when things were going wrong, who stuck with you in the heat of the battle. These friends are the ones who offer you constructive criticism. They don't offer it pointing a finger at your chest but with an arm around your shoulder. They don't yell at you in front of people, they find a quiet private moment and have a chat with you in low, assertive tones. And they don't nag; they don't tell you "I told you so." They understand there's no need for finger pointing and playing the "backseat blame game." You know what you did wrong, and they know it. The message is delivered once, and it sticks.

Constructive criticism from a real friend is *never* about one bad pass you threw either. It's never about any one thing going wrong. It's never about details. It's about the big picture, important things. It's not about blame or "I told you so." It's about learning from that mistake and doing it better next time.

So now I ask you the reader, after reading and understanding the philosophy of a true Contrarian, which role do you choose? Would you rather spend your life listening to critics and experts telling you the "right way" to do things? Or would you rather live the life of your dreams, always against the grain, against the current, against the cattle following each other to slaughter? Remember, you'll be a bit lonely if you ignore the experts, and you'll always be on the road less traveled. But I guarantee you'll be lonely at the *top* of the mountain—successful, wealthy, and wise.

Maybe you would rather choose to spend your life surrounded by masses of asses who follow the experts right to slaughter, those who sit on the couch paralyzed by the dire predictions of the critics, paralyzed by a fear of taking action, afraid of going against the crowd and taking the road less traveled. Here you can choose to spend your life surrounded by friends who sympathize with your losing ways, simply because they lost right alongside you. You'll never be lonely. You'll never travel empty roads. You'll have plenty of shoulders to cry on, and plenty of "pity parties" to attend. After all, misery loves company. Given the choice between the road less traveled versus the road more traveled, I know which one I would choose every time. Do you?

If you're going to become a successful gambler and risk-taker—whether the gamble is to bet on sports, invest in stocks, start a relationship, or start a new career or business, in all cases, you'll need to avoid the critics, laugh at the experts, ignore the odds against you. You'll have to shun your own friends, think analytically, be willing to stand alone behind your convictions, and *always* think like a Contrarian. It's not a strategy—it's a new way of thinking. It's a way of life. If you want to become a Contrarian, a value investor, and a *winner*, have I got a book for you! Read on!

■

SEVEN

VALUE INVESTING

How Not to Follow the Crowd

Value investing is simply always investing contrary to the popular opinion of the day, doing the opposite of what seems obvious, being illogical instead of logical, running away from the crowds. Crowds are losers; masses are *always* cattle going to slaughter. They love to invest or bet on what's sexy and appealing, the flavor of the moment. Crowds love sure things. But you and I both know there are no easy winners or sure things in life.

Where did I get my value sports-betting philosophy? From the guru of Wall Street value investing, Benjamin Graham. In fact, I have the honor of having been called by none other than *Fortune* magazine "the Benjamin Graham of Sports Gambling." Who is Benjamin Graham? What can you learn, as I did, from the master of value investing?

Benjamin Graham was born in 1894 and died in 1976, at the age of eighty-two. The third son of an immigrant family impoverished by his father's death, he grew up in New York and attended Columbia University. Sound like a familiar background? You bet!

In 1915, at the youthful age of twenty-one, he was working for a Wall Street brokerage. At that time, he saw an opportunity to buy the stock of a bankrupt railroad. He reasoned that the railroad was worth more than the stock price—that it had value above what the public perception was. The Contrarian thinking starts to emerge. Furthermore, his bosses—the experts—said this was a bad buy. What was he thinking of? they asked. Graham insisted on his assessment and convinced the partners to follow his advice. In a few years they were able to sell that "bad buy" bankrupt railroad stock at *six times* what they had paid for it!

That was before Benjamin Graham learned how to get better from the stock market crash of 1929. Before he taught Warren Buffett at Columbia. Before investment kings like Peter Lynch, Mario Gabelli, John Neff, Michael Price, and John Bogle were influenced by his methods. It was nineteen years before he wrote the timeless work, *Security Analysis*, with David Dodd. And well before his 1947 investing masterpiece, *The Intelligent Investor*. At the age of twenty-one, Benjamin Graham had already figured out how *not* to follow the masses and the experts. After the stock market crash of 1929, he learned how *not* to listen to the critics.

Let's look at how Benjamin Graham's philosophy applies to sports gambling. Here is a quote from a 1946 lecture Benjamin Graham gave, with my comments in parentheses:

Well, it stands to reason that if you define selectivity as picking out a stock (the teams to bet on) which is going to go up a good deal later on (win)—or more than the rest—you are going to benefit. But it is too obvious by definition. (Just as I picked the railroad stock in 1915 because nobody was looking at its value, why should I buy something because everyone's doing it—and it's probably overvalued?) What the commentators mean, as is evident from their actual arguments, is that if you buy the securities which apparently have good earnings prospects (the marquee players), you will then benefit market-wise (win); whereas if you buy the others (the underdogs), you won't. History shows this to be a very plausible idea but an extremely misleading one (the facts don't support the speculative thinking by the masses and experts that the best team is a good value bet and that the worst team is a bad value bet).

Who is a Contrarian value investor in the sports world? How about the Oakland Athletics? Michael Lewis wrote a brilliant (and brilliantly titled) book, *Moneyball*, about the baseball Contrarian general manager, Billy Beane of the Oakland Athletics.

The Oakland A's have the fifth lowest payroll in baseball. Everybody believes (the masses, the experts, and the critics) you have to buy the marquee players to win. But Oakland lets them go. Why? Because they can't afford to pay the overvalued salaries of the marquee players.

But Oaklands' success isn't purely attributed to letting go the overpriced players and bringing in cheaper players, any more than Southwest Airlines is successful because they cut costs. Southwest delivers value. The Oakland Athletics have figured out that there are plenty of good buys in minor-league baseball (and some at the major-league level that they acquire through trades) to deliver a competitive team at a price they can afford. In other words, they have established a Benjamin Graham–style scouting system that intentionally looks for undervalued players. Sound familiar?

After the 2001 season, Jason Giambi, the star Oakland slugger, left for my beloved New York Yankees. Yes, I love the Yankees, but even I as a Contrarian have had to learn not to listen to myself (especially my heart!) on business and betting decisions. The doomsayers were saying that Oakland wouldn't make the playoffs without a slugger like Giambi, that he was irreplaceable and worth any asking price. *They were wrong!* Not only did Oakland win their division in 2002, but they won 103 games that year, the same number as the Yankees, which tied them for the most wins in baseball—more than any of the other twenty-eight teams!

What's the result of the A's philosophy? In the four years since implementing their Contrarian scouting/player value evaluation system, they've been to the playoffs four times. One year out of four is a fluke. Two out of four might be something to think about. Three out of four is definitely a pattern. But four out of four? Come on! Even the masses should be able to spot that trend—but amazingly, they can't!

Yet the experts and the critics still argue against the A's point. The critics say, "But the A's choke in the playoffs—they don't get out of the first round." What about the *other twenty-two teams who didn't make it* at all, most of which had *higher payrolls* than Oakland? Or the Minnesota Twins, a team that Bud Selig, the commissioner of baseball, was considering for "contraction," being *fired* as a franchise—another low-payroll team, with no marquee players that year after year is in the hunt come October.

And where is Texas in 2004, the team that traded the most expensive player on the planet—Alex Rodriguez—to the Yankees? Through their first forty-three games in 2003 with their "A-Rod" star, they had nineteen wins and twenty-four losses. They were in last place, a bunch of losers. In 2004, through the first forty-three games, without their star player, playing guys you have never heard of, their record is the *opposite:* twenty-five wins and eighteen losses! They're winning!

Here's another value-investing example. One of my longtime friends and original investors in GWIN, Inc. . . . we'll call him "M" for privacy reasons . . . is one of the brightest businessmen I know. A multimillionaire, he built a public company into an industry leader, and now is retired at fifty-two to a beautiful home in Florida. But his best story has to be his "September 12" story.

He was looking for a million-dollar condo in Manhattan the first week of September 2001. Then came that fateful day of the World Trade Center tragedy on 9/11. Emotions ran wild. "New York is done for" . . . "Wall

Street is destroyed" . . . "New York is the target . . . there will be many more attacks" . . . "We've got to get out of New York at any cost": that's what typical New Yorkers were saying—and who could blame them? They were in shock, and they were scared!

Not my friend M. He asked his realtor to call up the owners of every million-dollar Manhattan condo he had looked at and liked. He offered them all fire-sale prices. Most accepted *on the spot*. M bought up the most prestigious real estate in the world at rock-bottom prices. To him this disaster—this tragedy—was the greatest buying opportunity in the history of Manhattan. Not since the Indians sold Manhattan to the Dutch for a few trinkets had so much New York real estate been offered at such low prices.

Was M being unpatriotic? To the contrary—he was and is the *ultimate* patriot. And the ultimate proud New Yorker. He loves America. He loves New York. He had faith in New York (and, most of all, in New Yorkers) even after the worst tragedy ever in American history. It was because of this faith that he took the risk of a lifetime, despite the fact that *everyone* knew that Manhattan was *the* terrorist target. When I asked M how he could rationalize risking millions of dollars (money he needed for his retirement) buying real estate in the midst of such fear and uncertainty, he gave the reply of a true Contrarian. "Who cares," he said. "New York is the greatest city in the world and it will never fall. If it falls . . . if Wall Street falls . . . *all* of America falls. It will not happen. America won't let it happen." M of course was right on the money.

That's not taking advantage of a tragedy. That's chutzpah. To spend millions buying up real estate when prices seem to have no bottom takes courage, confidence, vision, and most of all, *guts!* And it takes a heck of a Contrarian to buy when everyone is selling in panic . . . especially in an area under *enemy attack!* How many of you would have risked millions on September 12, 2001? I dare say *none.* That's why risk-takers get rich in America—to the victor go the spoils!

Fast-forward to 2004. In just the few years since the tragedy of September 11, Manhattan real estate has hit all-time highs. Prices have doubled and tripled. While most Americans would be thrilled to retire with one million dollars (but most *never* will), M has made a fortune in only a three-year period on his Manhattan residential real estate investments from September 12 alone!

That's why the man is retired at age fifty-two. He's a genius; he's a risk taker, a patriot, and the *ultimate* Contrarian. The same Contrarian principles apply to any investment—the richest men in the world were the "robber barons" of America who *bought stocks with both fists immediately after the great crash of 1929.* They made *billions.* Again, were they taking advantage of tragedy? Most Americans lost everything and the world slumped into depression. But the Rockefellers and Morgans and Carnegies had the courage and confidence to risk everything they had on buying "worthless American stocks." That's not unpatriotic—that's actually the very *definition* of patriotic. And *gutsy* beyond reason. They had faith in America and risked on the future of America when no one else would!

Like my friend M, that's the ultimate in courage, confidence, risk-taking and chutzpah. And the definition of Contrarian thinking. Always *buy* when people are selling, buy even *more* when they are selling in a panic, at the very moment when they'd pay *you* to take the investment off their hands. And *sell* when everyone else is buying and price is no object!

On the surface, people buy stocks because "everyone's doing it." On the surface, M was "taking advantage" of a poor real estate market. But how could he have predicted the upswing in real estate prices when everyone else was running for their lives? New Yorkers weren't running from a real estate collapse, they were running from large-scale terrorist attacks! But M was being a value investor, just like Benjamin Graham on Wall Street and yours truly in the sports-betting world. And if he had been wrong and prices had never rebounded, then he was really doing the right thing for those people by buying their real estate before it went down further (as the doom-and-gloomers predicted). However, M never wavered in his confidence that Manhattan real estate would come back, and he put his money where his belief was.

What's truly amazing is that so few investors would have the guts to buy in the face of a real estate collapse or a terrorist attack (at the moment they should), but *everyone* steps up to the plate to buy when real estate is flying off the shelf and overvalued! People get confidence from the very thing that should give them pause. But again, it's all part of my "misery loves company" theory. If everyone else is doing it, you feel you must do it too. The masses love misery—and company! Whether in real estate, stocks, or sports gambling, smart Contrarians buck the crowd and go it alone. It's lonely at the top, but boy it's *wealthy* too!

Look at the airline industry. While the big airlines were flying monster 747s, paying inflated salaries to personnel and lavishing customers with first-class luxuries, a little Texas airline started by a lawyer began offering cheap airfares, low-cost service (peanuts, no less), lower employee wages, and smaller planes (little 737s). What did Southwest Airlines think it could possibly do to succeed, competing against the "experts"? What did that lawyer know that everyone else in the airline industry didn't? "You can't make money doing it that way" the industry experts and insiders scoffed.

Well, along comes September 11, 2001, and all the big airlines start screaming for government aid. Except one. That little itty-bitty airline that for sure was going to fail kicked the big boys' asses! And what did all these big airlines start to do? Copy Southwest. Well, how do you like that? The experts were wrong again? What a shocking development.

But do you know what? A lot of them are going to *fail anyway*. Why? Because they don't *philosophically believe* in the Southwest business model—they are merely trying to copy it. They aren't true Contrarians. All they see on the *surface* is lower employee wages, a smaller first-class section, and peanuts.

That's what many people see—only the surface. This is what bean counters, overeducated MBAs, and arrogant executives (the "experts") often see. What they don't see is what's behind the numbers. They don't see the years and years of slowly developing the Southwest Airlines' industry counterculture. Employees were paid less but were also told up front that the reason for the lower pay is that the focus was on hiring good people who want to work in a good work environment, with other good people. Passenger loyalty was earned not only by on-time departures but by the feeling that they were a part of the Southwest "family" of employees, who both care about their passengers and have fun at work. Southwest used paper clips instead of staples *when times were good* because paper clips can be reused. Southwest is not a bunch of miserly penny-pinchers—just smart Contrarians looking for *good value!*

Frugality in good times didn't make Southwest shove it down everybody's throat in bad times. Southwest Airlines is a value-driven airline in everything it does, from hiring frugal people who like working in a positive team environment to making sure that the most important things— getting people to where they want to go on time and safely with their luggage—work right. They don't get distracted by the "industry crowd" that says they should use larger planes, pay more money to (theoretically) get the best employees, and fly empty airplanes around the country serving food nobody eats anyway.

One last piece of proof of how Southwest is a value investor: Try calling any airline, then call Southwest. Southwest doesn't have the automated answering system that everyone else (the masses of airline "experts") says you need to have to cut costs. They value their people and their people relationships.

You can't imitate that—the superficial stuff—and succeed. Not as a value investor, either. You have to *believe* in this approach, like Southwest and M do. You have to believe, because when it's time to make a decision with this belief, you won't have time to copy someone else (like the airlines are doing with Southwest). You have to know in your heart and then take action. The only way to know is to believe in the philosophy of value investing.

There is a price to pay for everything. Sexy investments are fun to own but are rarely profitable. I like nice, boring, plodding investments. I bet on teams that put fans to sleep! I bet on teams that look like sure losers. I bet on teams that no crowd would ever unanimously agree to wager their money on. I bet mostly on *ugly* underdogs—and the result is, I get great odds most every time.

In the long haul, I win consistently, day in and day out, week in and week out. Not 100 percent, not 80 percent, not even 70 percent (although for short periods of time I catch fire and hit streaks of high winning percentages like that). But all you need to have to win money betting on sports is a small edge. Fifty-three percent makes you money. Fifty-five percent makes you very successful. Fifty-eight percent makes you *wealthy*. Hit 58 percent consistently day in and day out and you will die a very wealthy and happy man or woman!

Only Contrarian sports bettors, otherwise known as value investors, can achieve that edge on the bookmaker. The funny thing is, as I'm walking into my bank, quietly and confidently carrying my substantial winnings (remember, as the bettor always on the "wrong" side, I always get great odds), the crowds of cattle are always walking out shaking their heads, ash-white, sad, lost, disheveled, wondering what hit them, with that look of a deer caught in the headlights of an oncoming car! They have just made a substantial withdrawal. Life has not been kind to them. They are *not* in control, and they know it. But these masses can be thankful for at least one thing: Following the advice of friends and "experts" means they'll never have to cry alone. There will always be plenty of other losers to cry with.

EIGHT

■

MY PERSONAL STORY

The World's Greatest Riverboat Gambler

Following the masses, the experts, and the critics is the downfall of people who take risk foolishly. This is one end of the spectrum when it comes to failing to improve your lifestyle. At the other end of the spectrum is the fear of risk and failure—the total fear of taking chances to better your life. This chapter is the true story of my journey from S.O.B. (son of a butcher) to world-class gambler, risk-taker, and entrepreneur.

I believe that becoming comfortable with and successful at risk can and will transform your life, just as it has mine. This book is not just about showing you how to win at gambling. It's truly about transforming you into a successful and fearless risk-taker. Because whether the topic is gambling or investing on Wall Street, building a career or opening a new business, growing a family or looking for a personal relationship, the odds are always long. They are always against you. Only a courageous and fearless risk-taker and Contrarian can succeed. This is my story. I hope it educates and inspires you.

We all start out as gamblers. We crawl, and then we take a risk to stand up, knowing we might fall. Then the obvious happens. We fall. Do we quit? No. So why do we quit taking necessary risks when we become adults? Because, ironically, we're afraid to fall. Yet if we had that same mind-set as children, we'd have never learned to walk in the first place! So, if the definition of "growing up" was gambling to take our first steps (the odds being very high that we would fall), what are we doing now if we aren't willing to take risks to improve our lives? Stagnating? Dying?

I've often thought about what I have attained and what my dad *could have attained*. I realize that from my dad's perspective this is why people come to Las Vegas to gamble—it is their way of doing something they can't do in the current trap of a life they have created for themselves. They're butchers (or bakers, or middle managers), and they hate it. So they work hard, save their money, and then go throw it away on a slot machine, or at the blackjack tables in Las Vegas. Gambling is their release. Their time to let loose and finally risk. Then, ironically, they learn the wrong lesson: They get on a plane and go back home to the butcher shop.

They gambled with no knowledge, no smarts, no experience, no money-management skills, and no game plan. They never expected to win. They arrived at the casino with "money I can afford to blow." Then they made every amateur mistake in the book, lost it all quickly, laughed about it, and decided gambling is not winnable. "It's only for fun." Then they get back on the airplane and go home to their boring, unhappy, risk-free lives; more certain than ever that risk is bad and they were right in their decision to settle instead of taking chances and risking failure and the possibility of feeling pain. A true cycle of misery and idiocy! Bad psychology, bad decisions, bad conclusions from start to finish.

That's the connection the average person doesn't understand. *You have to risk failure on the front end in order to succeed on the back end.* It's the difference between living a fulfilled life or just sitting around waiting to die. Do you know how much I've risked and failed in order to succeed? I'm just talking about my own personal and business life, not the 50,000 sports predictions and the 20,000 losses I've experienced in my career as a professional sports handicapper! Before I ever became a professional handicapper, before I even turned twenty-five, I had failed more than a dozen times trying my hand at a legal career, politics, real estate, restaurants, nightclubs, health/fitness training, a cleaning business, and a dating service. I was in debt and living at home with my parents, but I knew I didn't want to be a butcher (or anything else that didn't define me). I *had* to keep risking until I found something that worked, something that made me feel alive!

It was at this juncture that a positive change in direction occurred. I had dinner with a friend and mentor, Douglas Miller, a distinguished corporate CEO. Older, wiser, and experienced at the ways of business and life, Doug took pity on me. He asked me a series of crucial questions: What did I want out of life? What were my specific goals? How would I get there? What was my game plan? Did I even have a game plan? It was out of this discussion at a small Chinese restaurant in Manhattan that my dream began to take shape.

Doug believed that success was tied to a three-step process. Step one was simple: Establish your goals. We both agreed that my new goal was clear: to become the Jimmy "the Greek" of my generation. Jimmy "the Greek" Snyder was America's most famous football prognosticator. (He starred on NFL pre-game shows on CBS.) I knew that I loved sports—specifically football. I knew that I loved to gamble on sports. I loved talking about sports and gambling. I wanted to do it on television. I was a natural born communicator and I had a knack for predicting the winners of major sporting events. I decided that day that I would combine my talents into a lucrative and glamorous career talking sports gambling on TV. Besides, I figured "the Greek" was old and would retire soon. It was time for a new Jimmy the Greek for my generation. I decided that I was it! This goal also fit my personality. For once I was doing something that I loved, and I had a plan. That's a powerful combination!

Step two was facing the formidable obstacles that stood in my way. I was broke and had no connections, experience, or education in my field. I'd never taken a single broadcast journalism class in my life. I'd never spent five minutes in front of a television camera. And as far as connections, my father was a butcher. So if I wanted a nice piece of corned beef or bologna, I was hitting on all cylinders. As far as knowing news directors or producers at major television networks, I was starting from ground zero.

That brought Doug and I to step three: designing a game plan to overcome the seemingly insurmountable obstacles I faced. Put the odds in our favor. Our plan: Attack, attack, and attack some more! I had no idea how much rejection and failure I was about to experience. I could have never imagined that everything I had done to this point would seem easy compared to what lay ahead. It's lucky that I didn't comprehend the difficulty of the journey I was about to begin, because if I did, I probably would never have even tried!

I started by printing up a fancy brochure describing my talents and credentials as the Jimmy the Greek of my generation. I then sent out five hundred of these brochures to radio, TV, and print media outlets touting Wayne Allyn Root as the "greatest sports prognosticator in the world." Doug and I both believed that attracting the attention of the press and building name recognition would be my best plan of attack. Five hundred brochures and press releases out, and not one single bite—only five hundred rejections. (One TV producer actually did call—just to inform us that we'd spelled Jimmy "the Greek" Snyder's name incorrectly. Great start.)

So I sent out five hundred more. This time I tried follow-up phone calls. I received 499 rejections but one bite. One small local paper in Westchester County ran a story on my budding career. They called me the new Jimmy the Greek, and they even called Jimmy to ask him what he thought of my chances to succeed. Jimmy said, and I quote: "Tell this Root guy that in every town, village, and city in America, there are five hundred guys lined up to become the Greek. Get in line!"

Back to the salt mines. Photocopy the article (hey, it was the first time I could point to *someone else* saying something nice about my career instead of me). Type a new press release. Lick and seal. Send out five hundred copies again. No response, five hundred rejections. Try sending out five hundred more. Four hundred and ninety-nine rejections, but once again, one bite. This time I hooked a whale—the New York *Daily News*—at the time (1986) the largest urban newspaper in America. The *Daily News* ran a full page story in the sports section on "Wayne Root: The Sports Prognosticator of the Miami Vice Generation."

It was the first big break I needed. I was determined not to let it slip away, so I begged, pleaded, and cajoled fifty of my nearest and dearest friends and relatives to write laudatory letters to the *Daily News* sports editor about Wayne Root. And of course, I coached them a bit. "What a story. We want to see more of Wayne Root," was how most of the letters started.

Within two weeks, the phone rang. It was a *Daily News* reporter, Filip Bondy, asking for another interview. "My editor has never received so many letters about a story before. So we'd like to do a follow-up story." Once again, as soon as the article was printed I went to work—fifty more letters from friends and family were sent to the editor demanding to see Wayne Root on a regular basis. Two weeks later the phone rang again. This time it was the *Daily News* sports editor, Vic Ziegel, offering me my own column!

Now, the description "column" would be a great exaggeration in my opinion. It was really a box, about three inches wide and four inches long. It simply contained my NFL predictions each Sunday. My pay: a whopping $50 per week. I remember Doug Miller negotiating *hard* for that $50. I believe Ziegel was offering $40 per week. We won! Hey, it wasn't much, but it was a start. It may have been only a box, but it was *my* box and it had a byline with my name on it. Over a million new Yorkers could read it. That tiny box changed my life!

Back to the copy machines. I made hundreds of copies of my first column, along with a press release announcing that "Wayne Root, the world's greatest sports prognosticator, is hired by America's largest newspaper." Once again, I faced hundreds of rejections, but one "yes." Are you starting to see a pattern here? No risk, no success. Hundreds of rejections and failures are meaningless. But one yes can change your life. The key to the life of your dreams is taking the risks necessary to find that one yes! This time the one yes was NBC radio in New York. I was offered the job of predicting NFL winners on the popular *Joey Reynolds Show* each Friday afternoon.

The pay was even worse than the *Daily News: nothing!* But the show offered me more exposure, more credibility, and, of course, the opportunity for more press releases! Once again, I was busy writing up and sending out releases with the following headline "NY *Daily News* Prognosticator Root Joins NBC Radio." For a guy earning a grand total of $50 per week, I sure *sounded* impressive!

It seems ridiculous to even look back at the situation nowadays, but I was a married man living in a small room in my parents' house, living on $50 a week . . . and a dream. I was building mountains of debt to publicize my career, but I had high hopes, lots of energy, and tons of unbridled enthusiasm. I was in constant motion and things were happening. It was the most exciting time of my life. I don't think I've ever had more fun!

My NBC press release paid off. Within a few weeks NBC radio in Chicago came calling. Would I be willing to talk about my football picks on *The Jonathon Brandmeier Show*—the number-one morning show in Chicago? This was not a tough decision.

The pay was par for the course: zero. But you couldn't beat the exposure! I knew I had another stepping stone in my journey—and another press release headline! At this point, I've now got over a million listeners in New York, over a million in Chicago, and over a million New York readers. I'm a miniconglomerate, yet my combined income is still $50 per week! My debts are escalating, but so is my career!

I was only on NBC Chicago for a few short weeks when opportunity came knocking—*loudly*. Radio host Jonathon Brandmeier asked me to predict the outcome of a big ABC Monday Night Football game between his hometown Chicago Bears and the San Francisco 49ers. When I predicted a 49ers rout, Brandmeier came to the defense of his hometown heroes, suggesting that I was being rather foolish and shortsighted "biting the hand that feeds me." He went on to suggest that the entire city of Chicago would publicly humiliate me if I was wrong.

I immediately sensed an opportunity to turn this disagreement into a big opportunity. I responded, "I'll take a chance on a public humiliation, if you will too. Do I smell a bet?" Brandmeier took the bait. He suggested—unrehearsed, live on the air—that we devise a unique punishment for the loser of this bet. With a large portion of the city of Chicago listening, he decided that if I was wrong about his beloved Bears on Monday Night, I'd have to fly to Chicago to cohost his show in my underwear, outdoors, in the midst of a freezing Chicago December morning, in front of a crowd of hundreds of his screaming, taunting Chicago listeners. Now that's public humiliation. But to me, it was also more publicity, more headlines, and most importantly, a "can't lose bet" that couldn't help but supercharge my career. Besides, when you're living on $50 a week, you've got to take a few chances!

Without missing a beat, I accepted and asked him if he'd be willing to do the same. He agreed that if he lost, he'd fly to New York to host his show in his underwear, outdoors, on a nasty New York December morning, in front of world-famous Rockefeller Plaza. And he agreed that I'd be right by his side, cohosting the festivities. The bet was agreed to, live on the air. The team I predicted to rout the Chicago Bears—the 49ers—won by one of the most lopsided scores in Monday Night Football history: 41-0.

Brandmeier flew to New York to host his radio show live from Rocke-feller Plaza. True to his word, he stripped down to only his polka-dot boxer shorts and appeared outside in ten-degree weather, with me by his side. He figured he'd have a little fun, amuse his listeners back home, and gain a few headlines for himself in Chicago. What he hadn't counted on was my turning his appearance into a major media event.

I sensed an opportunity to take my career to a new level, and I wasn't about to let this opportunity slide away. I emptied my bank account of my entire life savings—a grand total of $2,000—and hired a major New York public relations firm to publicize the event. When Johnny B. stepped outside Rockefeller Plaza in his boxers, he was met by dozens of news organizations from around the country—UPI, AP, Entertainment Tonight, all the TV tabloids, newspaper photographers, television cam-eramen, and reporters from virtually every TV news channel in New York.

I had created an event! And since it was my PR firm that was direct-ing the event, I was the star! Headlines that night on every New York newscast sounded like this: "Chicago's biggest radio host hit town today, stripped of his pride and his clothing by famous New York sports prog-nosticator, Wayne Root!" One newscaster reported, "It's easy to tell which one is Mr. Root and which one is Mr. Brandmeier. Root is the sharp-dressed New Yorker, smiling, and looking like a winner. Brand-meier's the guy standing in the freezing cold without his clothes on!"

Overnight, I had made a name for myself! I was identified as a "win-ner" and a "famous New Yorker." Only hours before I was a broke no-body, living in my parents' house, working for $50 per week!

Within days my phone rang. It was an executive at the NBC Source Radio Network—a group of over 125 NBC radio stations appealing to young adult listeners. A group of NBC radio executives had been in the audience outside Rockefeller Plaza and watched me ham it up in front of the cameras with Johnny B. One of these executives was Stephen Soule, president of NBC Source Radio. Soule liked what he saw and offered me a job as a sports talk show host on their 125 NBC radio stations! I was offered a fat salary—not to mention a limousine to and from the radio station. My life had just changed forever! But the odds were still against me. My days of risking and failing were not over by a long shot.

For several months I was limoed to and from my NBC radio job. In between I was whisked around the country to make publicity appearances at various NBC radio stations. I was given the star treatment wherever I went. My parents and my wife were incredulous.

Unfortunately, my bubble was about to burst. NBC unexpectedly announced the signing of America's Top 40 radio superstar Casey Kasem to a multimillion-dollar contract. My producer hastily explained to me that those millions had to be cut elsewhere. They had decided to cut my entire department. That meant I was terminated only three months after I had started! Easy come, easy go.

I had gone from the outhouse to the penthouse and back to the outhouse again, all in a few months. But all wasn't lost. I've always had a unique ability to look at the bright side of things. Even though my job was axed, I still had a contract with NBC. That meant they'd have to keep paying me. And that constant source of income meant lots of money to promote my career. I wasn't through—I was just getting started!

I knew television was where I wanted to be, so I took my NBC radio income and produced a TV highlight tape at a professional studio. I then acquired a list of every local television station and national cable network in America and began sending out tapes via Federal Express. I thought executive producers and news directors would stop and take notice of a FedEx package, that it would stand out from the crowd of packages and papers on their desks.

Unfortunately the only things that stood out were my bills for overnight shipping, copies, stationery, business cards, videos, messengers, and follow-up phone calls to all corners of the country. I was eating up my entire NBC salary and then some! My debts were growing faster than my career—much faster!

All that money I was spending wasn't even paying off. The responses I got were more than just negative—they were downright humiliating. Mostly I heard deafening silence. Very few producers or news directors would even come to the phone. The few that did either said, "Don't call us; if we're interested, we'll call you," or "I've seen your resume and you didn't even graduate from broadcast journalism school. You have no chance in this business. Stop wasting your time," or "I watched your highlight tape. It was amateurish and unprofessional. Why don't you quit before you humiliate yourself further?"

It was at this time that I decided I needed a good agent. I was getting nowhere representing myself. Unfortunately my search for an agent met with more rejection. I was rejected by every agent in the sports, news, and entertainment business—no decent professional would even consider representing someone as raw and inexperienced as I was.

My only choice was to pose as my own agent. With his permission, I began using Doug Miller's name. The humiliations continued unabated. Out of the hundreds of rejections I received over the next few months, one stood out above all the others; I still remember it like it was yesterday: An ABC Television producer actually called upon receiving my tape. He said: "Your client Wayne Root is a joke. This man has no talent of any kind. You should be embarrassed sending out such garbage as his highlight tape. Hell will freeze over before this guy ever gets a job as a television sportscaster!" He didn't know it of course, but he was talking to me. Ouch!

Looking back, this was the low point of my long journey. It was also one of many occasions when I came close to deciding to give up my dream. At this point, the odds looked more than long—they looked downright impossible.

However, each time I considered giving up, some little victory materialized that kept me going. My tapes weren't exactly lighting up the television world, but those same promotional and video materials were attracting interest from investors. I was offered an opportunity to start a business where I'd provide my sports predictions to bettors for a fee.

I raised $150,000 and started a sports handicapping business called Pure Profit. My goals were simple: stay active, stay visible, keep fighting, keep moving forward. Hopefully the exposure would lead to the TV career I coveted. Unfortunately, Pure Profit was pure debt. The business closed. Add just one more failure to the long list.

At this point, my long series of failures was beginning to take its toll. I didn't have a dime in the bank, and my personal debts were approaching $150,000. That was a lot of money in 1988—especially when my weekly income was $50. It was soon after this last disaster that I was forced to declare personal bankruptcy. Within months my first marriage was over as well. My wife announced she was leaving me for another man. Ouch again!

I wasn't just failing—I was finding new and innovative ways to fail. And the failures seemed to be getting bigger, more expensive, and more depressing. But a *thriver* doesn't give up or hide under the covers. I trudged forward. I risked some more. Risk creates opportunity. Or so I hoped. And prayed!

Just as I hit rock bottom, I was saved again. My business may have been out of luck, my television career going nowhere, my marriage in shambles, and my bank accounts busted, but my nonstop promotions and press releases were paying off. Bantam Books, one of America's largest and most prestigious publishers, agreed to publish my first book, *Root on Risk: Betting to Win on Sports*. It was a small and short-lived morale boost. The book was a flop. Add one more failure to the long list.

But being a published author opened up another door for me. *Robb Report* magazine named me contributing sports editor. The *Robb* is like a toy store for the world's wealthiest men and women—the average reader earns almost a million dollars per year. My name was positioned in front of the movers and shakers of the business world. I was able to interview many of the biggest names in sports—Mark Spitz, Bruce Jenner, Mario Andretti, Lyle Alzado, Steve Garvey, Dallas Cowboys' owner Jerry Jones—and the commissioners of the NBA, NFL, and PGA. Despite setback after setback, I was making a name for myself, gaining credibility, and most importantly, staying in the game. I was literally risking and failing my way to the top!

I was also attracting the attention of some major television networks. First I was called by Bill MacPhail, the legendary boss of CNN Sports. He had an opening for a sportscaster at CNN and I was on his short list. I immediately flew to Atlanta to audition for the job. I didn't get it, but it was an honor to be considered. It gave me a boost of confidence and convinced me that my goal was finally within reach.

Within days of my return from Atlanta, FOX Television executive Michael Binkow called and invited me to fly to Los Angeles to interview for the host position of a new national television sports show. The show was aimed at a young, hip, urban audience, and Binkow made it clear that I fit the bill perfectly. I was so excited and sure this was the break I'd been waiting for, I even paid for my friend and mentor Doug Miller to fly to Los Angeles with me, to act as my agent.

Once I got to Los Angeles, it became clear that this was just another false alarm. The show was merely at the "exploration stage." I would soon learn that in Hollywood that's television talk for "pipe dream." I had flown across the country for nothing. More money wasted—money that I didn't have. Yet I remained undaunted. Instead of getting discouraged, I grew more determined. Here I was with my "agent" in Los Angeles—all dressed up with no place to go.

The trip was already paid for, and I wasn't about to fly home with my tail between my legs. I decided to start "dialing for dollars." I began dialing every television station in Los Angeles. I vowed to turn a wasted cross-country trip and the biggest disappointment of my young career into the biggest break of my life—and I did!

Doug and I sat in our hotel room for two full days waiting for the phone to ring. It never did. At one point even Doug, the eternal optimist, suggested giving up and heading back home. His exact words were (we still laugh about this conversation to this day): "Wayne, it's one thing to be a positive thinker. It's another to be a glutton for punishment. You've got to know when to give up. You're humiliating yourself. Please stop. I can't stand seeing you put yourself through so much pain."

Instead of listening to reason, Doug's words inspired and angered me. I was an underdog with a chip on my shoulder. I made another few dozen calls. Just like the old days, I experienced 99 percent rejection— but one bite. After over a year of effort and more than a dozen calls (all unanswered) to Arnie Rosenthal, general manager of Financial News Network (FNN) Sports, I decided I had nothing to lose by taking one more shot—to place that thirteenth bet after twelve consecutive losses. Thank God that I'm a gambler. Lucky number thirteen changed my life forever.

I was shocked when *Rosenthal himself* actually got on the phone. "Where are you?" he asked. When I told him I was in Los Angeles, his response was like music to my ears. "Wow, what great timing. Our number-one anchorman, Todd Donoho, just announced this morning that he's leaving for ABC. How soon can you be here?"

Doug and I probably set the cross-town speed record that day! Within an hour I found myself sitting in the executive offices of FNN, negotiating a deal that would put me on national television in front of over 33 million viewers. We shook hands that day.

The official deal was negotiated by Doug over the next month. I flew home to New York, told my family that I'd been hired by Financial News Network as an anchorman and TV host, packed my bags, got into my car, and drove cross-country to Los Angeles to start my new life.

I'll never forget it. I arrived in L.A. on a Wednesday; on Thursday I was walking into my new office in the FNN newsroom; by Friday I was standing on the field at Dodger Stadium interviewing Tommy Lasorda!

Broke and living in a bedroom in my parents' house one day . . . a few days later living in a Hollywood Hills home overlooking the twinkling lights of Los Angeles and hanging out with superstar ballplayers and Tommy Lasorda. Pinch me—this was surreal.

But wait, it gets better. About a week later I was called into my general manager's office. When I walked in, Arnie Rosenthal said, "Wayne Root, meet your new cohost, Jimmy 'the Greek' Snyder." Talk about full circle! I had started all those many years and risks and rejections ago with a dream to become the new Jimmy the Greek. Here I was standing next to the legend himself, talking about the plans for our new TV show.

A couple of weeks later Arnie called me into his office again. He told me that I would spend the month of July flying across America to every NFL training camp, to interview the biggest stars of the NFL. When I returned, I'd start hosting my new NFL pre-game show with Jimmy the Greek. The kid that loved football and gambling was now going to get paid to interview NFL stars, talk football, and talk gambling, all on national TV!

Was all that risk and rejection worth it? You're darn right it was! What is it that the fitness fanatics say? "Without pain, there is no gain." Well I had experienced lots of pain, rejection, failure, even humiliation ("Hell will freeze over before Wayne Root lands on TV") and bankruptcy. But now I was living "the gain." I was living the American Dream, exactly as I had imagined it. The S.O.B. (son of a butcher) was a TV star, and talking about NFL football and sports gambling was my life. I had finally made it big-time.

All those critics were *wrong*. All the people who believed my dream was a joke had been proven wrong. I had risked and failed thousands of times. But I had found the one *yes* that changed my life. It had been quite a ride. And quite a payoff at the end.

Except for one small detail. I wasn't at the end. This was just the beginning. After two years of hosting and anchoring as well as picking NFL point-spread winners as FNN network oddsmaker and prognosticator (in my first year on TV I hit a respectable 59 percent winners; in my second year I hit a blazing 67 percent winners; both years combined I won a spectacular 77 percent of my best bets), I decided to take the biggest gamble of my life. Yes, bigger than all the others combined! I decided to quit FNN to become a full time professional sports handicapper. How big was the risk?

I had gone from bankrupt and living in my parents' home to popular national TV host. And now I was risking everything I had just achieved on a new gamble, a new dream. Anchorman and host had never been my dream. Nor was collecting a weekly paycheck. I'm a gambler—a Riverboat Gambler. Always have been, always will be.

To me the "brass ring" was to earn my living as the most famous professional handicapper and gambler in America. Turning my gambling advice into a business. *Big* business. So I left FNN to join a football handicapping show called *Proline* on the USA TV network. Even riskier, I went from an anchorman's salary to no salary. I'd work for only a commission—on the revenues earned by my handicapping advice.

And what did the critics (and my friends and family) say this time around? Any encouragement? Anything positive? I heard: "Are you out of your mind? You're leaving a job as a famous TV host and anchor to become a professional gambler?" "You're leaving Financial News Network for a gambling infomercial?" "You're self-destructive. You must want to ruin your career." "You're leaving a fat weekly paycheck and the security of a big TV network for a commission with no guarantee? You've gone nuts." "You're a reckless gambler."

The critics are always out there, looking to make you doubt yourself; looking to discourage you, depress you, destroy your confidence, ruin your plans. My best attribute is I never listen. I just keep moving forward, making things happen, taking chances to improve my life. And it worked again!

When I left FNN to sell my football handicapping advice on TV for a fee (on a 900 number), few had ever heard of the fledgling 900 business. Those that had heard of it didn't think much of it. It sure was "risky." It certainly didn't compare to the status of being an anchorman—or so my fellow anchormen thought (along with everyone else).

That was, however, before I became a self-made millionaire by selling my handicapping picks to sports gamblers on TV. That was before I attracted about *one million* television callers paying $25, $50, and $100 per call for my advice. That was before I bought my first home on the beach in Malibu. Once again, I had risked and won big. Once again, I had proven my critics, naysayers, and detractors dead wrong.

But once again, this was a beginning rather than an end. The money was great for the next decade, but after ten years of success and more calls from American sports gamblers than any TV handicapper ever, I decided to risk again.

I left *Proline*, the company that turned me into a professional sports handicapper. I left behind a life that no normal person could imagine ever leaving (just like I had at FNN). I walked away from a huge guaranteed revenue stream (I had become so successful that I was given a big fat annual guarantee); and financial security (the Las Vegas company that I worked for was the leader in the handicapping industry and had been in business for over twenty years). With my record-breaking success, the job was mine for life.

But more than the money, I was leaving behind one heck of a lifestyle. My job was to fly first-class to Las Vegas, get picked up at the airport by limo, driven to a luxury suite at a four-star hotel, star on my TV show, and then fly first-class back to my Malibu beachfront home to get paid to pick football winners sitting poolside in the sunshine. Then sit back all weekend to watch football. And all this while bringing in a guaranteed annual income bigger than normal people make in a decade. How many sane people in the world would risk everything to *leave* that life?

I gave it all up—with a new child on the way and a huge mortgage in Malibu (that beachfront lifestyle comes with a big price tag). But the Contrarian gambler had a gut instinct again. No matter how much money I was guaranteed or how great my lifestyle, I hated working for others. It was time to start my own business. It was the biggest risk of my life—*again*. From this point on, nothing would be guaranteed. I had no idea how I'd finance my new business—it would require around $10 million. I was scared. But I knew I had to take another risk—to start my own handicapping company. I was willing to risk everything to be my own boss. New dream, new risk. No pain, no gain. Another word for gambler: "entrepreneur."

I wanted it all. I'd aimed for Jimmy the Greek and made my dream come true. I'd aimed for national TV and made my dream come true. I'd aimed to turn my football prediction skills into big money and I'd succeeded. My new dream was to build my own personal mini-empire, to leave all my financial security behind to create a TV show from ground zero, to start a business from ground zero, become CEO instead of handicapper, take the company public on Wall Street, and turn it into an industry leader. Lofty goals.

Instead of a huge guaranteed income, I walked away for nothing guaranteed but debt. No guarantees, plus the risk of losing everything I had in this world. I invested my own money, put my home on the line as a financial guarantee. My partner in the venture would be Doug Miller, my mentor and lifelong friend. He warned me that business start-ups are hell. That we'd work 24/7, 365 days a year. That there would be lots of days when I'd curse my decision. But I'd be the boss. Sounded good to me.

There was the problem, however, of those pesky critics again (the knives are always out, no matter what your status in life). My old employers had some interesting parting gifts: "You'll *never* make it without us." "You'll *never* make it without our money." "You'll *never* make it without our TV show." "What we built took us twenty-five years. You can't replicate this in *fifty!* You've got no chance."

The TV experts said, "You'll never get a handicapping show on TV. Other than *Proline*, there are no handicapping shows on TV for a reason—networks will not accept them." The financial experts said, "You'll never raise the money necessary to build this niche business from ground zero." I wanted to take my company public. Nobody believed I could do it. The Wall Street experts all said, "Are you joking? Sports handicapping, public? It will *never* happen!"

All these cynics, critics, and naysayers were negative even *before* the Internet Revolution imploded and the stock market crashed in April of 2000. I needed to raise as much as $10 million, and the stock market was in the middle of its worst slump since 1929, venture capital had dried up, investors were nowhere to be found, and the economy was plunging into a recession. I had burned my bridges with my old employer. I could not go back. I was in the middle of a never-ending nightmare. So what happened? How did the Houdini of risk turn out?

- The experts said I'd never raise the money. They were right in one sense—I was looking for $6 to $10 million, but since the inception of GWIN, Inc., I've raised almost $20 million.
- The experts said I'd never get a football handicapping show on a national TV network. They were right again. I got my show on three networks! First PAX, then FOX Sports Net, and now Spike TV, the first TV network for men. Not only did the TV experts predict that a gambling-oriented show would not get on TV, they were *positive* it could never get on a network that broadcast NFL games. With our launch on FOX Sports Net, the experts were proven wrong again. Now with the debut of *Wayne Allyn Root's WinningEDGE* on Spike TV, we are reaching a total of 87 million viewers. Our show is broadcast into literally every cable home in America!

- The experts said I'd never be able to create a high-quality handicapping show—one that looked like a network pre-game football show more than a gambling show. I can see why they doubted me. I had starred on TV all those years, but only as a handicapper. But I'd never created a show from scratch, nor executive produced one. They were wrong again. In our first year we hired Bob Levy, the director of the FOX Sports NFL pre-game show (starring Terry Bradshaw and Howie Long) to direct our show. We designed a state-of-the-art set. We were able to sign NFL Hall of Famers John Riggins, Randy White, and Dan Hampton, along with NY Giant Phil McConkey. Over the last couple of years we've added two-time AFC coach-of-the-year Ron Meyers and Sporting News Radio host and Emmy Award winner Chet Coppock. I can now state with pride that *Wayne Allyn Root's WinningEDGE* is the most highly rated handicapping show ever on American television.
- The experts said we'd never be able to take our company public on Wall Street. They were *really* certain of this one. Today, we are America's only publicly traded sports-handicapping firm.
- The experts said sports handicapping had nothing in common with Wall Street. I created a company modeled almost identically after a Wall Street brokerage firm. Our TV show is similar to *Wall Street Week*, with experts discussing and debating their favorite "investments." The stars of my show are positioned just like the analysts at major mutual funds or hedge funds. Our clients call to speak to our sports-brokers (identical to stockbrokers). Our brokers sit in state-of-the-art offices complete with the latest computer and telemarketing equipment—offices that look just like a Merrill Lynch brokerage office. I was profiled in *Fortune*—the magazine of American business. I have become a regular guest on CNBC—the financial authority on American television. I'd say we have definitely changed the image of sports gambling!
- My last goal is about to be achieved as well. I said from day one that we'd expand globally to cover international gambling sports like soc-

cer, cricket, rugby and formula one. I just returned from London. We are making plans to expand to Europe soon. If Merrill Lynch can be global, then so can GWIN, Inc.

So how did I do it? How did I beat the odds? How did I do what so many experts said could not be done? And the really important question—how can *you* do the same? Can my success be emulated?

1. First, I was a Contrarian. I went against the crowd and ignored the experts.
2. Second, I was willing to take risks to achieve my goals. Again and again, I walked away from what most everyone would call financial security (a "sure" thing). Again and again, I was willing to invest my own money and put my assets at risk.
3. Third, I did *not* take crazy risks, but rather calculated risks. High-percentage plays—just like my gambling picks. I put the odds in my favor: My old boss may have had twenty-five years' experience in the business, but I saw dozens of things I could do to improve the way he ran his business and his TV show, and then I applied them to my own business. I did my homework. That puts the odds in your favor.
4. Fourth, I am a Zen Gambler. I sustained my efforts despite the fact that literally everyone and everything was against me. I made positive healthy choices in reacting to stress and challenge (more on that in later chapters). Those choices often determine whether you will succeed or fail in the face of long odds. No matter how smart or talented you are.

The average person risks a business venture once, fails, quits, and goes back to being a butcher. They settle. They make the same mistake with relationships. Meet somebody nice, it doesn't work out, then they quit dating for the next two years (or forever). Or they take up golf big-time, join the country club, buy the best clubs, get private lessons from the top instructor, and then go out and lose a dozen balls on their first round or two, then decide never to play again. They want to buy their way into Tiger Woods's level of play.

What they don't understand is that Tiger works at it every day, all day, and actually even he hasn't won too many tournaments lately (as I write this book, Tiger is in the biggest slump of his career). But he still gets up every day and hits a thousand practice balls. He still works with his personal swing coach every day. He still studies film of his mistakes, to analyze what went wrong and how to correct it. He still plans out in his mind how he'll play every hole in that day's tournament. He has a game plan—one honed by a lifetime of experience and success.

Many people won't take the risks. Many others take the risks, but without a game plan, or practice, or the psychology to back it up. When they fail, they have nothing to fall back on and therefore they quit. They give up too soon, because they don't have the tools, experience, or understanding to deal with rejection or failure.

As you can tell by now, risking and failing has never deterred me. Every time I lose a bet, I sit down and analyze what I did wrong. I figure out how to do it right the next time. Sometimes I analyze a wager and figure out that a freak circumstance happened and all my pre-bet analysis was right but unique circumstances beat me.

Many people don't look at a bet this way; they just look at the result. They never check to see if the analysis of the result has any connection whatsoever to the reasoning behind the bet. They think their lesson is to "not do that again." Wrong! Then they pick the opposite of their good logic the next time and lose again! So now they come to the wrong conclusion again—they make a really dumb decision and quit altogether. They storm off and say, "I'm a loser. I quit." Or, "The odds are stacked against you in gambling. There's no point in wasting my money." Or, "I will no longer risk humiliating myself. Gambling is not for me. I'm going to settle rather than experience rejection, failure, and pain."

Yes, I am unique. I am a successful professional sports handicapper and gambler. And I am a successful entrepreneur. This chapter points out that these disparate successes are no coincidence—they are synergistic. Success at gambling and risking, combined with seeing the world from the eyes of a Contrarian, have allowed me to succeed in both the business and television worlds. Apply my philosophy and strategy to your personal and business lives, and you too can morph from survivor into a daring, risk-taking *thriver.* A Riverboat Gambler extraordinaire.

NINE

■

ROOT'S RULES
FOR SUCCESS

Remember, I'm an S.O.B.—the son of a butcher. I started with nothing. It has taken me twenty long, tedious, tenacious, roller-coaster years to become an "overnight success," rising from obscurity in a dead-end, blue-collar town on the border of the Bronx, with no money, no connections, and no education in my field; to become a self-made millionaire, CEO of a public company, television celebrity, and the "King of Vegas."

It's been quite a journey, but I wouldn't change a thing. When I give speeches and seminars at corporations across America, I always end with my fifteen Rules for Success. The foundation of my success is certainly Contrarian thinking and calculated, high-percentage risk-taking. But there are so many important rules and principles that have led me to achieve my goals and overcome such astronomical odds. Here are a few of the key ones that have empowered me every step of the way:

RULE #1: RISK IS GOOD.

All entrepreneurs are *huge* risk-takers. Daring risk-takers. I call them Riverboat Gamblers. Without daring to risk big and even fail big, you can never succeed big! I wish I could say that I'm smarter than most ordinary people I meet, but I'm not. The only real difference I see between myself and all those poor souls that despise their jobs and lives is that I aimed much higher and wasn't afraid to take daring risks to get there.

When I study superachievers, most seem to succeed based on those same two principles. Aim high; do not settle for an ordinary life. And once you decide on that dream, go after it with such gusto, passion, and dynamic daring that you can't help but succeed.

RULE #2: HAVE CHUTZPAH.

Chutzpah refers to *balls*. Having the courage or guts to aim for the stars. The courage to take *daring* risks to reach your goals, and even the courage to fail. So many of the superachievers I've studied have failed many times before finally hitting it big. But they had *chutzpah;* they were always willing to take one more risk. They understood that one single solitary *yes* erases all the *no's,* and changes your life.

Chutzpah also means having the balls to think highly of yourself. Great superachievers are rarely humble. They are rarely wallflowers. They are usually super-confident self-promoters. They understand that if you don't believe in you, no one else will either. In my opinion, chutzpah is more important than brains and talent combined!

RULE #3: AIM FOR THE SKY.

My goals have always been aimed at the stars. I aim for *greatness*. If you aim for ordinary dreams, you'll be stuck your whole life in a mediocre job, with a mediocre marriage. This is the mistake most of us make—we aim too *low*. We *settle*. When you aim for the stars, if you miss, you can still land on the moon. But when you aim low and you miss, where do you land? *Newark?*

Ninety-nine percent of the world aims *far* too low. Their only goal is to survive, while superachievers aim to *thrive*. I've always been hungry and ambitious. Actually, hungry doesn't describe my attitude—I'm *starving!*

RULE #4: TAKE ACTION.

Don't think about it, don't talk about it, *do it!* Don't wait for the phone to ring, *make* it ring. My phone rings over one hundred times a day, I receive over two hundred e-mails a day. Why? Because I *make* one hundred calls a day and *send* over two hundred e-mails! If I did not aggressively *attack* all day every day, my phones would stop ringing.

There is no worse sound than silence! I hope my phones and e-mails keep coming until the day I die. Most people I meet who are not super successful, have spent their lives talking, but not taking action. Talking, complaining, making excuses—all those accomplish *nothing*. As Nike says, just do it! And you can't help but achieve and succeed.

RULE #5: BE TENACIOUS.

I have the resolve of a bulldog *combined* with that of a cornered wolverine. As Winston Churchill said to hold his country together in the face of sure defeat: "Never, never, never, never, never give in!" Nothing can stop me. No one can discourage me or slow me. Failure and rejection mean nothing. As a matter of fact, they are good. They motivate me. They educate me. I learn from each failure and rejection. Then I'm right back at 'em again. No one and nothing keeps Wayne Allyn Root down.

RULE #6: THINK CONTRARIAN.

You *knew* this one was coming, didn't you? Yes, the masses are asses. Stop following the crowd. Stop fearing being alone in your convictions. The crowd is poor, dumb, and dumber. They follow the masses like sheep to slaughter. Be glad you are different, unique, and willing to question authority. Those traits will lead you to the promised land. They will make you a *winner.*

The time to start worrying is if the things you are thinking or saying sound like everyone else. You can only find success on the road *less* traveled. Bet on teams no one else wants. Buy real estate or stocks that no one else wants. Ignore the critics, cynics, and know-it-alls. They are *always* wrong. All the great opportunities of life are missed because we let others talk us out of them.

RULE #7: EGO RULES.

Ego is good. It always amazes me when I hear people criticize ego. Funny, but I've never met a superachiever *without* ego. Show me a great real estate developer, I'll show you an ego the size of Texas! Show me a great stockbroker on Wall Street, I'll show you an ego the size of Manhattan! Show me a great actor in Hollywood, I'll show you an ego the size of California. Show me a successful politician, I'll show you an ego the size of the Capitol Building! Show me a great sports gambler, I'll show you an ego as bright as the lights of Las Vegas!

You've got to be an aggressive self-promoter, a P. T. Barnum for your career, business, or products. If you don't believe 180 percent in you, *no one else will.* Besides, as Mohammed Ali often said, "It ain't bragging if you can back it up!" Without confidence and sky-high self-esteem, you can accomplish nothing *great* in this world. The masses aim to just survive—to keep a job, to collect a paycheck—but superachievers expect to *thrive.* I repeat: *Ego is good.*

RULE #8: SCREW THE CRITICS.

They're always *wrong* anyway! That's precisely why you need *ego.* To be able to stay confident in the face of all your critics, cynics, naysayers, and jealous competitors.

RULE #9: LUCK IS THE RESIDUE OF DESIGN.

This rule is all about *discipline.* To me, discipline means being detail-oriented, goal-oriented, meticulous, *intense* like a laser-guided missile. I call that being a *list maniac.* Make lists of all your short-term and long-term goals, lists of what you want to accomplish today, this week, this month. Schedule your life to the minute, hour, day, week, month. Create detailed plans for how you will achieve your goals. Luck is the residue of design.

Funny how the people with lots of lists, and a detailed plan, and who *work* their plan by making two hundred phone calls a day, just happen to get "lucky." These discipline details are what *back up* a big ego. Find me someone who has a big ego but is undisciplined—I'll show you a windbag who talks a big game, but achieves nothing. But put ego together with action and discipline, and there's a winning combination that cannot be stopped.

RULE #10: THE BEST DEFENSE IS A GOOD OFFENSE.

Unlike gambling, where I taught you that defense rules, in the real world you need to be on the *constant* attack. You need to be hyper-aggressive 24/7. Aggressive to the 100th power! There is *nothing* I won't do to sell or promote or market me or my products. The word "defense" isn't in my vocabulary. Neither is the word "rest."

RULE #11: PASSION RULES.

Enthusiasm is *not* silly or corny or fake. People respond to energy and enthusiasm and *passion*. People who have these things are called "leaders." Leaders are not born, they are *made*. First find something you love to do. Then follow my "Positive Addictions" program (discussed in Chapter 10) to create the energy, creativity, and focus you need to give 180 percent!

You can *cultivate* passion—no drugs, alcohol, cigarettes, junk food. Your body is your temple. Instead, fill your body and life with meditation, yoga, prayer, organic food, exercise, vitamins. Now go after your dreams with such intensity that you either succeed or explode!

RULE #12: CREATE YOUR OWN RULES.

Too many people wait their whole lives for permission to succeed. In case you haven't figured it out yet, no one will *ever* give you permission to succeed. You have to *make* it happen yourself. You have to *take* it yourself. If you ask for permission, what you'll hear 98 percent of the time is *no*.

You'll never get that permission from the government. Government only gets in the way. Government will only give you enough help to *cripple* you for life, to make you a survivor (at best). Government doesn't create *thrivers*.

You'll never get permission from a boss. Successful entrepreneurs are their *own* bosses—they make their own rules, come to their own conclusions. They don't wait for permission or ask for consensus. They are Contrarians and world-class risk-takers. They never take *no* for an answer. They laugh at critics. They move on from failure or rejection without missing a beat. Trust me, in life it's *always* easier to ask for forgiveness than to ask for permission.

RULE #13: STAY POSITIVE.

Good things just seem to happen to positive people (at least those who *combine* optimism with tenacity and action). Stay positive your whole life. Stay positive about your own goals. Be appreciative of the blessings in your life. Be optimistic that you can and will overcome the challenges standing in your way. Be positive about you and your future.

No, I cannot guarantee that your life will be perfect—no one's ever is. But I do *guarantee* that you will achieve more success and happiness than people who are negative, cynical, critical, complaining, or jealous of the success of others.

RULE #14: ROLE MODELS.

Read voraciously the biographies of great superachievers. My personal favorites: Jesus Christ, Moses, Sir Winston Churchill, Ronald Reagan,

Bill Clinton, Abraham Lincoln, George Washington, Benjamin Franklin and all the founding fathers of the American Revolution, General Robert E. Lee, General George S. Patton, Nelson Mandela, Sir William Wallace (Braveheart), Oprah Winfrey, Joan of Arc, Golda Meir (former prime minister of Israel), Steve Wynn (the visionary who created modern Las Vegas and changed the image of gambling). These were great leaders who accomplished great things.

None of their achievements could have happened without incredible *chutzpah!* If you want to be inspired and motivated to think big dreams and achieve great things, constantly read the stories of superachievers like these.

RULE #15: FAITH, FAMILY, AND FREEDOM.

First of all, I thank God for all that I am, and all that I have achieved. I am a *spiritual* being. Without God I'd be nowhere. I give my goals, my ambitions, my worries, and all my many challenges to God. He takes the burden off my shoulders. Prayer is the foundation of my day, *every* day. It's having God by my side that gives me the confidence and optimism and chutzpah to succeed!

Second, I thank God for my family. They are the foundation of my life. If you study superachievers, virtually all of them base their lives around their spouses and children. My wife, Debra, and children Dakota, Hudson, and Remington are the reason I want to succeed, to *thrive.* They are the *root* of my ambition. Without them, I am *nothing.*

And finally, I come to freedom. I thank God for putting me in the greatest country in the world—the United States of America. A land of Contrarians and Riverboat Gamblers! A land of cockeyed optimists, with can-do spirit. A land of people who believe *nothing* is impossible. A land that gives its people *freedom* from government interference and artificial limits. Here, anything is possible. A land that quite naturally has always asked and *received* the blessings of God. From the days of the American Revolution to World War II to the Internet Revolution, America has always seemed blessed by God. My foundation for success as a professional gambler, handicapper, businessman, husband, father, and human being has always been and will always be a deep and abiding *faith* in God, family, and the amazing freedoms only found in America!

TEN

THE SPIRITUAL
GAMBLER

Cultivating Positive Addictions

A s a type-A personality, I have a lot of energy. It's this nonstop energy that helps propel me through the tough times, the times of constant rejection, humiliation, and barrages of negativity from the critics. It's this energy that gives me confidence, tenacity, creativity, and enthusiasm when the so-called "experts" tell me that something is impossible. And that same energy fuels me when I'm taking all those high-stress risks. But that energy alone hasn't gotten me to where I am today, nor will it alone get me to where I want to go tomorrow. My physical energy is how God made me (to some degree, although the program you'll read about in this chapter can increase energy levels for virtually anybody). God blessed me with a tool to use. The key is to use it wisely.

High energy can be an extreme negative if it is focused in the wrong direction. I must balance the stress and strain of my physical energy with spiritual well-being, the foundation of building a successful, well-balanced me. Also, I have to take the time to pause, to meditate and allow myself to channel my energy in the right direction with a clear mind. Meditation cleanses my mind of negative clutter and helps me to realize my positive potential. Finally, I cannot maintain my energy level without putting good fuel in my "physical engine" and making sure it is tuned up daily with good exercise.

This chapter is a look at my "system" for building confidence and defeating stress. Hey, if professional gamblers can utilize handicapping systems for picking winners, why not also utilize spiritual systems for creating a healthy, positive, balanced mind-body-spirit connection? If you can master this system I call "Positive Addictions," you can achieve phenomenal success at anything (gambling, business, career, and personal and professional life). The keys to my system are stress management, self-mastery, physical fitness, positive thinking, and personal development. In this chapter, I prove myself to be anything but a stereotypical gambler. I showcase my love of family, fitness, spirituality, healthy habits, and holistic living. A Zen Gambler—now that's truly Contrarian!

Most people think of the typical gambler as the stereotype you might see in Las Vegas: the overweight, chain-smoking, alcoholic, sixty-year-old macho guy with five gold chains around his neck and a tacky, gum-chewing, twenty-year-old stripper on his arm. You can see them walking around the casinos on a regular basis. And when these stereotypical gamblers lose, they drink more, smoke more, eat more junk foods, and practice loads of other negative, self-destructive habits. Their daily exercise consists of rolling their fat butt down to the buffet, gorging on too much fried and fatty food, then waddling over to the casino, strapping themselves into a chair to lose, lose, lose. Instead of yoga, their version of stretching is when they pull the lever of the slot machine.

To make matters worse (*much* worse), let's add a little stress into the equation—stress *not* brought on by losing at gambling. Stress from everyday life—work, family, or driving around town. Most people react to negative situations or fearful (stressful) situations by feeding that stressful feeling (or empty feeling, or depressed feeling) with negative habits—drinking, smoking, drugs, and other bad diet and lifestyle choices. So now this stressed-out person gets loaded on booze, cigarettes, drugs, and bad food, and only then does he or she head to the casino to start gambling. Good luck!

My Contrarian reaction is quite the opposite (what a surprise!). I practice *positive habits* to counteract the destructive effects of a stressful life. I think holistically and positively, start my day with a daily nature walk, pray, meditate, practice yoga, exercise, eat healthy foods, and add megavitamin supplementation, and these Positive Addictions help me think through tough situations (and think creatively and intuitively) to a positive conclusion.

The only way to overcome a losing slump as a professional gambler, handicapper, entrepreneur, or human being is to have real confidence to go out and take the next calculated, high-percentage risk (i.e., make the next bet, or make the next sales call, or ask out that next beautiful woman, or invest in that next exciting opportunity). How can I have confidence if I have confused my mind and slowed my body with too much booze, too many cigarettes, and too much poison junk food? I have no focus, no energy, no creativity, no confidence, no clarity, and per-haps most importantly, no tenacity, if I do numb myself with negative habits. A person with those kind of negative habits isn't a gambler—he's a *loser*. Imagine if the CEO of any major corporation reacted to stress this way. What do you think would happen to the performance of that company?

Type-As like myself typically don't live a *balanced* lifestyle. The same type-A attributes that lead to our high levels of intelligence, energy, and success often lead to many negative habits, which eventually slow or un-ravel our success. That's precisely why I figured out how to slow down a part of my day in order to maintain or even increase my high-energy pace the rest of the day. The whole purpose of my Positive Addictions program is to counteract the negative aspects of being an ultra-Type-A personality. For example, I meet a lot of type-A people who by financial standards are extremely wealthy—their business lives are a success—but they are absolutely miserable and unhappy in their personal lives. They aren't satisfied.

These are people who have money but also three ex-wives and kids who don't speak to them (or like them) anymore. Or they have a serious illness or disease. Some people point to all the examples like that and say, "Money can't buy happiness." I say that money has nothing to do with it one way or the other. If you gave up your soul to get there, all the money in the world will not make you happy. It isn't the money that made you unhappy, or sick, or divorced—*it was you!*

I also meet many people who are spiritually content, absolutely satisfied in their personal lives, but weak financially. I look at that in a different way. Although they've figured out that money can't buy them happiness, there is still something missing. Oh right, they're broke!

You can rationalize it all you want, but life without wealth sucks! I mean *really* sucks. Unfortunately, many (if not most) of the spiritual people I meet are in an economic rut. Let's face it—people who want to aspire to greatness don't look down, they look up. Living contently in mediocrity isn't my definition of success either. There is nothing great or balanced about living a life of mediocrity or desperation. I know that doing without the things you want (or deserve) in life would certainly never satisfy me.

The key, then, is simple: balance. Is it possible to have your cake and eat it too? Absolutely! How can I strive for economic stature and success, without sacrificing my soul, health, and personal happiness doing it? To answer that question, I offer my Positive Addictions (healthy habits to counteract stress), which, combined with my Contrarian strategy, can lead you to financial security and mega-success. Let's look at the Positive Addictions more closely.

SPIRITUAL NURTURING AND MEDITATIVE POSITIVE ADDICTIONS

I pray every morning within minutes of awakening. I know that if I don't schedule it and do it—first thing in the morning and last thing at night— it won't get done. I need that foundation before beginning a long, stressful day of work. Without prayer, I'm lost, I'm angry, I'm quick-tempered, I'm stressed out. When I start my day with prayer, I'm a different person—more loving, more compassionate, more focused, more creative, less apt to snap at others. Prayer is so important to my mental well-being, I cannot skip it. So I schedule it and I do it—period!

Another way to effectively utilize prayer is to schedule it throughout the day to alleviate stress. Praying at the start of the day may reduce stress, but you'll need to pray more often during times of intense pressure. When I receive bad news, get into heated discussions, or face stressful deadlines (like writing this book), I pray several times throughout the day, even if only for a few seconds or minutes.

What do I pray for? Compassion, understanding, and the inner strength to endure difficult and challenging times. Prayer allows me to pause when things are not clear, or not going "right." It grounds me so that I don't lose my balance. Most of all, prayer helps me stay focused on the bigger picture of life when a momentary distraction (such as a losing streak) is threatening to unravel me.

You may think I'm successful, but actually I'm weak. All humans are. My shoulders (no matter how many weights I lift) are not strong enough to carry all the stress, burdens, and challenges of every day. Neither are yours. I give my problems to God and let him bear the weight. That's a heck of a weight off my shoulders. That leaves me free to pursue excellence.

If you're interested in a powerful one-two punch, it doesn't get more powerful than prayer combined with meditation. I perform both of these Positive Addictions each morning when I rise. They are so important to my mental health and well-being, they are the first two things I do after I open my eyes!

Is meditation complicated or difficult? Not at all! I keep it simple. Most of us do not have thirty to sixty minutes to meditate. I'm not a yogi or a samurai. I do not have time to dedicate my life to reflection and inner peace. But the good news is you don't need that much time. You can get the benefits of meditation from just a few minutes a day! And you can refresh and reenergize your spirits with short two- to three-minute mini-meditations throughout the day. You can meditate anywhere—at home, in your office, in the pool or Jacuzzi, in the bathtub, or on your bed—and like prayer it doesn't cost a dime! As long as you can find a place to sit quietly and breathe, you can meditate!

How do you do meditate? It's easy. Let me show you how I do it.

First, you find a quiet place or room in your house. I recommend doing it first thing in the morning, before your children, spouse, or the business world wake up. You can also meditate during the day—it's a great daytime break. You can do it at your office if you can close the door and ask for no interruptions for ten or fifteen minutes.

Next, put on a tape or CD of music that soothes, relaxes, and inspires. I use nature sounds (ocean, forest, or stream) or classical music. Set a timer or alarm clock for ten to fifteen minutes for your main daily meditation. I'd recommend starting at ten and building up to fifteen minutes, which is plenty of time.

Sit up straight in your chair or lie down flat on your back. Keep a straight line with your head and spine. Start by saying a short prayer. Ask God for help in calming and focusing yourself. Ask for the concentration to go deep within. Ask for the ability to hear the wisdom and messages coming from God. This is the transition you will need to make the difficult jump from a stressful day to a place of inner peace and mental calmness.

Next, close your eyes. Become aware of your body. Begin to breathe in deeply and slowly. Feel your breath. Concentrate on each breath. You might want to count to eight on the inhale, hold for eight beats, then count to eight on the exhale. Or you might be more comfortable focusing on an unspoken word, sound, or thought with each breath: amen, God, love, safe and secure, serenity, or anything that makes you feel positive and calm. Repeat the word(s) slowly on each breath in and each breath out. That's it. That is how you meditate! It's not complicated or mysterious. Simply do it until the timer or clock rings. You will feel refreshed, energized, motivated, positive, and focused. The positive feelings you experience will get stronger each time you meditate. And the results will last longer each time, too. Meditation is much like playing sports—the more you practice it, the better you'll get at it, and the more you'll get out of it.

What does meditation do? It simply stops the negative chatter going on in your subconscious mind all day long. Your mind is busy—a nonstop talking machine. Meditation blocks out those distracting thoughts. It simply relaxes and quiets your mind. Studies have proven that a few minutes of meditation are equal to a hour (or more) of quality sleep. Your mind is tired and overused. It needs the rest. A lifetime of meditation will take years of wear and tear off your mind. You'll reduce stress and anxiety. You'll look better and feel better. You'll get sick less often, because stress damages your immune system and causes most sickness and disease. You'll add years to your lifespan. Nothing we can do to improve our lives is more important than finding a positive and healthy way to deal with stress. Meditation is such a way.

There is a complication to all this, though. Sitting still, even for only ten minutes, is not always as easy as it sounds. You may start tapping your feet, twitching your legs, or itching. Your mind will definitely wander—it's never been quieted or controlled before. It will rebel and try to gain back control from you (yes, your mind has a mind of its own). Your mind doesn't want to be quiet—it wants to chatter endlessly and incessantly. That's what it's done since you were born; now it wants its freedom back. It will try to win the battle of wills by distracting you; it will wander into thoughts about your business, relationships, bills, worries, children, etc.

Your mind is smart; it knows how to get your attention. Don't get angry or frustrated. Simply ignore the thoughts and go back to concentrating on your breathing. After a few seconds, the thoughts will disappear. Then the chatter and distractions will start all over again. Simply ignore the distractions and breathe deep again. Let them float gently away.

The more you meditate, the easier it will be to eliminate the interruptions. Your subconscious mind will eventually put aside the noisy, negative, stressful chatter. After a while your mind will come to enjoy the quiet—it will crave the time off! That's when you'll start to access your most positive, loving, insightful, creative (and *profitable*) thoughts.

Be patient and kind to yourself. Don't expect miracles the first few times out of the box. Keep practicing. Like any new activity, meditation will start to feel natural over time. The benefits will be extraordinary. I'd suggest keeping a pen and pad or tape recorder nearby. *After your alarm goes off and you open your eyes, write down the first few thoughts that come to your mind.* Many of the most creative and unique ideas of my life have come to me after praying or meditating.

As I end this section on meditation, please take note that only a type-A like me could suggest *scheduling* meditation. To many New Agers the point of meditation is that you are getting away from schedules. But I schedule meditation every day—that's the organized, disciplined, micro-managing businessman in me. And it works, so why knock it? Most successful business people never meditate. The few who understand and appreciate the benefits do it, but sporadically. They forget, or get busy, or just aren't disciplined enough to do it daily. Yet they never miss a business appointment. They never miss a doctor's appointment. They never miss a business lunch. Why? Because these appointments are scheduled. They've put them in their daily planner. So they are committed. Why not treat your Positive Addictions like a business meeting? Schedule them and stay committed.

Meditation is great for your body, mind, spirit, and soul. It makes you happy. It makes you positive. It makes you confident. It helps you to stay focused. And these are all traits that help you to make more money, too! These are all good things. So what's wrong with adding a little type-A American ingenuity to be sure it gets done? Schedule your meditations daily—and stick to the schedule. It will change your life for the better.

There's a third leg to my morning regimen. My one-two morning punch of prayer and meditation is followed closely by my morning nature walk. After praying and meditating, I go on my daily walk with my faithful German shepherd, Maverick. It's how I start every day, come rain or shine, warm or cold. That walk with nature (as I call it) has been "the rock" of my entire adult life. No matter the problems in my life or the disappointments or the stress, that walk at the start of my day grounds me. It gives me a feeling of appreciation for nature, for my life, and for the blessings bestowed on me by God. I get to spend time with my faithful companion (dogs are truly man's best friend), with nature (I walk in a beautiful park filled with trees, plants, flowers, lakes, fountains, streams, and ducks), and with God. And I get quiet time with myself— to think clearly, to reflect, to talk to God. Often my wife or children (or both) join me—a great treat, and a great way to bond with family. Just a great way to start a day.

Just as with prayer and meditation, many of my greatest (and most profitable) ideas have come to me on my morning nature walks! My suggestion: Bring along a recorder and save those ideas. The best ideas always come during quiet times of reflection: prayer, meditation, and nature walks. It amazes me that most people *never* start their days with any of "the big three." I *never* start my day without all three.

I'm a rabid reader. I love to read biographies of great American heroes and superachievers. And many (if not most) of our greatest superachievers report starting their days with a walk. Many boast of their greatest ideas (that changed their lives) coming to them during those quiet walks with nature. Like prayer and meditation, a morning nature walk is free. It doesn't cost a cent. Anyone can do it. Yet few take advantage of one of life's greatest gifts. I've been walking at 6 a.m., for over twenty years now, and I rarely ever run into another human being. Whether you want to be happier or healthier, more successful as a gambler or as an entrepreneur, a morning walk is an integral part of any Positive Addictions program.

In addition to applying the spiritual and meditative aspects of Positive Addictions, you need to build self-esteem. Why is self-esteem so crucial? The answer is simple. The way you choose to see yourself, virtually without exception, is also the way others will see you. If you do not believe in you, who else will? If you can't think of qualities that sell you, who else will? If you don't believe you're a unique asset to any business, who else will? If you don't think you make a great friend or spouse, who else will? *The answer is nobody.* You must first believe in your own success, before anyone else will. Your self-image and self-esteem will affect the way you approach your goals, your career, your investments, your gambling, your relationships, and your life. In order to succeed, you must first believe you are capable of achieving success. Positive self-esteem is at the core of any program designed to make you successful at anything!

TEN WAYS TO BUILD POSITIVE SELF-ESTEEM

- **Create positive self-esteem internally.**

Everyone has strengths. Recognize yours. Write them down and recite them out loud before bedtime. Remind yourself of the greatness within. Remind yourself of what you've achieved. The human mind is a funny thing—it believes whatever it hears. Feed it positive affirmations.

- **Create positive self-esteem externally.**

The external world judges you on how you look, feel, and act. If you feel good about yourself and you look like a happy, healthy, positive person, people will have a more upbeat, positive impression of you and treat you accordingly. People want to spend time around winners—period. It is essential that you project the image of a winner. It is amazing how many people dress like losers, like slobs, like they just don't care. How many people are groomed poorly? How many people talk like losers, complain and talk about how bad their life is? Guess what? No one cares! Shut up and turn your life around. But if you tell others how unhappy or unlucky or broke or jinxed you are, they will run for the hills. That I guarantee.

- **Look for ways to make others feel good about themselves.**

When you "pass it on," you not only make others feel good about themselves, but you nurture your own well-being in a positive way.

- **Educate yourself.**

Life is an ever-changing learning experience. It's amazing how many people are stuck in dead-end jobs but do nothing to improve their minds or lives. Coming home to watch *Oprah* or *The Bachelor* does not improve your mind. Going back to school for a master's or business degree does! Reading the biographies of great leaders will make you more interesting. Taking classes and learning new hobbies will make you a more interesting person. Watching the Learning, History, and Biography channels will make you smarter. Going to business-networking events will open up your circle of friends. Nourish your mind. Experience new things. Read.

- **Be prepared.**

Preparation helps reduce the stress of reactive uncertainty. Write down each night before bedtime all the possible things you might be faced with at an important meeting tomorrow. Play the whole meeting out. Plan out your reactions and answers until you design the best reactions and responses possible.

• **Make yourself feel good!**

Reward yourself with time to relax, read, get a massage or facial, pay yourself a positive compliment, buy yourself a gift as a reward for little successes, and continue to build on the positive aspects as well as the positive balance of your total self.

• **Donate your time and money to others less fortunate.**

The smile on a poor child's face when they get a book or the tears of joy from a father who can move his family into their first home are great moments of charitable giving that make you feel good about yourself and your contribution to the world you live in. Give to others and you'll glow! Don't tell me you don't have the time. A wealthy friend of mine put it best. He said, "Some people have the time to sit with cancer patients. I don't. So I donate enough money so one thousand people can sit with cancer patients!" So whether it's time or money, no matter—just find a way to give to others less fortunate. Just so you know that you are reading a book by an author who walks his walk—I personally donated over $100,000 to charity last year (2005).

• **Build health with a positive and healthy lifestyle.**

I will go into more detail on this later, but without question a healthy you can and will create a wealthy you.

• **Surround yourself with positive friends.**

Ever wonder why sports teams call their home field an "advantage"? It's because it *is*, when they are surrounded by thousands of applauding, cheering, and positive-reinforcing people—their hometown fans! Too many of us surround ourselves with negative, critical people. People with bad habits that drag us down too. Misery loves company. Find positive people and spend your time around them. Eliminate the toxic people in your life.

• **Face your fears.**

Have you ever been afraid to tell a good friend or a loved one something that you were absolutely fearful of? Then, when you did it, it was a great burden lifted from your shoulders—and actually not that bad? Your fears are one of the great things that will hold you back. The more you are willing to challenge them and conquer them, the more self-confidence you will build. Write down your fears and decide what is the worst thing that would happen if they came true. Now come up with a solution. Do this for a while and I'll bet you find you're not afraid anymore. You need to take control over your fears—not the other way around.

AFFIRMATION AND VISUALIZATION

Affirmation is a way to give yourself verbal messages that support your success. Visualization allows you to create an image of how your successful life will look in the future (near or far)—to literally see yourself turning your dreams into a wonderful, magical, extraordinary reality!

Become aware of the negative messages you are sending yourself. Most of us have a constant low-level murmur going on deep inside the recesses of our brains. Unfortunately, this murmur is usually pretty negative. If you really concentrate on what your subconscious mind is telling you, you'll probably hear many negative things. Why is this? Because of all those critics, so-called experts, and naysayers I've been talking about for much of this book!

You've heard negative predictions, criticisms, doubts, and fears your whole life. For example, studies prove that parents say *no* and other negative words thousands of times for every positive word they say to their kids: "No, you can't do this." "No, you can't do that." "Bad boy." "Bad girl." "Are you an idiot?" "Why don't you listen?" "Don't do that, you're going to hurt yourself." These are the negative and toxic messages that you've heard hundreds of thousands of times throughout your whole life. Becoming aware of how you bully yourself and promote your own failures (because your subconscious is simply repeating all the negativity and toxic attacks you've heard) is the first step toward changing.

Your next step is to create alternative positive messages. These are called *affirmations*. They are the antidote to that low-level negative murmur going on in your mind. You're now going to reprogram your subconscious to think positively. You will repeat these positive messages again and again, to recondition your subconscious mind.

You cannot solve a problem, overcome challenging odds, achieve a goal, or win a bet without *believing* you can do it. When you believe you *can*, you think about solutions, not excuses. One of the ways I keep myself positive and confident, as well as focused (like a laser) on the the solution (besides prayer, of course) is to affirm and visualize it. So think of all your goals and dreams; then think of your problems and challenges. Write down positive affirmations that encourage your goals and dreams, and that overcome your challenges. Now say them out loud (preferably into a mirror) each day. I prefer to say them before bedtime, so all night, while I'm dreaming, my subconscious will be flooded with positive thoughts and images.

How do you visualize? First you sit in a comfortable and quiet place, free of distractions. The more relaxed you are, the more powerful the image you are able to create in your mind's eye. Next you create a picture of yourself in the situation you desire. Be as specific as you can. See the objects, companions, clothing, activities, and surroundings as you want them to be in your dream life. It's like watching your own personal movie or television show. You're now watching yourself in that show. Be sure you have everything you want. You don't want to visualize (and therefore mentally create) the *wrong* dream. You are now *creating* your future. Your mind believes what it sees. Unfortunately, most of us deep down see only negativity and failure. We carry that negative and damaging baggage our whole lives. Visualization is a way to change the subconscious image.

Now sit comfortably for five minutes (set a timer), "acting" out the scene. Create as many details as possible—bring in all your senses. See the pattern on the jacket and the tie you are wearing. See the expressions on the faces of the people in your visualization. The more realistic your visualization, the more deeply your mind will begin to believe that this situation really exists!

After you've added all the details you can to your visualization, simply enjoy the internal experience you've created for yourself. When you're done, you'll feel energized, refreshed, positive, and confident in your success. Most important, you'll start to believe in *you* deep down. That's the start of all success.

THE DISCIPLINE PRINCIPLE

You can be the brightest person on the planet, possess the greatest ideas, shoot for the highest goals—but without *discipline*, you will never carry out those goals. Without discipline, all the commitment, confidence, and tenacity in the world is for naught. You can dream big dreams, but without discipline, that's all they'll ever be!

Occasionally, individuals without discipline succeed, but their success is usually fleeting. They wind up losing it as quickly as they achieved it. (Or it's just due to blind luck, but that happens only very, very rarely.) Do you want to rely on the whims of fate to win the life of your dreams? Are you waiting for a prince (or princess) on a white horse to turn your fantasy into reality? Are you banking on winning the lottery? If so, this was the wrong book for you in the first place.

Discipline is essential to putting the odds in your favor. Discipline wins wars. Discipline keeps soldiers alive on battlefields—the success of armies since the beginning of time has been based on discipline. But why? What do sit-ups, push-ups, and ten-mile jogs have to do with success on the battlefield? What do spit-shined shoes and spotlessly clean barracks have to do with winning wars? What do physical fitness and personal grooming habits have to do with courage and valor? The answer is *everything*.

A disciplined soldier will be better focused, better organized under fire, better able to cope with life-and-death challenges. A disciplined solder will be better prepared to think creatively under adverse conditions. A disciplined soldier will react like a professional while others run for their lives. He or she will show courage and valor under intense fire. A disciplined soldier will automatically feel better about him- or herself, showing more confidence and pride. That automatically translates into tenacity, loyalty, and commitment, even in the midst of the most adverse conditions. War is a test of a soldier's ability to think and perform clearly and successfully when facing challenge and adversity. Like life, it isn't a question of *whether* you'll face challenge, adversity, and failure; it is only a question of *when* you'll face it, how *much* you'll face, and *how* you'll react. Discipline is what determines your reaction in the face of negativity, fear, and failure.

The modern world we all live in today very much resembles a battlefield. We all face tremendous stress and challenge on a variety of fronts. Raising healthy children is a daily battle. So is keeping a marriage together. The business world most closely resembles a battlefield—getting to the top is like fighting a war! Staying at the top is even harder. The landscape is littered with the casualties of the dead and wounded—the unemployed, the homeless, the bankrupt, the emotionally scarred, the billions who have chosen to settle and hate their mediocre lives.

Like it or not, life is like war—it is a daily test of your will; a battle for survival of the fittest. You will fight this battle every day of your life. Every time you walk into a job interview; every time a client auditions your firm, or a new customer walks into your store; every time you walk into a party looking for Mr. or Ms. Right; every time you pick up the phone to make a business call that could change your income or your level of achievement; every time you make a bet or take a risk, *you are being tested*. You are in a competition. Only the most disciplined will win. Only the best of the best will *thrive!*

How do you encourage discipline? Well here's my program:

• First and foremost, get up early each and every day.

Remember the old saying, "The early bird catches the worm"? It's true. Make it a regular part of your regimen to get up early and jump-start your day. I credit much of my success to the fact that I get more done by 10 a.m. than most people do in an entire day. Why? Because I've been working since 5:30 a.m. without interruption. Kids aren't up. Phones aren't ringing. I've already done my morning one-two-three punch with prayer-meditation-nature walk, so I'm energized, focused, and motivated.

This early-morning time is my "clearheaded" time. It's my advantage or "edge" over my competitors. Let them sleep late—I'm beating them to the punch before they've even awakened! Getting up early is a disciplined way of turning energy and enthusiasm into opportunity and success. Changes like this won't happen all at once, but they'll work successfully if you gradually implement them. I recommend setting your alarm clock to wake up one minute earlier every day for four months. Doesn't sound like much, but at the end of two months you've gained an extra hour. At the end of four months you've gained two extra hours. Now use that extra time wisely.

• Face your fears—write them all down.

Once you acknowledge them and face them, you've taken their power away. The confidence you get from facing your fears will allow you to achieve any goal you set for the rest of your life.

• Become a list maniac.

Make lists of everything you need or want to accomplish today, this week, this month, this year. *Now make them happen!* Don't procrastinate or make excuses. If you put it off, it will not get done. Lists allow you to focus, and to be truthful with yourself. Either you took action, or you didn't. If it was done, you can cross it off the list. If not, move it to tomorrow's list. It stays on your "to do list" until it's done—period. Lists have ruled and changed my life. Everything I accomplish, I owe to my lists. I am proud to call myself a list maniac.

• Create a daily diary.

Creating a diary is the best way to analyze what you did right or wrong today. Spend five minutes before bedtime writing about your day—your positives and successes, as well as the mistakes and failures. Now analyze and write down the why's. Go back and review the last ten days of a losing streak and I'll bet you'll find a pattern. That discovery will change your life. It works with gambling, business, personal relationships, health—literally anything and everything.

This daily diary is your black box. Like the device in an airplane that tells FAA investigators what went wrong in the last moments before a crash, this diary will record all your triumphs and failures and the reasoning behind them. It is my most valuable tool for success in gambling, business, and life.

• Schedule your appointments.

Start each day by planning out your day. Have a detailed plan for what you want to accomplish, what you'll be doing, where you'll be going. Will you make every "appointment"? No. Will you meet every goal? No. But putting a goal in writing makes it real. If you don't get to all your goals or appointments today, don't fret. Add them to tomorrow's schedule.

Your subconscious mind believes it is possible. Try your best to keep to that schedule, and soon your goals will start to become achievements. If you simply meet a few of your goals each day, you'll enjoy a dramatic improvement in your efficiency level, success level, and time-management level. The result will be a whole new quality of life.

• Sign a contract with yourself.

Do you break contracts? I sure hope not. If you do, you're probably bankrupt or in prison. A contract is the law. When you sign a mortgage or car payment, you become obligated. Those are contracts. I want you to feel mentally obligated to achieve your goals, too. Create a written contract listing your goals, dreams, and timetable for success. Sign and date it. Frame it in your office. Review it daily.

• Create a dream book.

As important as the written word is, so is the visual. People only achieve what they can clearly see. Think of what you want in life, then cut out those images (from magazines, newspapers, books) of homes, cars, businesses, destinations, people you want in your life. Your personal definitions of success. Put them in a photo album. Review these positive and motivating images every week for a few minutes. That's *your* future flashing before your eyes.

Slowly but surely, you'll start to make those images your reality. As you achieve one or two, change the goals and update your dream book. It has worked like magic for me again and again. I've gone through entire books as I've achieved every image and goal in my dream book. At that point, I always invent a whole new dream!

If you can institute all the Discipline Principles above into your daily schedule, you will see a dramatic change in your life. The reason is discipline. Those who have it succeed beyond their wildest expectations! Those who don't fall by the wayside (and then complain that life is unfair).

EXERCISE

I've discussed the mental approach to a better, more focused, you. But there are two other aspects to work with: exercise and diet. First, exercise. I've experimented for years and found three hard and fast rules that apply to exercise:

1. Do it every day, without exception.
2. Do it in the morning when your energy is highest.
3. Do it at home. In the time it takes most gym rats to drive to their gym and back, I've already finished most of my workout. And why do you think most people buy gym memberships, then never use them? Because they actually have to get to the gym! They find excuses, and they never go. So exercising at home eliminates the possibility of excuses. And by eliminating the thirty- to sixty-minute roundtrip drive to the gym, you've freed up the time necessary to exercise in the first place. Now you have no excuses!

Exercising adds years to your life—so you get the extra time to do the things you love to do! And the extra money to do those things, too! What do exercise and healthy lifestyle have to do with money? Allow me to explain.

A study on cigarettes from about a decade ago revealed the lifetime costs of smoking—purchase of cigarettes, higher medical bills, higher life- and health-insurance rates, missed time at work due to illness, and the interest charges over a lifetime on all those extra bills. The average cost of smoking over a lifetime: $1 million (and that was a decade ago). Interesting, too, that the scientists who conducted the study added their own opinion at the end of the study: that $1 million of wasted money is enough to buy a mansion and put an exotic car in the driveway (so that's where the term "up in smoke" comes from). Now add in the cost of alcohol (I'll bet it's another $1 million over the typical lifetime) and drugs.

This leads me to an interesting observation: I've never smoked, drunk, or done drugs. And since I reached the age of thirty, I've always had a mansion and an exotic car in the driveway. Interesting coincidence, don't you think? Most people waste their money on negative and unhealthy habits, then wonder why they don't have any money.

If you have the money for cigarettes, alcohol, or drugs, you have the money to exercise, raise your self-esteem, and change your life. If you'd stop drinking or smoking for just a few months, you'd save enough to buy a piece of exercise equipment for your home. And if you'd use that equipment religiously every morning for a few months, you'd become more addicted to a new sense of accomplishment and self-esteem than you ever were to drugs, alcohol, or cigarettes! That new positive feeling would translate to millions of dollars over the course of a lifetime. You'd gain $1 million (or more) for quitting your negative addictions, plus gain $1 million (or more) by adding your new Positive Addictions! That's enough for a mansion at the beach, *plus* a mansion on the ski slope. With enough left over for two Jaguars!

I treat exercise as a two-part process: natural and planned. Natural exercise takes advantage of nature. We were not created by God to sit in chairs all day looking at computer screens, followed by lying on the couch all night watching television. Our lifestyles have changed, but not our bodies. Our bodies were created to walk everywhere, work with our hands, hunt in the woods, work in the fields, and sleep under the stars. I believe all of us must find ways to put more physical activity (especially *outdoor* activity) into our everyday lives. Here are a few simple ideas for making your daily life more physically and naturally active:

- Start every day with a nature walk (see above).
- Take the stairs instead of the elevator at work.

- Bring a workout outfit to the office and skip lunch. Take an hour's walk or work out in the gym instead. Then snack on small healthy meals throughout the workday (studies prove that eating six small meals per day is far preferable to eating three large meals).
- Organize outdoor outings with family and friends. Spend your time together hiking, biking, swimming, skating, skiing—instead of sitting on sofas talking, gossiping, or watching television.
- Organize business functions and seminars around outdoor, goal-oriented, and team-building events—mountain climbing, rappelling, biking, hiking, camping, kayaking, etc.
- Use weekends to discover new sports and hobbies designed to get you off the sofa and out of the house. Or if you're a gambler (which you probably are if you're reading this book) and love watching games morning, noon, and night, great! Train your mind and body to think of TV sports time as *exercise time!* I watch more sports on TV than most anyone—it's my job! But I watch those games while working out on my exercise bike or treadmill or elliptical trainer. Or I lift weights in front of the TV screen. In that way, sports and gambling are no longer for "couch potatoes." *Sports gambling can create fitness fanatics!* I never watch a game anymore without exercising during all or part of the game. So for me, gambling is the key to a longer and healthier life! *How's that for Contrarian?*
- Make a connection between "family time" and physical activities: Play volleyball, or basketball, hike, bike, swim—all together as a family unit. A family bike ride every Saturday morning is much more beneficial than a family outing to the fast-food restaurant.

Planned exercise, as its name suggests, refers to exercise that you schedule (yes I do schedule everything!—I have a busy life and that's the only way it gets done). Usually this is done indoors, in a controlled and timed setting. There are three types of beneficial planned exercise:

Number one is *aerobic*. This is exercise that gets your heart rate and breathing up and keeps them there long enough to have a strengthening effect on your cardiovascular and respiratory systems (and your immune system). Some good examples are running (on a treadmill or outdoors), skiing (cross-country or on a ski machine), rowing (outdoors or on a rowing machine), stair climbing (on real stairs or on a machine), bike riding (outdoors or on a stationary bike), or simply a good aerobics class.

Number two is *strength* training. This is exercise that builds muscle strength and mass. It includes exercise done with weight machines (or free weights) and calisthenics (push-ups, pull-ups, sit-ups, etc.). This kind of exercise has some of the same benefits as aerobic exercise, but it also has benefits all its own: It helps you burn fat more efficiently, decreases the risk of bone loss with aging, improves your appearance, and reduces the risk of injuring underdeveloped muscles. Recent studies prove that the benefits of weight training apply at any age—even eighty- and ninety-year-olds experienced dramatic improvements in heart rate and strength within weeks of undertaking a weight-training program!

Number three is *flexibility* conditioning. This is exercise that increases your range of motion, making it possible for you to use each of your joints fully and effectively. Leg- and back-muscle stretching helps prevent back pain.

Yoga is the best exercise I have found to increase flexibility. The benefits of flexibility conditioning are improved grace and balance and reduced risk of sports injuries caused by muscle tightness. You can get a book on yoga at any library or bookstore, or you can take a yoga class in virtually any major city. Simply learn ten to fifteen basic exercises and then do them at home before or after you exercise. What makes yoga one of my personal favorites is that the mental benefit is equal to or better than the physical benefit. Yoga reduces stress and uplifts my spirits! Yoga is my fourth "must" in my daily morning ritual. Starting any day with prayer, meditation, nature walk, and yoga is guaranteed to change your attitude and supercharge your life.

Ideally, a person should get at least thirty to forty-five minutes of aerobic exercise four to six times a week, a half-hour of strength training two to three times a week, and fifteen minutes of flexibility conditioning two to three times per week. Does that sound like a lot of exercise? All it adds up to is about *one hour* every day of the week.

You don't have to start off like gangbusters. Start with a walk every day. Build up to a jog. Now add in weights a couple of days a week. Then start to add in or substitute other aerobic, strength, and flexibility exercises. Soon you will be addicted. And in a world where addictions usually revolve around cigarettes, coffee, alcohol, recreational drugs, prescription drugs, and junk food, *these are addictions to be proud of.*

Author's Note: Be sure to consult your physician before making any significant changes in your physical habits (exercise, diet, or nutritional supplementation). Please understand that the recommendations in this book are not intended as a substitute for the regular care of your family doctor or other medical practitioner.

HEALTHY DIET

You'll need energy and enthusiasm to achieve your goals. A healthy diet and lifestyle lead to enormous amounts of energy, vitality, and pure get up 'n' go! Think of your body as a $150,000 Ferrari convertible. An expensive foreign sports car doesn't run on cheap, low-octane fuel. A Ferrari requires special handling and maintenance. It requires some old-fashioned TLC—tender loving care. So do you! Your body is like a delicate racing machine. In addition to getting out on the road frequently (exercise), your body requires special fuel: healthy food. Junk food, fast food, frozen dinners, high-fat food, and foods laced with chemicals, preservatives, pesticides, hormones, and antibiotics (which is pretty much all food not grown organically) will damage and decay your engine. The result will be a lack of energy, enthusiasm, and optimism; a lack of focus and creativity; and eventually illness and disease.

My healthy-diet addiction is a simple, practical approach to better eating. I'm *not*—I repeat, *not*—going to ask you to give up steak, hot dogs, hamburgers, pasta, pizza, soda, desserts, pretzels, French fries, pancakes, bacon, and all of those other delicious but "bad for you" foods. You won't get any dramatic lectures from me demanding you make extreme changes to your diet. I won't ask you to spend the rest of your life eating salads, carrot sticks, tofu, soy hot dogs, veggie burgers, and bean sprouts. You and I both know that for most people, that's never going to happen. First of all, very few of us can stick to a diet that's boring and unappetizing. Second, to eat a diet like that would require willpower very few of us are born with—especially in a society that advertises and promotes junk food everywhere we turn. Finally, that diet would require that you abandon all your friends and business acquaintances—who'd want to spend time with you if all you ate was tofu and bean sprouts? If you're a sports gambler, that goes *double* for you!

What I'm asking you to do is to *moderate* your eating habits. *Make small changes:*

- **First, lower your fat and limit your carbs.** If you only made these two changes and nothing else, you would most certainly lose weight; reduce your risk of heart disease, diabetes, and cancer; and feel healthier and more energetic. The average American gets about 40 percent of his or her daily calories from fat. Most scientific studies recommend about half that amount—around 20 to 25 percent. So how do you reduce the fat in your diet without sacrificing taste and satisfaction? Here are some suggestions to get you started:

- Find alternatives to frying (for example, chicken can be baked or grilled).

- Exchange high-fat items for lower-fat ones that still please you (for example, try a fresh whole-grain bagel with low-fat cream cheese instead of a high-fat morning muffin with butter; try pretzels instead of chips).
- Reduce cooking oils and fats (for example, use half the amount of oil recommended in a stir-fry recipe and add a bit of chicken broth or water for extra moisture). Use only organic, cold-pressed oil.
- Find lower-carb versions of items you enjoy. Low- or no-carb stores are sprouting up (excuse the pun) everywhere, and these low-carb products now have their own aisles in supermarkets. There are now delicious low- and no-carb breads, dressings, pizza, pasta, and desserts. Two years ago they tasted lousy—now they've made great strides and low-carb food tastes great!

- **Find organic, healthy versions of your favorite comfort foods.** As an example, I still eat pizza, but it's made with organic crust, organic cheese, organic vegetables, and topped with organic chicken-hot-dog pieces. I still eat hot dogs, but they're made with organic chicken or turkey, on an organic bun, with organic mayo, organic mustard, organic ketchup, and even organic pickles. I still eat cheeseburgers and fries, but they're made with organic beef, organic cheese, organic mayo, and organic ketchup, along with organic *baked* French fries. I still eat bologna sandwiches, but they're made with natural chicken bologna (no hormones, antibiotics, or nitrates) on a low-carb whole-grain bun, with organic mayo. I still enjoy pretzels and chips while watching a football game, but they are organic pretzels (with sea salt) and organic chips, dipped in organic guacamole. I might top off those meals with dessert—organic soy ice cream with organic chocolate topping and organic sprinkles, on top of a no-carb vanilla cake. I still love a glass of ice cold milk, but I drink organic rice milk. All these foods taste *better* than the unhealthy originals, because I know that with each bite, I'm making myself *healthier and wealthier* (a healthy, fit mind and body equal better energy, creativity, focus, and decision-making capabilities). And organic foods are no longer hard to find. They are *everywhere*. Giant health-food supermarkets like Whole Foods and Wild Oats are spreading across the nation. Many traditional supermarkets have a fully-stocked organic/health-food aisle, and often it's right next to the low-carb aisle. Spend your time in those two aisles.

You'll find that as you eat less fat, less carbs, and less junk, you'll start to crave them less. After a few months, rich sauces, premium ice cream, and fried foods will start to taste greasy and unappealing, and will feel heavy and indigestible in your stomach. That may be hard to believe, but try it and see!

▪ **Eat more:** No, not more food, but *more often*. A number of clinical studies have shown that when animals eat less, they live much longer, maintain youthful vigor and metabolism, and seem better able to ward off age-related diseases. The easiest way to eat less is to eat smaller meals several times throughout the day. That way you are never too hungry and are less likely to pig out on huge quantities of food. You'll feel light, satisfied, and full of energy. You won't experience heartburn, upset stomach, or those middle-of-the-day power outages anymore! Your energy will stay consistently high all day long.

▪ **Don't be too extreme:** Our eating habits are built up over a whole lifetime. For most of us, tastes, textures, specific foods, and food-connected rituals have deep associations with family, love, comfort, and fulfillment. Changing your eating habits (even when it makes sense and you feel motivated) isn't an overnight thing. I encourage you to make changes at a rate that you can sustain. Explore the world of healthy food. Don't think you have to renounce pleasure to be healthy! Take it from me—healthy and delicious are no longer mutually exclusive. Healthy, organic food tastes better than it has at any previous time in history. It has taken twenty years, but healthy foods have closed the "taste gap." All your old stereotypes that have kept you away from healthy food no longer apply. If it tastes great and it's good for you, what's holding you back? Healthy diet is now a "sure thing."

- **Increase your intake of natural, unprocessed foods.** As I reported above, virtually everything you eat is now available in a healthy alternative at a health-food store or supermarket. This includes whole-grain flours and the products made from them (bread, crackers, pretzels, cereals, and pastas), grains (brown rice, millet, barley, oats, and dried corn), legumes (beans and peas), vegetables (potatoes, peppers, broccoli, and carrots), and whole sweeteners (rice syrup, malt syrup, molasses, sorghum, and maple syrup). Unlike simple carbohydrates like white flour and refined sugars, these whole foods are digested slowly, providing steady energy rather than a quick energy rush (and let-down). Most complex carbohydrates also have lots of fiber, which reduces your risk of cancer, helps your digestion and elimination, and keeps you feeling satisfied longer after you eat. So if you refuse to cut carbs, at least eat organic carb products chock full of fiber.

This whole section is another good example of how Contrarian thinking can change or save your life. Almost everything you see advertised to eat on mainstream TV is poison! It's toxic to your immune system. The corn flakes, dairy products, sodas, ice cream, pork, beef, fast food, junk food, cookies, and cakes you see advertised on TV are all bad for your health, energy levels, and brain power. Only a true Contrarian could watch all this subconscious brainwashing (called TV commercials) and choose to buy none of it. I can't remember the last time I bought anything advertised on television. My food choices are all Contrarian. I buy them in organic-health-food stores only. Once again, I'm healthy because I choose the road less traveled. The masses may be asses when it comes to gambling choices, but they are even *bigger* fools when it comes to the garbage they choose to put into their mouths.

SUPPLEMENTAL VITAMINS

Vitamins work—period! Today I look better, feel younger, work and play harder, and stay healthier than ever before. I've got more energy than when I was a teenager! I rarely, if ever, get sick. I couldn't afford to get sick—I run a publicly traded company, I executive produce and host multiple television and radio shows, I write books and serve as head of a household (now with three little Roots). Who has time to get sick?

Many doctors will tell you that we do not need vitamin supplements. Well, they are wrong. First of all, doctors know little to nothing about nutrition. Sound Contrarian? But it's true (isn't it starting to seem like Contrarian is *always* true?). The typical doctor takes one single nutrition course in all of their years in medical school. *One.* The typical doctor knows as much about vitamins as I know about being a midwife (the answer is *nothing*). Second, take a look at doctors. Do they look healthy? Enough said. If we all lived a low-stress life, in a pollution-free environment, eating completely natural food and drinking pure water, perhaps we wouldn't need vitamin supplements. But modern life being what it is, taking high-quality vitamin supplements is essential to optimum health, high energy, and vitality. Look around you—people are sick. We are experiencing epidemics of cancer, heart disease, stroke, high blood pressure, chronic fatigue syndrome, and many other deadly diseases. Obviously we are *not* getting the proper nutrition or vitamins from our diets.

A subgroup of vitamins called antioxidants can also retard aging and help prevent cancer and immune-system damage. Floating through our bodies are "free radicals"—molecules with unpaired electrons that can interfere with the functioning of our vital organs—and that can lead to disease and premature aging. Scientific studies have shown that antioxidants neutralize free radicals, thereby preventing cellular damage. Powerful key antioxidants include vitamins C, E, and A; selenium; glutathione; grape seed extract; and olive leaf extract.

For years, vitamin and nutritional supplementation was considered controversial by the medical establishment. Finally, after decades of attacks, the Western medical establishment is starting to wake up to the power and effectiveness of nontraditional and unconventional medicine. (There's my Contrarian thinking at work again.) Yes, the gambler was ahead of the doctors in sensing a need for healthy diet and lifestyle! Oh so Contrarian! Scientists, medical researchers (and at least a few progressive doctors) are today confirming the enormous health benefits of vitamins and healthy diet. Antioxidants in particular are drawing rave reviews.

Even insurance companies are starting to explore the option of allowing visits to chiropractors, acupuncturists, holistic healers, and homeopaths. It's taken several centuries too long, but Western medicine is finally coming around to a holistic way of thinking. In the past year, I've read or watched hundreds of news reports on the power of vitamins to heal illness, slow aging, and prevent disease.

My suggestion to each of you is to do some research to find out which supplements might be the most beneficial for your personal and unique needs. Never pop pills indiscriminately. Experiment slowly and carefully. Be aware of food allergies, and by all means, stop taking any supplement that makes you feel bad or causes a negative reaction. *But get ready for the energy high of your life!* If you want to keep your energy high, your stress low, your attitude positive, and your good health intact, I believe that you have no choice but to supplement your diet with mega-doses of vitamins. You, my friend, are now a Zen Gambler!

> **Author's Note:** Let's talk turkey. I'll bet some of you (especially
> the hard-core gamblers) are thinking I've lost my mind. You think
> healthy diet, exercise, yoga, prayer, and meditation have nothing
> to do with picking winners in the gambling world. Well, I disagree
> strongly. But I've explained all that already. No matter. Let's as-sume you are correct—a healthy lifestyle will not help you pick
> more winners. A recent study concluded that fully *one third* of all
> deaths globally are a direct result of obesity (being overweight),
> lack of exercise, and smoking.

So if nothing else, implement the Contrarian betting strategy you'll read about in Part Two of this book to pick winners. Then implement the Positive Addictions program above to create a healthier, longer-living you! That's one heck of a combination. Why would you even want to pick winners if you're going to die young because of obesity or disease? Is that your idea of a good life? What good is picking winners, if at the same time you're dying of cancer? Do you want to die at fifty, instead of seventy-five? In the end, healthy diet and lifestyle are *not* Contrarian. They are simply common sense. Unfortunately, in this complicated, con-fusing, fast-paced and stressed-out world, it often takes a Contrarian to figure out common sense!

FINAL COMMENTS

Sometimes the day starts before I do, or ends after I do—the phone rings at 5 a.m. or midnight (or both) and I answer it; someone from Europe or the East Coast is calling. Then another phone call comes in, or the first phone call initiates some action on my part. I get so busy, I forget to do my morning essentials—prayer, meditation, nature walk, yoga, and exercise. Right about noon my wife says to me, "You know Wayne, you are acting negatively and erratically. Your energy is much lower than normal. Let me guess. You didn't exercise or meditate this morning." And of course, she's always right.

When I'm having a bad day, or enduring a tough losing streak, it's almost always because I didn't start the day out right by doing my Positive Addictions. Winners (in gambling, business, or life in general) understand the mind-body connection. In the middle of an eight-loss slump, the typical amateur gambler will make a bad gamble on game number nine that day. Not me, because if I have done my physical, mental, and spiritual conditioning, I have increased my odds—put them in my favor—of breaking the slump and starting a winning streak because I am thinking positively about solutions, not reacting negatively to problems.

Most gamblers (as well as individuals in all walks of life) never quite get the connection between what you think and eat and do for your mind and body adding up to success or failure. But then again, the masses are asses. You are now a Contrarian. And a winner.

PART TWO

A COMPLETE GUIDE TO CONTRARIAN SPORTS BETTING

ELEVEN

■

WHY BET
ON SPORTS?

Okay, so Americans like to gamble. But why is sports gambling in particular so popular? Because we are also a nation of couch potatoes. Sports allows us to gamble to our heart's content from the comfort and safety of our homes. You don't even have to leave your couch or bed to bet on sports! You just call your local bookie, or log onto your favorite online sportsbook, turn on the TV, and sit down in your favorite chair.

With other forms of gambling you need to get in your car to drive to a racetrack or casino or poker room, or maybe just to buy a Lotto ticket, but sports gambling is enjoyed in the comfort of your home, office, or favorite sports bar. Sports betting is the most convenient form of gambling. And it is tied to America's favorite form of recreation—television! No surprise, then, that it is also the most widespread.

And, of course, we are a nation of sports lovers, as well as a nation that loves competition. We certainly have a love affair with money. *Sports betting allows us to put all three loves together!* Like Wall Street, you get to bet on something and watch it go up or down—make money or lose money. You get to match wits with the competition, both amateur and professional.

Plus, in sports betting the payoff is much sweeter. Instead of watching CNBC's complicated ticker all day or following the boring press releases of IBM and Microsoft or reading the boring *Wall Street Journal*, sports bettors get to watch their investments toss a touchdown or sack the quarterback or kick a game-winning field goal as time expires! They get to watch ESPN *Sportscenter* instead of *Wall Street Week* and read *Sports Illustrated* instead of *Barron's* or *BusinessWeek*. Isn't the life of a sports gambler just a tad more stimulating than the lives of the Ivy League big shots on Wall Street?

And then there's the TV set—America's favorite piece of furniture. Of course, to sports fans it's more than a TV—it's a big screen. Television and gambling go hand in hand. America's love of the TV set has enabled sports gambling to grow like no other form of gambling.

Let's examine the ratings of TV and how they apply to the growth of sports gambling. The highest-rated TV event in America? The Super Bowl. It's also the highest-rated betting event of each year. Over $6 billion is bet on that one day—most illegally. The second-highest-rated TV sports event? March Madness. Once again, it just happens to be the second-highest-rated betting event. Are you getting the idea that these are *not* coincidences? The highest-rated sport on TV? Again, an easy winner: NFL Football is the *king* of TV ratings. Did you know that a rather ordinary NFL match-up between the Dallas Cowboys and New England Patriots during the 2003 NFL regular season became the highest-rated cable TV program in history? Not the highest-rated sports program in cable history, but *the highest-rated program of any kind, ever.* Does that give you some idea of how popular the NFL has become?

It is no coincidence that the number-one betting sport *by far* is NFL football. NFL football was made for betting. Point spreads and high scoring make every single game interesting (and bettable) to bettors.

Finally, what sporting event is a TV institution that has made the top twenty of American TV ratings for over three decades? Monday Night Football. I guess you won't be surprised to hear that Monday Night Football is also an American *betting* institution! Betting is so fast and furious on Mondays that bookmakers were forced to change collection day— the day all betting accounts are settled—to Tuesdays, to allow America's bettors to make one last big bet on Monday night.

And bettors don't disappoint. Most sports gamblers bet all or nothing on Monday nights. If they're up money from the weekend to the bookmaker, they try to double their profits on that last game. If they're down money to the bookie, they also play double or nothing!

Perhaps that's why it has been said that betting literally "made" both the NFL and Madison Avenue. All those billion-dollar advertising agencies and their clients certainly have scored big because of the point spread. After all, if not for point spreads, who but gamblers would be tuned in to meaningless late-season games between also-rans? Why would the viewers be watching Charles Schwab or Mercedes-Benz advertisements in the fourth quarter of Monday Night Football blowouts if fourteen-point point spreads did not exist? Because of gambling and gamblers, viewers are still watching TV in every minute of every game, thereby benefiting the NFL's TV contract, the TV networks, Madison Avenue, and of course advertisers like Charles Schwab, Merrill Lynch, Microsoft, Coors beer, Coca-Cola, Gatorade, Hummer, Cadillac, and Mercedes-Benz. All those global corporate institutions have gambling to thank for their ever-expanding revenues!

But wait—there's even more psychology behind the explosion of sports gambling. You see, sports gambling isn't really gambling at all, it is *entertainment*. Allow me to explain. If you take your significant other (spouse, girlfriend, lover, best friend) to dinner and a Broadway play in

Manhattan, you are in for a $300 evening. Do you complain? No, not if you were entertained. If you enjoyed yourself, you got your money's worth.

Now let's compare that entertainment experience with betting on sports. You and your three best friends bet $300 on Monday Night Football. You all gather at your home, in front of the big screen, with your favorite foods and your remote control at your fingertips. And you now get to enjoy three to four hours of pure, unadulterated, macho male joy! There is yelling, screaming, ups and downs, amazing peaks and valleys, high fives, nail-biting, edge-of-your-seat suspense. Pure adrenaline, combined with testosterone!

Then, when it's over, if you've lost your bet, you've spent the same $300 on entertainment, as your buddy and his wife did at the Broadway play. But if you win (and with the help of this book, *you* now have the winning edge) you have the opportunity to profit while being entertained by others. Sports gambling is therefore the only form of entertainment in the world that pays you to enjoy yourself! And critics wonder why sports gambling is exploding?

Yes, sports gambling is the "new national pastime," and as you can see above, for good reason! Now it's time for you to profit from the success and popularity of sports gambling. Whether you want to earn a full-time living through sports betting or whether it's just a fun hobby that you'd like to make at least mildly profitable or whether you just want to learn how to be a successful Contrarian thinker and world-class risk-taker by using the lessons learned from sports gambling as your business model for any business or career you choose, you've come to the right place. Read on.

TWELVE

■

ROOT'S RULES FOR SPORTS BETTING

ROOT CONTRARIAN RULE #1: THE PUBLIC PLAYS NONSTOP FAVORITES—A *HUGE* MISTAKE.

Here's an important fact to always remember: Favorites lose. Last year (Football 2003) I picked *outright* winners (forget about the spread) a remarkable fifty-eight times with underdogs. Every one of these underdog winners was independently monitored and documented for authenticity. That's fifty-eight times that my inferior, pathetic underdog picks won the game without even needing the points. Over a seventeen-week college and NFL football season, that's an average of a little over three underdogs winning for me *outright* every week!

But football 2003 was not a dream season—it was a typical season for the King of Underdogs! Believe me, as a career underdog that has continuously beaten the odds, I am the patron saint of lost causes. My teams are in most cases pathetic losers with no public support, and as far as bookmakers, bettors, and experts are concerned, they have no chance to win. Yet they managed to win *outright* for me a little over three times a week (out of about six to eight top plays released per week).

If a bettor had bet my underdogs on the moneyline (taking 2 to 1, or 3 to 1 odds, instead of points), he or she would have made a killing. But in the end, it's the points that give underdog bettors the edge they need to beat the bookmakers. The heavy tariff (otherwise known as points) will kill a bettor who bets favorites—even if the selected favorites do manage to win the game. But in many cases, favorites will suffer a letdown and lose outright, thereby adding insult to injury, burning both your money and your pride. The moral to the story: In sports betting, *you cannot make money betting on favorites.*

Three Major Reasons the Favorites Lose So Often

Let me state first that favorites don't lose in all situations. In fact, statistics over the last twenty years prove that favorites and underdogs are actually quite even versus the point spread. So if you picked *all* the favorites on the schedule in any given week, you might go fifty-fifty or so.

The problem isn't betting *all* the favorites. The house (or bookmaker) owns the real edge when you choose to bet certain favorites: *public favorites,* teams everyone loves and sees as infallible. It's specifically the most popular favorites, playing games where the betting public cannot picture the favorite losing under any circumstances, that wind up destroying the bankrolls of the masses. Why is this true? Let me explain.

Reason #1: Lopsided Betting Action

Bookmakers adjust lines to keep the betting as equal as possible. Why? Because if there's equal money, the bookmaker takes no risk; he wins no matter what. Bookmakers automatically collect a 10 percent commission (called the "vigorish"). So twenty-four hours a day, all a bookmaker wants in life is even money on every game. That's your edge as a bettor! Since 80 percent or more of the public bets almost exclusively on favorites, the bookmakers and oddsmakers have no choice but to constantly slant the lines *against* the favorites to get some betting action on the underdog.

This is especially true with the public favorites (teams beloved by the largest number of masses of asses). So if a bookmaker thinks a team will attract big betting action, they often add 1, 2, or even 3 points to the line. This is to inflict maximum pain on the favored team's bettors, and to encourage more bettors to bet on the underdog. Thus, there will be even money on both sides. Despite that point-spread edge in the underdog's favor, the betting public often ignores the extra points (or tariff) they must pay to play their public teams. So money pours in on that favorite anyway (ignoring the bloated spread), and *in reaction the point spread moves even higher* to punish the masses of ignorant asses.

By game time, the favored team's fans are paying such a ridiculous premium that the odds are astronomically against them from the moment of the opening kickoff. Your job as a smart bettor is to recognize those situations where you have a significant edge. On Wall Street this strategy is called value investing. Sound familiar?

Reason #2: Better Teams Are Overrated

The second major reason favorites lose so often is that the betting public often overrates the better teams. This is a classic example of perception distorting reality. In the NFL or NBA, the difference between the best team in the league and the worst is often razor thin. On any given Sunday (as the saying goes) any team, no matter how pathetic, can finally put a flawless performance together and beat a far superior team. No matter how dominant a team appears, even an unbeaten team, for example, they are capable of being upset in the right situation by what appears to be a far inferior team.

Now factor in the points. The point spread is set to accommodate the perception—not the reality. If the public perception is that a team is unbeatable, the points rise dramatically. So this perception has created an even bigger betting edge for the underdog bettor.

Reason #3: Underdog Psychology

The favorite is usually embraced by the public for good reason—they're on a hot streak. They have won four in a row; and five of their last six. They are scoring remarkably high point totals (the public loves glamorous, high-octane offensive juggernauts that score and score and score some more). They aren't just squeaking by their opponents, either—the favorite has been *dominating* (winning games by 20 or even 30 points).

The reason they're winning is because they have marquee players that attract high-profile media attention. While their pathetic opponent is being panned or savaged (or worse, ignored) by the media, our public darling (the favorite) is being lauded in headlines from coast to coast.

So here's the perfect situation for a Contrarian like me: One team is underachieving and being ripped apart in the press. Their fans are booing and questioning their manhood. Even their friends, families, girlfriends, and wives are starting to doubt and criticize them. So the natural result is that this underdog is angry, motivated to finally win a game, and insanely jealous of their far superior, more glamorous media-blessed opponent.

And you wonder why pathetic underdogs regularly win games against dominant favorites? The underdog has been waiting all week for this game. The dog has a chip on his shoulder; he has something to prove. He resents the glamorous, pampered marquee players on the other sideline, complete with their entourage traveling in tow. The underdog is sick of losing and seeing his name savaged by the media. He wants revenge, and he wants desperately to taste victory. He wants to rub that victory in the other team's face. As a result, he is practicing harder and with more emotion than he ever has in his life. He is focused, motivated, and ready to rip his opponent's head off!

Likewise, the big favorite is overconfident. He has acquired a big head after being told all week by fans, his agent, his personal assistant, his teammates, his girlfriends, and the media that he is unbeatable. And he no longer cares about practice. "Why practice? We're the best team in the world. We don't need practice to beat those chumps." The big favorite with the big ego is ripe for a beating. I don't know about you, but I'd put my money on David versus Goliath every time. Even better—David never got points! Here your angry, hungry, jealous, motivated underdog has been given an edge—they are getting a bunch of points versus an overconfident, fatheaded opponent.

I'll take the underdog every time! Does betting underdogs work? Certainly not every time. But underdogs provide a slight edge to the smart professional bettor. In almost twenty years as a professional gambler and sports handicapper, I've never yet met a winning gambler who did not make underdogs the cornerstone of his betting strategy. Now you know why this world-class Contrarian is the King of the Underdogs.

ROOT CONTRARIAN RULE #2: THE PUBLIC BETS WITH THEIR HEARTS INSTEAD OF THEIR HEADS—A *HUGE* MISTAKE.

The typical amateur bettor (or "square," as professional gamblers call them) bets not only favorites (meaning point spread favorites) but their personal favorite teams. The public often bets, for example, on home teams—New Yorkers bet on the Giants or the Jets, *no matter what the price.* San Francisco bettors wager on the 49ers or Oakland Raiders, no matter what the price. Chicago sports bettors are willing to bet the Bears, Cubs, Bulls, or Notre Dame, no matter what the price.

This home-team bias is one of the biggest and most obvious mistakes in all of gambling. Perhaps even more popular is the habit for college football and basketball fans to bet their alma mater. (Except for me, of course. I went to Columbia University! My Columbia Lions football team suffered the longest losing streak in college football history while I attended school there. Suffice to say, Columbia grads from that era do *not* have any interest in betting on their alma mater!)

In all of these cases, the bettor is unwittingly being taken to the cleaners by bookmakers. Knowing that most New Yorkers will naturally bet on the Giants, New York bookmakers automatically slant the line against the New York bettors every time. If your bookmaker knows you are a Michigan alumnus and you're willing to bet Michigan come rain or shine every week, he too will slant the line (or point spread) against you. Bookies the world over always move lines against popular teams (for example, the New York Yankees, the L.A. Lakers, Notre Dame, the Dallas Cowboys—otherwise known as "America's Team"—and the Oakland Raiders, just to name a few) or popular superstar players (such as, over the years, Michael Jordan, Shaquille O'Neal, Kobe Bryant, John Elway, Peyton Manning, Joe Montana, and Roger Clemens) and their fans and bettors. You will always pay a premium to bet popular teams, your hometown team, your alma mater (bookmakers keep track of your patterns), or your personal favorites.

If you choose to bet this way, you will *always* be getting the short end of the stick. How can you capitalize on this newly acquired knowledge of smart betting strategy? If you live in Boston, bet *against* your hometown teams. If you live in New York or L.A. or Philly or Chicago, bet *against* your hometown teams. Bet against popular public teams like Notre Dame, the Oakland Raiders, or the L.A. Lakers on a regular basis. (Wagering on the Detroit Pistons as 7 to 1 underdogs in the 2004 NBA Championships versus the L.A. Lakers might have been a good investment, don't you think?) At the very least, make yourself a promise to never bet on any game involving your hometown team or favorite team. That way you can just sit back, relax, and root for your favorites—without making stupid money decisions based on them.

If you're going to risk your hard-earned cash, save it for high-percentage betting opportunities. But don't bet on your college alma mater or hometown heroes (unless of course, everyone else is betting against them!). Start thinking and *betting with your head—not your heart.* It's the only way to win in the sports-betting business.

ROOT CONTRARIAN RULE #3: THE PUBLIC PLAYS LONG SHOTS—A *HUGE* MISTAKE.

I recently sat in a taxi in traffic in London, England. I was in the United Kingdom to spread my sports handicapping mini-empire to the European continent. The taxi driver asked where I was from and what I did. I told him. He wanted to jump out of his seat! He had a big-time professional gambler from America in his backseat, as a captive audience. He began to tell me how much he and his friends loved to bet sports— mostly soccer and rugby.

In England, betting on sports is perfectly legal and acceptable. As a result, there are sports betting shops on nearly every corner! I asked the taxi driver about his betting strategy. "Well there's certainly no point in betting five pounds and winning only five pounds," he said. "I play long shots. Big odds. Big payoffs. I want bang for my buck! If I bet five pounds, I want to get back one hundred pounds. What would be the fun of winning only five pounds?"

"Interesting strategy," I thought to myself. Sounds like most of the American sports gamblers I meet, too. They all want to strike it rich with one big bet. And the result is they bet parlays, teasers, and other exotic wagers. Wagers in which they have little or no chance at winning. But "going for broke" is stupid, reckless, and most of all *hopeless.*

Going for broke with long shots can only get you broke fast! The average bettor just doesn't understand how hard it is to win one single solitary bet. Just one—even for me, one of the most successful sports handicapping experts ever. If I bet on two games and win one, I'm even for the day (minus the vigorish, or bookmaker's commission, of course). At least I live to fight another day, when the odds might be more in my favor.

But if I bet a two-team parlay and go one win and one loss, I lose the bet. I'm punished for breaking even (winning one and losing one). That's not my definition of putting the odds in my favor. As a matter of fact, I'd call that kind of bet downright stupid.

Trying to win two bets in a two-team parlay is just complicating your efforts, and the odds against your winning rise dramatically. A three-team parlay is even harder. And the really exotic bets—the five-team parlays, ten-team parlays, teasers, reverses, and proposition bets are all but impossible to win. You might as well set fire to your money, then flush the burning remains down the toilet. That's how badly betting parlays and other exotic bets screw up your chances of coming out ahead—all for the sake of those supposed big payoffs.

By the way, that's why the payoffs are so big in the first place—to entice you into throwing your hard-earned money away on fruitless, reckless, hopeless bets, bets you just have virtually no shot at winning—bets that come with payoffs that literally make your eyes bulge. These are the kind of promised payoffs that turn amateur bettors into dreamers.

But even those big payoffs are a mirage. Let me explain. On a two-team parlay, the payoffs look big. But the true odds of winning a two-team parlay are 3 to 1 against you. So the payout should be 3 to 1 (or 15 to 5). But casinos only pay 13 to 5. That's their edge. But it's a huge edge. They're stacking the decks against you. Your odds are even worse on a three-team parlay. Your true odds of winning are 8 to 1 against you. However, casinos only payoff with odds of 6 to 1. Starting to get the picture? You're getting (legally) ripped off!

The most common form of betting in America is not with a bookmaker or a legal Las Vegas sportsbook. It's in the workplace on a parlay sheet—the office pool. Millions of these parlay sheets are handed out at offices across America.

The odds these office parlay sheets pay are even worse than with the sportsbook. Their edge over the bettor can range from 25 percent (enormous) to 50 percent (ridiculous and hard to fathom). Yes, I said 50 percent. And that last parlay with the 50 percent edge to the bookmaker is the bet so many amateur gamblers love to make—a ten-team teaser. The attractive number that entices amateurs to bet on a ten-team parlay is the gigantic payoff of 500 to 1. But based on the odds, the true payoff should be a tad over 1,000 to 1. So you're getting ripped off on every bet you place. The "house" has a 50 percent edge over you.

And I've got a news flash for you: You're not going ten for ten anyway. I can't go ten for ten and I'm one of the best gamblers in the world. Trying to go ten for ten is like blowing your money up with a laser-guided missile. You might as well—you have no chance of winning. And even if you do, you'll be ripped off badly on the payoff.

Yet the masses of amateur gamblers make these stupid bets every day. They must be related to the day traders of Wall Street. They both live for "action" (lots of bets per day) without realizing that action will eat up your bankroll and leave you bankrupt in record time. These amateurs ignore the fact that a simple bet on one team in one game offers the best odds of any bet you can make—which means the best chance of winning.

Give me, the professional gambler, simple, straightforward 11 to 10 odds, with a fifty-fifty shot of winning. One game to sit back and enjoy with your favorite food in hand and best friends as supporting cast. And, most importantly, a great shot at winning. If you cannot enjoy this bet, knowing it's your best chance to profit, you are either a fool, self-destructive, delusional, or a gambling addict who is out of control and destined for the poorhouse.

Keep it simple, keep it safe, bet only a very few high-percentage games, grind the bookmaker out, and you'll laugh all the way to the bank (in your new Mercedes). But try to "break the bank" with parlays, exotic bets, and long-shot payoffs, and I'd advise setting aside the money right now to pay your bankruptcy attorney.

Just like on Wall Street, winning in sports gambling is all about being patient and grinding it out. Being willing to accept small profits, then stringing together a few small profits in a row. Just like on Wall Street, in the sports-betting world pigs get fat, but hogs get slaughtered!

ROOT CONTRARIAN RULE #4: THE PUBLIC RARELY HAS SUFFICIENT STAYING POWER— A *HUGE* MISTAKE.

The idea of grinding out a profit starts with a sufficient bankroll. That's a bettor's foundation for success.

But most amateur gamblers start off from day one with insufficient funds. So what else is new? They start with too little money, have no game plan, possess no discipline, and as a result quickly become desperate— and are therefore forced to go for long-shot homeruns to try to get rich quick. The invariable result is that they go bust virtually every time.

The key to "grinding out" a profit is having a large enough starting bankroll to overcome the inevitable losing streaks. If you are insufficiently bankrolled, you'll either be out of money before the streak turns around or you'll try to save yourself by taking huge risks (making stupid, low-percentage long-shot bets you have almost no shot at winning). Every gambler, including the best professionals in the world, will encounter losing streaks, slumps, last-second losses, and simple bad luck. These things are all part of gambling (and also of investing).

The proper and smart way to bet for fun and profit is simple.

- Start with a sufficient bankroll.
- Bet the same amount on every game. Only break this rule and step

up your bets if you're ahead; *never* when behind. That way you're only risking with the bookmaker's money, not yours.

- Be patient, bet only a few high-percentage plays a week.
- Take no huge risks.
- Never try to get it all back at once if you're down money.
- Play a safe, "grind it out" game.

Sound familiar? I'll keep repeating these important points, because they are the only ways to put the odds in your favor and turn "gambling" into a profitable investment.

ROOT CONTRARIAN RULE #5: THE PUBLIC BETS HELTER-SKELTER WITH NO GAME PLAN OR MONEY-MANAGEMENT SKILLS—A *HUGE* MISTAKE.

Here's a familiar pattern for the typical amateur sports gambler: He bets $100 each on ten college football games on Saturday (too many bets—virtually no chance of winning). Then he bets $100 each on ten NFL games on Sunday (too many bets—virtually no chance of winning). After a two-day nonstop orgy of gambling, our friend is lucky to be down only $250 to the bookmaker. Now he decides to bet the whole $250 plus another $250 (so he has a profit, of course) on the Monday Night Football game. He loses. He has turned a small losing weekend into a disaster.

Now our friend is down $800 in all (the $50 extra is for the vigorish). He's not sure how he'll pay for the mortgage next week. Or his kid's tuition. A nice weekend of entertainment has been turned into a financial train wreck because of poor money-management skills and a lack of patience.

Why was the Monday Night Football game worth $500? What made it *five times* bigger than any other bet of the weekend? Was any planning involved in this decision to go for broke? This is the simple but costly mistake most sports bettors make all the time. It's part of the same mind-set that makes an amateur sports bettor decide to bet a five- or ten-team parlay—he has no patience or discipline, and he wants the "big payoff."

It's the same reason that a bettor decides to bet ten separate games at $100 each, when in fact he'd be better off betting the entire $1,000 on one high-percentage game. It's the same reason that a bettor bets everything (and then some) on Monday Night Football. He wants the glory. But guess what? Gambling is much like war—the hero (the guy going for the glory) usually dies!

Take it from a world-champion professional handicapper: The only way to show a profit betting on sports (or anything else for that matter) is to grind out the bookmaker. Bet only a few select games. Bet the same amount on each game. Monday Night Football is *not* worth four times more than any other game. Never bet "double or nothing" when you're down. If you're going to step up and take a shot, only do it when you're ahead and therefore risking only the bookmaker's money. Have a game plan designed ahead of each weekend of gambling, and stick to it.

Here's one more example of poor money-management skills and the disastrous results they can lead to: A typical sports bettor loses and loses and loses some more on his own. Then one day he sees me, Wayne Allyn Root, advertising on TV. A light bulb goes off. He thinks it might be a good idea to hire a professional sports handicapper to advise him. But he's still skeptical—is Wayne Allyn Root really as good as advertised?

So he bets a conservative $100 on my first recommendation. He wins and is impressed—enough to risk $250 on my second pick. It wins. Now he's really getting interested. He bets $500 on my third pick. It wins. He's jumping out of his seat with excitement. He bets $1,000 on my fourth pick. It wins. Now he's downright giddy. He's found the answer to his prayers. He bets $5,000 on my fifth pick. It wins. He's now convinced he's hit the mother lode. He sells off some stock and uses the proceeds to bet $25,000 on my sixth pick. It *loses*. He's angry, frustrated, disillusioned. "Wayne has ruined my life! I never should have believed in him. What a fool I am." He quits my service.

What's wrong with this picture? *Money management—or the lack of it—has ruined this poor fellow.* I gave him six plays. My advice was a spectacular five wins and one loss, which adds up to 83 percent winners. This is as good as it gets. Eighty-three percent winners is beyond-belief good. A gambler who wins 55 to 60 percent of the time can make a fortune. But here our friend was a participant in a wonderful 83 percent winning streak on my part and he's managed to *lose* $20,650 (with vigorish). Do you now understand the importance of planning, grinding it out on high-percentage plays and disciplined money-management skills? It's the simple difference between winning and losing.

I've seen it again and again. A talented and disciplined professional gambler can "tread water" until a hot streak arrives, then bet big and make a fortune. Better yet, a really talented gambler can show a profit during a small losing streak. But an amateur with no game plan and poor money-management skills can lose money on even a hot winning streak. With the exact same advice, two gamblers can produce totally different results. That's the high-stakes value of good money-management skills.

ROOT CONTRARIAN RULE #6: THE PUBLIC ISN'T WILLING TO DO THEIR HOMEWORK— ANOTHER *HUGE* MISTAKE.

The average amateur gambler is either ill-informed or lazy. They believe that a win is a win. But it's not. A win for me (the professional) can easily become a ½ point loss for the amateur.

On any one game, one bookmaker may offer a 2-point spread, another bookie may offer 2½ points, and yet a third bookie may offer 3 points. The lines on many games will vary, and your job (if you want to win) is to find the best possible line on every game. Shop around for the best line. Winning is all about having access to the best possible point spread on every game and doing the homework necessary to find the best lines. Winning gamblers are always willing to do their homework. Losers always want the shortcut or easy way out.

Let me explain. Even for the most successful gamblers and handicappers in the world, many games are decided by ½ to 1 point. That's why it's so important to shop around for the best line. The key to success as a gambler is to always have multiple bookmakers—either three local bookies or three online sportsbooks, or three Las Vegas sportsbook accounts. In any of those cases, three is the *minimum* number of bookmakers a bettor should have. There will often be three different lines from three different bookies.

Now you have the ability to choose the best point spread on any given game *before* you place your hard-earned money on the line. So, for example, your favorite professional sports handicapper, Wayne Allyn Root, picks Dallas over Washington as a best bet. I personally shop around and find Dallas +3½ points and I place my personal bet. But my clients and fans don't shop around for the best price, and they place their bets on whatever line their bookmaker quotes them. The amateurs bet Dallas at only +3 points. Dallas loses by exactly 3 points. I win $1,000 (because I had Dallas +3½). My clients push (break even), thereby making *zero* and wasting a perfectly good profit opportunity. A profit opportunity that is lost forever. They can never get it back.

Let's take my example a step further. My clients get a line on that same game of +2½. I shop around and find Dallas +3. I use this opportunity to "buy" an extra ½ point (by paying 10 to 20 percent extra in vigorish, a bettor can buy an extra ½ point). So now my bet is +3½. The final result falls exactly on 3—Dallas loses by 3 points. Many of my clients lose because they were getting only +2½ points. I win $1,000 because I was getting +3½ points. They each lose $1,100 (the $1,000 bet plus the 10 percent vigorish). That's a dramatic $2,100 difference on one game. But worse, they lost on the exact same bet that proved a winner for me! That's the power of shopping around for the best price (or point spread)—it has the power to turn winners into losers or vice versa, all on the same bet.

More important than a possible $2,100 turnaround on one game is the effect "shopping around" for the best price has on a typical season. During a typical football season, for example, shopping and finding the best line will result in at least ten extra wins for a typical gambler. In some years, it adds as many as twenty extra wins.

Usually you can win one extra game (or at least turn a loss into a push) every two weeks during the course of a typical season. That may not sound like much, but turning ten losses into ten wins is actually a twenty-unit turnaround! If you're betting $1,000 per game, that's a $20,000 difference at the end of the season. If you're betting $10,000 per game (which many of my high-roller clients do) that's a $200,000 difference in your favor by betting on the exact same games!

It's amazing how many businesspeople are willing to leave no stone unturned to achieve success at their profession or business career—no detail too small, no opportunity to micro-manage passed up—yet when it comes to gambling on sports, they call that a "hobby" and disregard the very same skills that made them successful in the business world.

My advice: Do the homework. Put in the hours. Check the details. Shop for the best price—*comparison shopping* in the gambling world! As you do in your professional life, leave no stone unturned when you're gambling. My goal is to always put the odds in my favor. If you can do that, gambling is no longer "just gambling." It is an investment. A profitable investment. From this point on, treat it as one.

ROOT CONTRARIAN RULE #7:
THE PUBLIC TREATS GAMBLING
DIFFERENTLY THAN SHOPPING—
A *HUGE* MISTAKE.

Gambling, like shopping, always comes down to value. When you shop for groceries or clothing or a new car, don't you comparison shop? Don't you search for the best deal? Aren't you interested in the best value for your dollar? So why is gambling treated so differently? Whether you are making a wager on an underdog or on a favorite, you are "buying" that team for a set price.

As I've pointed out again and again, the price at which you buy the wager matters. It is often the difference between winning and losing. But the masses of bettors don't see it this way. If they like Team A, they will "buy" the wager at any price. If they want to buy Team A at –7 points, they will also buy at –8 points, –9 points or even –10 points. This is ridiculous. Anyone who does this is an idiot!

It's like saying you want to buy a new Hummer H2 (which happens to be my car!) and you don't care if the price is $55,000 or $71,000. How could you not care? That's a $16,000 difference. That might add $200 per month onto your monthly payment. Is that not significant? Will that price not factor into your decision? Is it not possible that you'd buy your shiny new Hummer H2 at $55,000, but might decide *not* to buy when you find out that the price has risen to $71,000? If you didn't think that way, you'd be a fool.

Sports betting is no different. Once you decide the New York Jets are a play, for example, at +4 points, you should look for the best line possible (remember my advice above for shopping around). But if you can only find the Jets at +2½ points, you should eliminate the bet. Don't press. Don't worry about losing out. Don't make your wager based on being down money to the bookmaker and desperately wanting to get your money back.

A bet is only a high-percentage play (a wager where you have the "edge") if it is "selling" at the right price. If it isn't, walk away! Besides, now that you've read my book and become a dedicated contrarian, you should *always* be getting the best price possible, on every wager. You are always in the minority, so your wager should automatically attract the value. Remember, the least supported team gets the most point-spread value, to encourage even money betting on both sides. If the spread is moving against you, you are doing something wrong. You have miscalculated public opinion. Walk away. A good shopper is always prepared to walk away—because price matters!

ROOT CONTRARIAN RULE #8: THE PUBLIC BELIEVES THEY CAN BECOME WINNERS BY LISTENING TO THE MEDIA EXPERTS—A *HUGE* MISTAKE.

There are three giant misconceptions here. First is the idea that members of the media are "experts." Second, that they posses "inside information." Third, that if they did have access to "inside info" they'd share it with you. None of these things is true.

First of all, there is no such thing as "inside information." To avoid gambling scandals due to unfair advantages and insiders' knowledge, pro and college sports demand the release of all pertinent information to the public. That way no one has an advantage—we all know the same things.

Where's your advantage by listening to sports talk radio? Or buying a 50-cent newspaper? Or watching ESPN SportsCenter? There is none. The media experts are merely repeating the same information already disclosed to the public—the same exact news everyone else knows; the same news used by Las Vegas oddsmakers to create the point spread.

All that news is already built into the very line you're betting on. By watching all those pre-game shows, you are learning *nothing* that can ever help you win a dime betting on sports. Zero. Zip. Zilch. Nada. Nothing. There is no "edge" to be gained by being "informed" by the media. The news you're getting is old news that has already been factored into the betting line, and therefore has no significant effect on betting.

Compare this to stocks. On Wall Street the average $10,000 investor gains access to nothing important. However, those with $1,000,000 stock accounts have access to the very best information, analysis, and advice. This is the arena where only the rich and powerful get assigned the smartest money managers, hedge-fund managers, investment bankers, or stockbrokers. You, the small-time investor, get nothing.

Money provides access; the rest of us get false hopes. It certainly is no different with sports gambling. If there were inside information, do you really believe you'd gain access to it for the price of a 50-cent newspaper? Or for free by tuning in your car radio to sports-talk screamers? Or simply for sitting in your La-Z-Boy watching SportsCenter? But no matter. There is none in the first place. Professional handicappers win because we do our homework. We put in the long hours necessary to isolate winners. In my case, I not only put in long hours, but I also have a staff of consultants and advisers who each put in fifty hours. I get all of their collective wisdom and homework.

My objective is to find the Contrarian picks that the public disregards, disrespects, and can't wait to bet against. And, of course, I bet on those very same teams with both fists! Unless you can spare fifty to eighty hours a week to find that "edge" or can employ a staff of consultants who each devotes fifty to eighty hours a week, my advice is to find a professional who can. But no matter what, please make me one solemn promise: Never again assume you're a sports-betting expert because you watch SportsCenter!

ROOT CONTRARIAN RULE #9: THE PUBLIC BELIEVES THERE IS SAFETY IN NUMBERS— A *HUGE* MISTAKE.

The typical amateur gambler is afraid to take the road less traveled. He lacks the confidence to risk his money on teams no one else wants. So he follows the crowd. Big mistake! Just like on Wall Street, in sports betting the herd mentality will get you slaughtered. Why?

First, because the gut instincts of the crowd are almost always wrong. By following them, you're jumping off the cliff with the masses of asses. Why bet on the advice of your friends, neighbors, cousins, or fellow drinkers at the bar? What do they know that you don't? If they are so successful, why are they always as broke as you? Why are they struggling just like you? Why aren't these experts driving Ferraris and living in mansions at the beach? The answer is that they know nothing (just like you) and they're guessing based on the bad information they heard on SportsCenter or sports talk radio (just like you).

Yes, it's a lot less lonely to follow the masses. It's more fun to be part of the crowd—all rooting for the same teams, yelling and cheering and high-fiving at the same plays, at the same time, as you watch on the boob tube. But think about the ending, when the games are over and you've lost as part of that crowd. Guess what? The party's over! Now the hangover begins. Trust me: Winning alone is more rewarding (and less lonely in the long run) than losing with friends. My friends are Benjamin Franklin (or at least his picture on the $100 bill), my family, and my banker. They keep me warm at night.

The second reason the herd mentality will get you slaughtered is because crowds make the point spread move the wrong way. Anytime you're betting with the majority, you can be assured you will be getting the worst value possible in the point spread. In plain English: If you're following the crowd in sports betting, you're screwed.

By taking the road less traveled and betting on teams that the masses would never support, you are always getting the best possible point-spread value. This is a huge advantage. It is the very definition of what I mean by playing only a very few high-percentage plays per week. The term "high-percentage" means (at least in my dictionary) teams that are out of favor and therefore are getting the maximum number of points from the bookmaker. The bookie wants to encourage some betting on that team because he wants equal money on both sides.

Being a Contrarian, you may be forced to sit quietly on the opposite side of the bar from all your buddies, but you're always getting value in the line. You now have the edge over the oddsmaker and bookmaker. You will "grind the bookmaker down" and win 55 to 60 percent of all your bets. You are now living proof that there is no safety in numbers. If there were, the masses would rule the world.

The common masses of humanity are not driving Ferraris, living in mansions, or retiring to Hawaii, Aspen, and Monte Carlo. In reality, the masses live lives of quiet desperation. They barely survive paycheck to paycheck. They rarely taste victory. They are living proof that there is no safety in numbers—just lots of losers.

If your goal is success and wealth, you must bet against the crowds, not with them. By the way, there's one more big benefit to betting (and living) like a Contrarian: In the end, you won't be lonely, either. As a matter of fact, you'll be the life of the party! The guy with all the money, buying the drinks, is always in demand!

ROOT CONTRARIAN RULE #10: THE PUBLIC DOESN'T UNDERSTAND THE IMPORTANCE OF TIMING—A *HUGE* MISTAKE.

Just like on Wall Street, timing in sports betting is everything! This concept is an offshoot of the herd mentality discussed above. Not only does following the crowd get you slaughtered—it also guarantees that you will fall victim to horrendous timing.

This is where Benjamin Graham comes in. Graham was one of the great stock pickers of all time and the inventor of the term "value investing." Graham's theory was simple: buy low, sell high. In other words, find value in stocks nobody is looking at . . . yet.

Value is all about timing. When a stock is at an all-time low of $10 per share, it is often indicative of an overreaction by investors. One or two bad announcements and the masses think the sky is falling. They will immediately knock a perfectly good stock down from $50 per share to $10. Suddenly an overvalued stock is undervalued. Why? Because no one wants the stock.

Ironically, now might be the ideal time to buy. When stocks are at their all-time lows, it's because no one wants to own them—yet if there is actual value in the stock, that is precisely when a smart investor buys! At the bottom, and against the crowds.

Why is the timing so ideal at this moment? Because when everyone is getting out of a stock, the price is low compared with its actual value. When the invariable good announcement about the stock happens—as it always does—there are lots of potential investors who want to buy back in, everyone (as a herd) decides that this same stock is a good buy again, and the price of the stock goes up. You got in at the bottom— perfect timing—at $10 per share. When it rises back to $30, you've made a small fortune.

However, the key wasn't the actual stock, or the management, or record corporate profits, or even new exciting products. The key was timing—often fluctuations in the price of a stock merely reflect public perception. The stock was a great value at $10 (when the perception was negative). It was undervalued. It had nowhere to go but up. But the same stock with the same story and earnings performance is *not* a buy at $28 (when the perception is positive), and by the time it gets to $48, the same stock is an automatic sell.

Do you now understand the value of timing? Those few points (up or down) will determine whether you earn a profit on your investment or a loss. We're talking about the same company, with the same earnings and management. Yet because of timing and the price of the stock at the moment of purchase, some investors will profit and some will get slaughtered over the next six months.

Betting on sports is *exactly* the same. The New York Jets might be a poor value at +4 points versus New England, but at +7 they are a great value. If they've lost three in a row and four of the last five games, you can bet that the Jets are out of favor with the public. They've lost the gambling public tens of millions of dollars over that span, and the betting public is angry with them. The bettors are disillusioned and will no longer trust the team to win.

In order to attract even money on the game (or anything even remotely close), the oddsmakers will change what should be a +4 point line to +6½ instead. There is now value in betting the Jets. By the day of the big game, the betting is still so lopsided on New England that the line has been adjusted to +7. Soon the line bursts thru to +7½.

Now is your opportunity! This is the very definition of value. The Jets are a good team that has played poorly for a short period of time. They've been denigrated in the press. They've suffered critical injuries to key players, but two of those key starters are recovered and playing today. The public has overreacted (as usual because of the negative reports they've read in the press). The public perception of the Jets is far too low. Besides that, the Jets have a chip on their shoulders. They have something to prove to their fans, the hated media, and to themselves. And as a bonus, they are playing their hated division rival, the New England Patriots. In my opinion, this is the perfect Contrarian betting opportunity. They have a good shot at pulling the upset and winning outright (as my underdog picks did fifty-eight times last season) under these ideal circumstances. But as insurance, you get 7½ points in the bargain. That's value, good market timing, and Contrarian opportunity all wrapped into one!

Now you understand the value of timing. The New York Jets—the same team that was *not* a buy last week when there were still too many "investors" who believed in them, trusted them, respected them, and wanted to bet on them, suddenly provides great value this week. Why? After yet another devastating defeat, the rats have left the sinking ship. The Jets have alienated all the masses of amateur bettors. They have no support left. Now the Jets define *value*. Still, we had to wait for the perfect point spread—one that reflects value. At +4 the Jets were not a buy. At +7 they are a good buy. At +7½ they are a steal. Same team, just a better price. Just like on Wall Street, where the same stock with the same fundamentals is only a buy based on the price. Betting on sports works the same way: Buy low, sell high!

ROOT CONTRARIAN RULE #11: THE PUBLIC DOESN'T UNDERSTAND THE PSYCHOLOGY OF GAMBLING—A *HUGE* MISTAKE.

Do you know the big difference between amateur gamblers who lose their shirts betting on sports and the best professional gamblers in the world? No, the answer is not that the professional gambler wins more often (although that's certainly true). It actually all comes down to how the professional prepares for and reacts to *losing*.

All gamblers lose. The best professional handicappers and gamblers hit 55 to 60 percent winners. That's all the edge you need to grind out a healthy profit—enough profit to make you wealthy and famous. But that means that the best gamblers in the world lose four (or more) out of every ten bets! That's a lot of losing. In my twenty-year career, my best estimate is that I've made over 50,000 predictions. I've won a little under 30,000 predictions, and lost a little over 20,000 predictions. That means that as one of the best professional sports handicappers in the world, I've lost about 20,000 times!

Perhaps now you can understand why I don't get crazy over a bad night or a bad week or a sub-par month. It's because I've been there before. That's the key to winning: Understand that every gambler (and investor) picks losers. Second, understand the "big picture." What happens in any one game, or in any one day (or week, or month) is insignificant. What matters is winning consistently over the long haul.

I've met a lot of gamblers over the years who thought they could earn a living as a professional gambler, like me. They thought they could become rich and famous. They were wrong. The difference in each and every case was that they couldn't handle the losing streaks. Within that 55 to 60 percent winning percentage over the long term, are many 0-5 NFL Sundays, many 2 for 15 streaks in college basketball, many 0 for 7 streaks to start the NBA playoffs, many losing months in baseball. They hurt—bad!—and that hurt can shake your confidence.

However, even after a no-win, seven-loss start, a top-ranked professional has the courage, confidence, and smarts to pull the trigger on game number eight. He or she has the guts to keep firing away with confidence, until fate turns things around and the next winning streak starts. Seven losses out of seven bets does not matter, especially if you win thirteen of the next fifteen. Add that record up and it combines to form an overall record of thirteen wins and nine losses—59 percent winners. That's just about my lifetime record over the last twenty years, spanning three decades. And that record makes me one of the best to ever walk into a Las Vegas sportsbook.

That example is pretty typical of the pattern of winners versus losers for a top-notch gambler. What I'm saying is that even a pro that wins 60 percent of the time does not win a consistent six out of every ten. There are losing streaks and winning streaks, as well as periods of breaking even. But add it all up and you get your 60 percent record. My record is often made up of a 0 for 7 losing streak, followed by a 13 for 15 hot streak.

Most amateurs don't have the patience, confidence, or courage to survive an 0 for 7 start. They fade away, never to be heard from again. And even if they had the courage and confidence, they don't have the bankroll or money-management skills to survive a long losing streak. They go bust just moments before a huge winning streak is set to begin. They are long gone by the time the 13 for 15 streak starts.

Only those with the right temperament can win at sports betting. As James Carville might put it, "It's not the winners that make you a winner in the sports gambling world; it's the psychology, stupid!"

ROOT CONTRARIAN RULE #12: THE PUBLIC DOESN'T UNDERSTAND HISTORY— A *HUGE* MISTAKE.

I'm a graduate of Columbia University. What I learned at that venerable Ivy League institution is that history repeats itself again and again. If we do not study history and learn from it, we are doomed to make the same mistakes with regularity.

The importance of history applies nowhere with more certainty than in sports gambling. I see the same bettors making the same mistakes season after season, year after year. It's almost as if the masses of bettors act together as a group to subconsciously block out their losses of the past. They return year after year, certain that this year they'll destroy the bookmaker, even though it has happened the other way around for ten or twenty straight years!

Logic would dictate that if bettors refuse to give up (a trait I admire), at least they should change their strategy. But collectively the masses of bettors seem to erase from their subconscious minds any shred of memory of past disasters, and start the new betting season by making the same mistakes all over again. Amazing!

I'm not a fan of team trends, so that's not the history I refer to here. I believe most of the team histories are either coincidental or anomalous and not worth studying. Players change teams because of free agency so often now that what happened five years ago is meaningless. A team's streak is bound to change direction at any time.

The history I refer to is the way *all* teams play in certain situations. For instance, year after year, in the last two weeks of the NFL season, the underdogs who are already eliminated from playoff contention consistently cover the point spread versus winning teams still fighting for playoff contention. Pretty simple. No thinking required. The losing team that is already eliminated is loose, relaxed, and carefree. They have nothing to lose—and they have a chip on their shoulder. That's a very potent psychological one-two punch for the underdog. The better team in this case is nervous and tight. They have everything to lose in this situation.

Give the already-eliminated team a bunch of points and you have the perfect combination for underdog upsets galore. Happens every year. I win money for my clients every year at this same holiday time. I call it my annual Christmas Fund!

So why do the masses of amateur bettors not know this, understand this, or remember this? Is history so hard to study? Is it so hard to remember? There are dozens of historical situations that I've compiled over the years. I'll talk more about them in Chapter 13, but the point in all this is simple: Don't make the same mistakes every season. Study past history, learn from your mistakes, and *profit* from history.

ROOT CONTRARIAN RULE #13: THE PUBLIC THINKS FOOTBALL IS KING—A *HUGE* MISTAKE.

America's sports bettors have a love affair with football. Sixty percent or more of all sports betting in this country is football related. Much of that casual betting is done all on one day—Super Bowl Sunday. Big mistake.

Football is my favorite sport to watch, but as far as betting, there is money to be made on *every* sport, in every season. As a matter of fact, basketball and baseball may present bigger and better profit opportunities than football. Once again, it's the follow-the-crowd theory at work. Since most sports bettors bet only football (the one big exception to this rule is March Madness, the NCAA basketball tournament, which is fast becoming a major betting institution), the others follow that same pattern. Once again, there is no safety (or intelligence) in numbers.

Betting sports should not be about only betting on TV games, or betting only on your favorite teams, or betting only on the sport you love to watch. It's an investment. Do Wall Street pros only bet on stocks of companies they root for, or only companies that own TV shows they watch? Of course not. Wall Street stock professionals invest for profit, not fun. It's a business, not a game. The same goes for serious sports gambling.

Basketball and baseball may not be as fun to watch, or even as fun to bet on (especially baseball because it has no point spreads), but they offer more profit opportunities simply because there are more games! Instead of games once a week, like in the NFL (Sunday) or NCAA football (Saturday), both basketball and baseball feature games (and therefore profit opportunities) every day of the week. Baseball offers seven months of these daily profit opportunities, and basketball offers an astounding nine months, while football lasts only five months. Because of daily play, with basketball and baseball there is seven times as much opportunity to profit each week over the one-day-per-week football. Add to that almost double the months of play time. So if you follow my Contrarian grind-'em-out strategies in basketball or baseball, you have many more opportunities by far than in football.

Gamblers tend to rush and panic during football season. After only a few weeks of football, it appears the season is almost over. Time seems to go so fast, and the opportunity to profit just slips away. That forces gamblers to bet too many games in one weekend (out of desperation), and to bet too much money on each game.

With basketball and baseball you have plenty of time to find high-percentage betting opportunities. You can afford to pass if the slate is weak—there are always more games tomorrow. You don't need to play catch-up by doubling your bets while you're down. You can afford to show patience and get it back a little at a time, day by day. In the ultimate salute to the grind-'em-out gambling strategy, in either basketball or baseball you can win one or two units a *day*, instead of the one or two a week you can win in football! For me, Wayne Allyn Root, the change of seasons is a breath of fresh air. Every season to me represents the color *green*.

ROOT CONTRARIAN RULE #14: THE PUBLIC HAS UNREALISTIC EXPECTATIONS—A *HUGE* MISTAKE.

Not only is the public as a whole unrealistic in their perceptions and expectations about the teams (favorites) they are betting on, they are just as unrealistic about their own chances for success as gamblers.

As a professional handicapper for almost twenty years now, I have an "edge" over the bookmaker—a small edge, but nonetheless an edge. On the other hand, I have a *huge* edge on the typical amateur bettor. That edge is the fact that I understand my odds of winning. I do not expect to get rich quick. Sports betting is not a get-rich-quick scheme. It is an investment vehicle, just like stocks, bonds, real estate, gold, or art.

A schoolteacher earning $45,000 a year cannot expect to triple his annual salary in one month through gambling. An accountant earning $75,000 per year cannot expect to become a millionaire overnight through gambling. All bettors are limited by what they can risk. It sounds unfair, but the richer you are when you start, the easier it is to multiply your stake.

So yes, what I'm saying is that the rich do get richer. They start with a bigger bankroll. They can make bigger bets. They can outlast losing streaks. They can afford to be more patient and wait for the high-percentage play. They can also afford to step up and take bigger risks without busting their bankroll. And they never have to risk the rent money.

Life is in fact unfair. But you, as the average gambler with financial limitations, can turn gambling into a profitable venture. You just have to be realistic, patient, disciplined, and most of all, a Contrarian! You can never expect to win 80 percent of your bets. It just doesn't happen. Not over the long haul, anyway.

However, the good news is that you do *not* need to win 80 percent of your bets. The break-even point is 52.38 percent. Few bettors even know this crucial statistic. Winning 58 percent of the time will double your bankroll in 110 wagers. Just a 2 percent increase to 60 percent winners will double your bankroll in sixty wagers—almost half the time! If you're betting ten games in a football weekend (five college games, five pro), that means you can double your bankroll in as little as six weeks, or in as long as eleven weeks. That's not bad.

Could you turn $10,000 into $20,000 in only six weeks on Wall Street? Remember that the top pros on Wall Street are thrilled with a 20 percent *annual* return. So that means that on a $10,000 investment, all you'd earn on Wall Street under the best of circumstances is $2,000 per year!

Yet truck drivers often expect to double their annual salary of $40,000 by betting on sports, which is an impossible expectation. Amateur bettors are often unhappy to learn that in ten weeks in the sports-betting world, they can only turn $10,000 into $20,000. Now that's the definition of unrealistic expectations!

What I'm trying to say here is that I can give you every edge in this world—and that's exactly what I'm doing in this book—but you're still not going to get rich overnight. There is no such thing. If you follow my advice, you will perform better as a gambler than you ever have in your life. You will grind out the bookmaker. You will win more than you'll lose. You will profit. If you apply my Contrarian philosophy to all areas of your life you will profit there, too. Hey, you're now a winning bettor, and as a bonus your life changed for the better. Not bad for reading one book!

ROOT CONTRARIAN RULE #15: THE PUBLIC OFTEN BELIEVES WHAT THEY SEE—A *HUGE* MISTAKE.

Most bettors watch sporting events and actually buy into what they see. If Team A crushes Team B, they now have formed an opinion that Team A is unbeatable and always a great bet, and that Team B is horrible and cannot be trusted in a betting situation. Wrong on both counts. What a TV viewer has just witnessed is today's reality. But today's result is not indicative of future performance.

The reality is quite to the contrary. Teams that play flawless games—the kind where everything goes perfectly—are playing above their heads. They may be playing the game of their lives. That kind of perfection cannot continue. Often, part of that "perfection" was luck—every ball and call bounced their way. That will not continue.

Often this so-called "perfection" is due to emotional intensity for an important game, or when facing a bitter rival. That intensity will not carry forward. To the contrary, that kind of emotional high often leads the following week to an emotional low. My point here: In the gambling world, even what you see with your own eyes is very often misleading (at least to a bettor).

With this tendency by bettors to overreact to whatever they watch, watching sports can be a real negative. The key to profiting from sports betting is to think like a Contrarian. If you just saw a team crush another team on Monday Night Football, so did the rest of the nation. Next week every bettor in the country will bet on that same "perfect team." You should be betting *against* them. The same holds true with the teams that were crushed last week because they played their worst game of the season. The masses of asses will all be against that "bad team" next week. You, as the Contrarian, should be betting on a rebound.

It works in every sport. Teams that win by 40-7 scores in football present good go-against betting opportunities the following week. In basketball, teams that win by 20 or more points are good go-against bets in the following game. If they win by 30, it's an even better go-against opportunity. In baseball, teams that win by scores like 18-5 or 16-2 (thereby setting season high records for hits and runs) usually lose 1-0 the following day.

The reverse is equally true. Find me a quality team that gets crushed (another word for that kind of loss is "embarrassed") and I'll show you a team that is ripe for a big win the next time they play. If they lose again in their next game, now public perception is even stronger that this team is a bad bet. A Contrarian's job is to make an even bigger wager on this same slumping team in game number three of the streak.

You are always going to be against the crowds of masses by betting on "cold teams" looking to get revenge or regain their honor, and betting against "hot" teams that seem unbeatable. You'll always be on the correct side of emotional intensity (teams that put forth big efforts are now due for an emotional letdown and vice versa). Better still, by betting this way, you'll always get the best odds from bookmakers.

So my advice: Your job as a contrarian gambler is to search for major national TV games, where one team plays an absolutely flawless (perfect) game in front of the nation (preferably the "betting nation") and the other plays horribly—as poorly as they've played all season. Isolate those betting opportunities all year long in all sports, and take advantage by betting against a repeat performance in their very next game! Isn't that simple (but against conventional wisdom)? Spend your gambling life betting on cold teams, against hot teams.

ROOT CONTRARIAN RULE #16: THE PUBLIC ALWAYS FALLS IN LOVE WITH A GOOD OFFENSE— A *HUGE* MISTAKE.

You'll read more about this one in Chapter 13. But this rule is so important it needs to be mentioned more than once. History repeats itself year after year, season after season, sport after sport: Good defense beats good offense every time. Yet that fact is ignored again and again, year after year, by the masses of sports bettors. This is amazing to me. The facts are staring them right in the face, but they just don't get it (or they choose to ignore it). The rule is so simple: Bet against flashy, glamorous, high-profile offensive juggernauts whenever they come up against good defensive teams with no star players.

The team that gets all the headlines is always the betting favorite. The line is always inflated. Public perception is always even more inflated.

The team that gets the headlines believes their own press—they think that their offense cannot be stopped. The quiet, no-name, defensive team has a chip on their shoulder. They may not get the headlines, but they work their butts off in practice. The team with all the headlines is too busy giving interviews and signing autographs to practice. Their attitude is "Who needs practice when you're as perfect as us? We can't be stopped." Guess who wins most every time?

The best offense in sports gambling is *always* a good defense! If you're a Contrarian (read: winning gambler), you'll want to bet on defense every time. It isn't as fun, it isn't as exciting, it isn't as glamorous, but it works. It gives you a betting edge. And like all my other rules, it enables you to always get the best odds and grind out a profit.

ROOT CONTRARIAN RULE #17: THE PUBLIC NEVER LEARNS FROM THEIR LAST BET— A *HUGE* MISTAKE.

In my business career, I've failed hundreds of times. Some were big failures. Others were just poor decisions quickly overcome and causing no lasting damage. The key to success, however, is studying these failures and learning from them.

Again, it is important to understand that history repeats itself again and again. Most people (including bettors) fail their whole lives because they've never learned their lessons. They fail, they ignore the failure, they move on, make the same mistake, and fail again. All the betting mistakes I've spoken about in this chapter fall under that category. People don't learn from their mistakes—and the typical bettor is even worse.

Hey, I'm not excluded either. The reason I know all this is because I've been there and made the exact same mistakes. I too wagered with the masses. I once bet on good teams and bet against bad teams. I doubled up on Monday Night Football to try to get even and bet on too many games each weekend. I bet on games just because they were featured on TV and I was watching. I made all those same mistakes in my betting career. I fell into the same traps as the masses of asses. But the difference between a winning professional gambler/handicapper and the typical masses of amateur losers is that I analyzed, studied, reflected, and *learned* from my mistakes.

A loss is not "just a loss." Any bet you lose is an opportunity to learn a lesson, create a new winning pattern, and profit. With a professional gambler, the bet does not end with the win or loss. Often that's just the beginning of the homework. A professional gambler studies what happened and why. Did I win because of pure luck or a good analysis? Was my thinking correct in the pick, or did I just get a lucky shot or a bogus referee's call late in the game? Is there a pattern in my last few selections? What am I missing?

I keep a diary to make notes on every bet I make, why it succeeded or failed, and how I can improve. I try to draw a conclusion from every selection I make as to what I can learn from the outcome, and what I could do better next time. That diary holds the clues to the puzzle of sports betting. Winning is about what's in that diary: the homework, the hours of study, the painstaking analysis, the psychology, the follow-up.

Much like the "black box" in an airplane, my betting diary is a way to turn tragedy into a positive, by learning from it, learning what happened, what went wrong, and thereby preventing it from ever happening again. That's the beauty of a black box. But it is only valuable if we study it and learn from our mistakes. Take notes on your bets, keep a diary, analyze what went wrong, isolate patterns, adjust your thinking. That diary is your black box!

The notes and thoughts in my diary and the lessons I learn from my follow-up analysis of every bet is the difference between winning and losing. Between making another mistake and finding a clue that turns defeat into victory. Between making a dumb guess and forming an educated opinion. Winners study history. Losers are doomed to ignore it, repeat it, and be beaten by it again and again.

As I close this chapter, let's review what we've learned.

- Never bet over your head (no bet is worth the rent money or the kid's tuition money).
- Grind the bookmakers out.
- Aim to win 55 to 60 percent of your bets.
- Shop around for the best lines.
- Look for value bets, where the circumstances, situation, and point spread all combine to create a high-percentage bet, where the odds are in your favor.
- Manage your money carefully.
- Utilize patience and discipline.
- Put the odds in your favor by betting mostly underdogs.

Do all this and you can expect to double your bankroll every 60 to 110 bets. And you can do this every sports season (football, basketball, baseball) throughout the year. Now add in the biggest bonus of all time: You can do all this while being entertained, watching your favorite teams play unforgettable games, sitting alongside your best friends or family. Ain't sports betting grand?

THIRTEEN

HISTORY MEETS CONTRARIAN STRATEGY

Historical Trends, Theories, and Systems
for Sports Gambling Success

Having shown you in the last chapter what *not* to do when betting on sports, I will now show you what a bettor *should* do—how to put the gambling odds in your favor. These historical trends and handicapping theories repeat virtually every year in the same situations. By understanding these trends, a sports gambler can win again and again in situations in which the vast majority of the public is ignorant of the historical precedents.

I learned very few things at Columbia University that have aided my career as a professional gambler and sports handicapper, but history was one of them. I learned that those who do not study history are doomed to repeat the same mistakes again and again. While I'm not a big fan of stats-based handicapping, there are a few significant pearls of wisdom in the numbers. The key is understanding which numbers.

Note that only those trends and systems that are "generic" work for me. By generic I mean trends that apply to *any* team (not a specific team) in certain historical situations. I believe that team-specific trends are phony, and I do not use them. What I mean by "team-specific," is that I do not trust or utilize a trend that says the Dallas Cowboys are 10-0 on the road versus teams from the NFC Central. Or Dallas is 0-7 the last seven times they've played on a Thursday.

First, a trend like that is most probably a statistical fluke—pure random chance. Second, there is a good likelihood that the trend is due for a turnaround, to bring the overall stat back to 50 percent (meaning Dallas is statistically "due" to go 7-0 the next seven times they play on Thursday, to bring the overall stat back to 7-7, or 50 percent). Third, a team-specific trend like this does not take dozens of other more important factors into consideration. Maybe the last seven times Dallas played on a Thursday, they were coming off brutal emotional rivalry games, and they had nothing left for the Thursday game that followed. Or maybe in each case Dallas was facing a superior team on that particular Thursday and was therefore at a disadvantage. Perhaps the next seven times the Cowboys play on Thursday, they'll be lucky enough to be playing inferior opponents, and after an easy win the week before that used up no emotional intensity. That should result in a 7-0 record over the next seven Thursday games.

And finally, my last reason for ignoring team-specific trends or systems is that because of the powerful effect of free agency in the NFL, teams change personnel drastically and often. A team-specific trend from five years ago is *meaningless*, because five years later the Dallas Cowboys are a whole new team! Heck, three years later they are a dramatically different team. As a matter of fact, only one year later it's possible they've had a 30 percent or more turnover in personnel. So how can you trust a trend based on the "old" Dallas Cowboy team, when none of those players are Cowboys any longer? The answer, of course, is that you can't. My point: Throw the team-specific trends in the wastebasket. They don't work.

What you can count on year after year are generic trends and theories that are useful in the same situations again and again. They are living proof that history does in fact repeat. All of them, by the way, are Contrarian in nature! Let's now examine a few I have used successfully for many years in multiple sports.

NFL FOOTBALL

The Heckle and Jeckle Theory

Here the bettor simply looks for a game match-up featuring two teams that played statistically outside the norm in last week's game. One played like Jeckle, the other like Heckle. One team must have won by 10 points or more better than the point spread (i.e. a 7-point favorite wins by 17 points or more), versus another team that lost by 10 points or more worse than the point spread (i.e. a 7-point underdog that loses by 17 or more).

Now these Jeckle and Heckle opposites are playing each other. Your job as the Contrarian is, of course, to wager on the team that just lost badly, to rebound. The bigger the disparity, the bigger the bet! As an example, if Team A won by 10 points better than the spread, and Team B lost by 14 points worse than the spread, that's a 24-point differential. You have a wagering opportunity.

An even more attractive opportunity would look like this: Team A won by 25 points better than the spread, and Team B lost by 20 points worse than the spread. That adds up to a 45-point disparity. Any game that adds up to 30 points or more is a great betting opportunity. If the disparity is 40 or more, that's my version of the *perfect* betting opportunity. You, of course, would take Team B (the team that was just destroyed and humiliated). The bigger the disparity in this Heckle and Jeckle theory, the stronger your wager.

The Perception Is Always Wrong Theory

Here we play our usual role as Contrarians. We look for teams that were *destroyed* (routed, overwhelmed, embarrassed, humiliated) on national TV last week and are in the role of the underdog this week. We wager on the wounded underdog and vice versa—we wager *against* the big winner of that national TV rout if, in their very next game, they are a favorite. In both cases, we gain the benefit of public perception (which is almost always wrong) on the side of our opponent. This gives us great value in our point spread.

Remember Contrarian Rule #15—your own eyes do often lie. What I mean is that a game you personally witness can actually be misleading. Whenever bettors watch a big national TV game and witness a rout, they come to the erroneous conclusion that the winner is unbeatable and the loser unbettable.

Both conclusions are dead wrong, and both are classic handicapping money burners. The team that you saw win big is often tired, emotionally spent, overconfident, or overrated by the public the following week. They are ripe to be upset. So they are a bad bet, even though they looked close to perfect in this week's game! On the other hand, the team you saw that got routed will be focused, motivated, angry, and looking for redemption the following week. They want to show the world that last week's humiliation was a one-time fluke. So they are a good bet the very next week.

Nothing is ever what it seems, or even the way it looks, in my Contrarian world! Always think Contrarian and wager against the masses, thereby betting on (or investing in) "the value." And root for routs—the more the merrier. The result is lots of new betting opportunities next week.

The Big Scorers Are Big Losers Theory

Go *against* teams that win and score over 30 points two weeks in a row if they are favored in their next game. Here we have the glamorous, high-profile, high-scoring juggernaut on a roll, and of course attracting all the betting public's attention and money. No surprise here—my Contrarian money always goes against these glamorous, high-scoring public favorites. I'll take the quiet, lonely underdog every time.

There is always value in betting against glamour and high-profile media darlings. Their heads are swelled, they have decided they no longer need to practice, while the weaker team (the one I'm asking you to wager on) is motivated, psyched, inspired, and ready to run through walls to pull off the upset. My kind of underdog. If this glamorous, high-octane scoring machine has scored 30 or more points two weeks in a row, history says they will slow down (or make mistakes) in that third consecutive game.

Even more important, oddsmakers will really raise the spread to punish those stupid enough to bet on the high-scoring favorite for the third week in a row. In short, if you take the glamorous favorite, you have the short end of the stick. Everything is aligned against you. You are fighting an uphill battle.

Will you win? Sometimes. But not in the long run. Over the course of time, all those historical factors and heavy-point spread traps will grind you down. That's precisely why bettors who constantly wager on favorites lose money. Are you starting to see a pattern here? My historical trends, systems, and angles are all Contrarian too! They take advantage of the same kind of situations and "market psychology" we've been looking at throughout this book. History is Contrarian!

The Best Offense Is Always a Good Defense Theory

I know I already covered this one in my Root's Rules for Sports Betting, but this is so important that it's worthy of a repeat here, too. And it deserves a repeat because it does double duty. This theory is a foundation of Contrarian strategy, as well as a strong historical trend that works again and again, year after year.

It's simple. Bettors love flashy teams with big high-profile stars that win a lot and score a lot. But those teams don't necessarily cover the point spread. And even worse, they don't win at all when facing boring, plodding defensive teams with no big-name star players. Wait for the several opportunities per season where a high-octane offense that "can't lose" faces a defensive powerhouse that gets no headlines and no respect. Bet defense every time.

Will you win every time? No. But you'll grind out winners (and profits) a high percentage of the time. Why? Because you'll always be betting opposite the masses of asses, always opposite public perception, always on the right side of the point spread, and therefore always get the value. And in the end, that's what successful gambling is all about!

The Three's a Crowd Theory

History repeats year after year when you see extensive winning and losing streaks. Again, we keep it simple. Just look for NFL teams that have won three in a row and bet against them in their very next game, and vice versa—bet on any NFL team that has lost three in a row.

These teams are professionals. This is not college or the minor leagues where great disparity exists. NFL stands for "Not For Long" league. In these hallowed ranks, even the best teams are not much better than the worst teams.

Yet the public thinks otherwise, year after year. They overrate the talent of those that win three in a row, and underestimate the talent of those that lose three in a row. Why complain?

You as the bettor can get the best value on either end of those misperceptions and misconceptions! Take the dogs versus the great teams on three-game winning streaks—you'll always get the bonus points that come with betting against public favorites. And take the dogs that have lost three in a row (those teams on a long losing streak will be the underdogs nine out of every ten times) and you'll also be getting bonus points by wagering on a team no one trusts or respects. Once again, high-percentage plays all the time. Once again, both Contrarian and historical!

The Triple Divisional Letdown Theory

Go against any team coming off three or more consecutive division games (playing against bitter rivals in their own division) and now favored versus a non-division opponent. Remember, the team coming off those three straight emotional games must be favored by the oddsmaker this week or all bets are off.

Your Contrarian play here takes advantage of a team that is about to suffer an emotional breakdown. No team can play three straight back-to-back bitter rivalry games with high emotion and intensity, then have any gas left in the tank for a non-division "nothing on the line" game. The result: You are wagering against a team that is too mentally and emotional exhausted to put up a top-notch effort. And the bonus is that by betting the more motivated underdog, you're getting points to boot! If the favorite in this situation is favored by a touchdown (7 points) or more, that makes the wager a best bet.

The Double Divisional Sandwich Theory

Another great go-against spot! Wager against teams coming off two or more consecutive division games in a row and now playing in the role of a favorite versus a non-divisional opponent, with two or more consecutive division games upcoming. "Sandwich" refers to the game in the middle. Here your team is in the middle of four important intradivision games. If the team in the sandwich role is favored by a touchdown (7 points) or more, that makes the wager a best bet.

The Circle the Calendar Theory

Revenge is a strong handicapping tool. But I believe it has been overrated and bastardized by handicappers. Revenge is useful only in the right circumstances. If you look at all revenge games (games where Team

A lost in their last game to Team B and this week they are playing the re-match), you'll find they average out to around 50 percent against the point spread. No advantage there.

But certain situations stick out like a sore thumb and make revenge a much bigger deal for the team that lost last year (or the last time they played). I look for only the worst loss of last season. Something so hu-miliating and embarrassing that the losing team has circled it on his cal-endar and has been waiting all off-season for a chance at revenge. But the game must stick out like a sore thumb: the single biggest loss margin of last year; a last-second loss to a bitter division rival that knocked a team out of the playoffs; the most points ever scored on that team's defense; the worst home loss of last year; the only time that team's offense was shut out in the last five years, etc. Isolate those "circle the calendar" games—losses that are sure to stick in a team's craw, losses they'll re-member forever.

Your job as a Contrarian bettor is, of course, to wager on the loser of last year's game in the rematch. In each of the memorable situations above, you will have emotional intensity and the highest level of revenge on your side every time. In each of these cases, you have isolated *super* revenge games in which it's guaranteed that the loser has circled their calendars and has been waiting for the rematch all year long!

The Highs and Lows of Life Theory

Pretty simple theory here. This theory works exactly the same way as the Circle the Calendar Theory above, but instead of waiting a whole year for revenge, here we look at the team's very next game.

The theory is simple: Things are never as good as they look, nor ever as bad as they look. Here we look for games where a team has been thrashed and humiliated. The humiliation can be offensive or defensive, but it needs to be record-setting in some way: the team gave up the most yards or points of the season; or lost by the biggest margin of the season; or offensively stank up the stadium, scoring the least points of the season or gaining the fewest yards or first downs. On either side of the ball, a total humiliation.

So what does a Contrarian do in response to this kind of humiliating, devastating defeat? Of course you now know my answer! You wager on the humiliated team in their very next game. And you do the exact *opposite* to teams that hit their highest totals for the season to date! In other words, bet against teams that offensively scored their highest point total of the year, racked up the most yards and first downs, or defensively had their best performance of the year or years. The better the performance, the stronger the bet against them the following week. Once again, Contrarian strategy meets significant historical opportunity.

The Perfection Doesn't Last Theory

The idea here is to look for big winning streaks by undefeated teams to start the season, and then wager against these seemingly invincible teams in the very next game after they suffer their first loss of the year. It works year after year. Watch teams that win five in a row, seven in a row, nine in a row finally lose their first game (outright) of the season.

They are now in shock and deep depression. "What? Me lose? How could we lose? We were unbeatable!" What is the result of this kind of shock (and hubris)? That "unbeatable" team many times loses again the following week, too. Even more certain, whether they win or lose, that shock of losing for the first time causes an emotional letdown.

The result in almost every case is a point-spread loss. Here you have a previously undefeated team that the betting public is still in love with, thereby creating a hugely inflated point spread, and to top it off, you have a team that is emotionally spent and mentally unfocused. Another great point-spread opportunity. Take the lightly regarded underdog and watch them cover the spread most every time!

This theory does double duty in another situation as well—it works (although not quite as effectively) to bet against any team on a long winning streak that finally loses one game. So instead of just looking at undefeated teams that lose their very first game of the season, a corollary says it pays to wager against any team at any point in the season that loses a game after winning five or more in a row. Bet against them in their very next game and watch them "sleepwalk" through a game as big favorites. After the game you have one thing left to do—collect your profits!

The Home-Cooking Theory

I've always liked home underdogs. But like revenge, this betting situation has been overused and overrated by the handicappers and so-called "experts." All home dogs don't win. If they did, all bettors would figure it out, bet them, and retire to a life of leisure at their beachfront mansions in Hawaii. Life never seems to work that way, does it?

Just like my revenge angle, there is one specific situation that isolates certain high-percentage home dogs, where the odds are in your favor. Like the infamous revenge factor, if you bet all home dogs, you'd go about fifty-fifty. No advantage there. I do, however, like betting home dogs that are home for the second consecutive week and who lost as home favorites last week.

In this case you have a very specific situation. The home dog was embarrassed last week—they lost a game they were expected to win (they were favored). And this embarrassing loss took place in front of their own home crowd. Now they are home for the second week in a row and have a chance to make amends to their fans.

I find that teams play much better in their second straight home game than in their first. Why? Simple: They're starting to feel at home. After fourteen straight nights of sleeping in their favorite bed and being around the people they love, they're in the groove. Plus, this time you're getting points in the bargain. Add in the fact that this team was favored last week, which indicates that they are at the very least a decent team in the eyes of professional oddsmakers.

What you have here is a set of high-percentage circumstances—a good team, at home, after a bitter loss (an upset), now getting points, needing to save face in front of their own fans. Once again, we've taken an overrated and losing proposition—betting home dogs—and isolated a *super* home-dog situation where the odds are in your favor.

The Post–Monday Night Blues Theory

Once again, we have an overrated situation. Handicappers and experts all seem to think that betting against the team that won on Monday Night Football the following week is a good bet. It is not. Like the revenge and home-dogs theories, this trend is highly overrated.

Again, in all situations, you'd go fifty-fifty betting against Monday Night's winners. But once again, I have isolated one high-percentage situation that does put the odds in your favor. Only look for Monday Night winners who played a division opponent (a bitter rival) and now, the following week, are playing a non-divisional opponent.

This creates a prime letdown situation. You have a team that played one of the (if not *the*) biggest games of the year last week, with the whole nation watching. They played on Monday Night, they played a bitter rival, and they won. Now, a short week later, they must find the emotional intensity to play well versus a much less meaningful opponent (non-divisional). In most cases, the Monday Night winner will be favored, too. (Why not? They just won in front of the whole nation.) So your bonus is that you get points in the bargain. Once again, we have isolated a high-percentage winning angle amidst an overrated trend.

The Boob Tube Lookahead/Letdown Theory

Study every NFL team's schedule before the season. I look for the two or three biggest TV matchups of the year, games where the whole nation is watching and the opponent is special—perhaps the prior season's Super Bowl champion, or a big Monday Night game, or a bitter divisional rival, or the opponent from a memorable game last year (a team that knocked them out of the playoffs).

Now I circle the games immediately before and after these big TV matchups. These are the potential land mines in every team's schedules—games where they are in danger of looking ahead (playing poorly in anticipation of a big game) or letting down (playing poorly after a big game). So every NFL team has at least four to six games circled on my schedule printouts. These are the games I now watch closely all season long.

I don't automatically bet against a team the week before or after a big TV rivalry game. It depends on how the season actually plays out. It depends on the point spread. It depends on public perception leading into or going out of the big TV game. It depends on the mental mind-set of the team, and their opponent. But one or two of these games per week will add up to solid wagering opportunities. You will catch a team at just the right or wrong moment and walk away a winner!

The Pre-season Boob-tube Theory

In pre-season NFL games, the TV factor is even stronger. Just like with the theory above, I look in advance at each team's pre-season schedule and circle all the national TV games. Three stations carry pre-season NFL games: ABC, ESPN, and FOX.

There are only two to three nationally televised games a week in pre-season. What else is there to get emotionally charged up for? So teams really look ahead before their one big, national TV pre-season game and let down after that same big game. This has been my most reliable pre-season angle for fifteen years now. Once again, this theory puts the odds (and team emotions and psychology) in your favor.

The Second-half Perception Theory

Here's a great one if you like action. I personally try to discourage making too many wagers. The vig (or bookmaker's commission on every bet) will wear you down and eat up your bankroll. But here is a trend that produces many betting opportunities per week. My advice is to pick and choose the two to five best at maximum, based on all the other factors and theories you've now read about in this book. But if you desire action, here's a way to find it.

The theory is simple: List all the teams at the halfway point of the NFL season that are 2-6 or worse (so only teams with a record of 2-6, 1-7, or 0-8), and 6-2 or better (so only teams with a record of 6-2, 7-1, or 8-0). You'll usually find four to six teams on each end of the spectrum. Now your job is to bet on every one of the "bad teams" for the rest of the season (the entire second half), and against every one of the "great teams" for the rest of the season. Often the bad teams play one of the great teams. This is an ideal wagering opportunity. You'll win a high-percentage of these matchups. Why?

The perception is on your side, while the betting public is always against you. First, oddsmakers are giving tons of extra points to these "bad teams" every week for the rest of the season. Even if they start to play better, public perception rarely catches up until it's too late. And play better they often do!

Bad teams in the first eight games of any NFL season are often bad because they are either stocked with young players or decimated by injuries (so replacements or backups are playing key skill positions). There is a learning curve in the NFL. It takes time for a young player to develop. But after half of a season, the younger players and backups start to catch on to the system. The balls they dropped earlier in the year start to get caught and result in touchdowns. So the bad teams start to improve (look at the Jacksonville Jaguars in '03—the worst team in football early, the most promising and improved team late in the season).

And it goes the other way as well: With the point spreads stacked against them by oddsmakers and a bull's-eye on their chest (the 8-0 and 7-1 teams are the ones every team in the NFL wants to beat to prove their manhood), the superstar teams often come back to earth in the second half of each season (look at the Kansas City Chiefs in '03, who started out unbeatable, then finished up defensively vulnerable and in disarray).

You will win week in and week out for the next twenty years by simply betting on the worst teams and against the best teams in the second half of the NFL season. Instead of a few key high-percentage plays per season, with this theory you get several plays every single week.

The End-of-Season Wounded Pride Theory

I've used this historical trend to profit at Christmastime for almost two decades. Once again, it relies heavily on public perception (or should I say public *mis*perception). The betting public makes the exact same mistake every single year in December. They overrate the best teams and underrate the worst teams. They assume that a team that *must* win to make the playoffs has a huge edge over a team that is already eliminated from playoff contention. Not true.

If anything, the edge belongs to the losing team that is out of contention! That team is loose, they have nothing to lose because their season is already over. They can't embarrass themselves more than they already have, and they're playing for pride and anger: "Our playoff hopes are ruined, so why not ruin our opponents' today too? Let's knock them out of the playoffs, so they can feel the same pain and bitterness and humiliation we feel."

On the other hand, the team that needs today's win is wound tight. Everything is on the line, and they are nervous and scared to even think about losing this important game. That kind of attitude results in "hands of stone"—receivers dropping easy passes, running backs fumbling, quarterbacks flubbing the center exchange, and punt returners muffing the return.

So here in the last three weeks of the NFL season, we have specific opportunities where teams the public loves (that need the win) are playing teams that the public ignores or despises (that are playing only for pride). And to top it off, this public perception once again distorts the point spread! So the "bad team" gets lots of points—far more than they deserve. Our play is, of course, to take the "bad team," the team that is out of the playoff race and is given no chance to win this game.

Do they usually pull the upset? Actually, no. The team that needs to win usually does win. But that team rarely covers the point spread! The "bad team" may lose the game, but they usually play their hearts out and keep it close enough to take home the money.

I've made money on this annual holiday gift for almost twenty years in a row! I've only seen it mentioned in one book in all my years of reading gambling literature—in Al O'Donnell's *Point Spread Playbook*. Al is a master of computerized stats, and he reports that the "bad teams" beat the spread at a rate of 65 percent winners over the past fifteen years! (That's despite the fact that Al reports those same "bad teams" lost 62 percent of those same games outright. So the point spread changes *everything*.)

Once again, underdogs win the money based on public perception. Once again, an ideal high-percentage wagering opportunity is created toward the end of every season, putting the odds in your favor.

The Late Season Home-Cooking Theory

Here's a specific situation where home underdogs prosper: Wager on home dogs playing a division opponent only on the last two weekends of the NFL season. I've been winning with this trend for almost twenty years. Another oldie but goody!

The reason it wins consistently over that time is simple: Here you have a home team, getting points, playing in its last home game in front of its beloved fans, against a longtime bitter foe. That's a lot of motivating factors. The home team you're betting on here is bound to be focused and emotionally intense for this game. If they're not, these players should all seek another profession! And you usually have a team that either is out of contention and only playing for pride (just like the trend above except at home—even better!), or is still in contention but playing one of the best teams in the NFL.

How do I know? Because if a team is in playoff contention but considered an underdog at home, they'd have to be playing one of the best teams in the NFL. And in both cases, the opponent is a better team (they're giving points) and a bitter rival (as a division foe, they've automatically played twice a year for decades). In all these cases, we have once again isolated a high-percentage play where the odds are in your favor.

The Early Season Coaching Disasters Theory

With all these late-season edges, I'm often asked if there's any early-season NFL betting edge. The answer is *yes!* While I've stressed again and again the parity among NFL teams (the fact that there is little difference between the best NFL team and the worst), early in the season, coaching can make a difference.

NFL game plans are *very* complicated. They take a long time to learn, let alone execute flawlessly. New head coaches bring with them new game plans and complex new defensive and offensive schemes. These new systems or schemes take time to master.

Over the years, I've enjoyed great early-season success when wagering against any team with a new head coach in its very first road game of the season. If they lose that game, as expected, then I'll go against the same team in their very next road game (the second one under the new head coach). If they lose again, I'll keep "testing them" until they beat me. The first time they cover the spread, I'm done.

Why does this angle work so well consistently over time? It's hard enough for NFL players to master a new game plan, but try doing it on the road in front of a huge, hostile crowd. That defines tough. And as expected, those rookie coaches and their new teams do not play well on the road early in the season. Teams are expected by fans, owners, TV viewers, and the media to get off to a fast start under a new regime. As always, the expectations are erroneous. History always repeats!

The Doug Fleming Theory

I've saved the best for last. These last three historical trends also define my Contrarian strategy. They are Contrarian, yet they repeat every year and never go out of style.

Doug Fleming has been a friend of mine for over twenty-five years. Back in the early eighties, he taught me two simple gambling rules. Rule number one: the oddsmakers are smarter than you or me. These professionals do not make mistakes, period. Rule number two: If the oddsmaker seems wrong, refer back to rule number one.

Doug taught me to look at the line set each day for football, basketball, baseball—any sport. Look for lines that look "bad." Whenever you find a line that looks like an obvious error or misjudgment (even if it's so bad it looks like a printer's error or a computer glitch), bet *with* that mistake. Assume the oddsmakers are correct and they know something you don't. *Because they do!* No one knows more than professional Las Vegas oddsmakers. Their entire life is figuring out the correct lines. If they are wrong, tens of millions of dollars could be lost. If they're wrong very often, they won't stay employed as oddsmakers for long.

Believe me, they don't make many mistakes. If it looks like a mistake, you've made a miscalculation or erroneous judgment. If you think the oddsmaker is being made the fool, trust me, it's *you* who's being played for the fool.

Every day you should analyze the line. You'll find one or two games that look as though the wrong team is favored, or a slightly better (or even a slightly inferior) team is favored by way too much. In each of these cases, my advice is to wager on the wrong team, or as I've always described it, "the side that makes no sense."

The Vegas oddsmaker is paid to spend 24/7 researching games, teams, players, situations, injuries. If something in the line looks wrong, you can bet they have found something crucial and significant to the outcome of the game that you never saw, never had access to, or, even if you did, would have never understood the significance of. For almost twenty years, I've tried to isolate oddsmaker's "mistakes" and bet with them—on the wrong side. And for almost twenty years I've been winning. Trust me—it's never a huge error in judgment to bet with the house. The house wins. Or as they say in poker, look around the table. If you don't know who the sucker is, it's *you*.

The My Cousin Vinny Theory

This theory was named after my good friend Cousin Vinny (name changed to protect the innocent). I phone Vinny daily to "pick his mind," to find out what he's thinking and betting. Vinny is, literally, "Mass Man." He thinks identically to the average amateur gambler, makes all the same obvious mistakes as the typical losing gambler, ignores history again and again, and bets nothing but favorites. He always bets what looks obvious and falls for traps—games that look too good to be true; he listens to the media experts and bets whatever they recommend, he follows trends and blindly believes them to be flawless, and he watches games and develops perceptions of teams. Those perceptions are in almost every case inaccurate.

And then, after a long day of losing—and pretty much every day for Vinny is a long day of losing—he bets double or nothing on the last game of the day. It loses every time. Vinny is Mass Man. What Vinny thinks, the whole world is thinking. The mistakes he makes, most amateur bettors are making. His perceptions are the public's perceptions.

Cousin Vinny is a one-man army. By talking to him, I can predict what 70 percent of the public will do or decide most every time. For a Contrarian sports handicapper like me, Vinny is the canary in the mine shaft! If he picks a team, I know every other amateur gambler is coming to the same destructive, moronic, suicidal conclusion, and they'll all walk off the cliff together like lemmings.

I, of course, take Vinny's advice and bet the opposite side. Works most every time. Everyone has a Cousin Vinny, or two or three. A know-it-all who knows nothing. A brilliant sports trivia expert who knows everything about every team, every player, every situation, yet he's a pathetic loser when it comes to gambling with all that brilliant knowledge. Vinny knows everything, and he knows it with complete confidence. Yet he's a pathetic loser who never met a dumb bet that he didn't fall in love with!

Find your own Cousin Vinny—or two or three of them. Ask their opinions. They're never shy about sharing them. Then match those opinions up with other idiots—oops, I mean other Cousin Vinnys—and run (don't walk) to the bookmaker to *bet the opposite way*. Yes, this is Contrarian strategy. But it's also historical trend betting because Cousin Vinnys the world over are always wrong, all the time. They repeat the same stupid thinking, strategy, and losing bets season after season, year after year. They are living, breathing barometers for what the masses of asses are thinking, betting, and losing!

The Gallup Poll Theory

Finally we come to my last historical NFL trend, and it is as Contrarian as you can get! To take advantage of all the Cousin Vinnys in the universe of amateur sports bettors, I recommend treating sports gambling like a political election.

Politicians incessantly poll their constituencies. Bill Clinton didn't make a decision without first finding out what the American people thought. Some have criticized him for that trait (including me), yet a recent poll (only fitting) finds that the American people consider Clinton one of the three greatest presidents in United States history—behind only Abraham Lincoln and George Washington. So using polls certainly turned out okay for President Clinton. (If only he had taken a poll to find out what the people thought of Monica Lewinsky, he could have saved himself a lot of aggravation!)

You, too, can take advantage of polls. Treat every NFL week like your own personal presidential election, and don't make a betting decision without first listening to sports talk radio, surfing sports handicapping web sites and chat rooms, reading major sports magazines, reading handicapping newsletters (available at any major newsstand), and watching ESPN SportsCenter and other sports TV shows. Take notes. *Then go the opposite way of everything that you have heard.* Go the opposite way of your own gut-instinct betting decisions after listening to all this "inside information," which, as we have seen, is actually not "inside" or insightful at all.

If you have the ability, take all this public polling a step further—conduct extensive polling among all your friends, e-mail chat-room buddies, and fantasy-football competitors. Or pay a buddy to give you the results of his office betting pool. Always go the *opposite* of the strongest plays (the ones the public agrees in unison on). This strategy is as historical as it gets—because it will work week in and week out all season long, for the next 100 years!

COLLEGE FOOTBALL

NCAA football is a totally different animal than NFL football. Using trends is virtually meaningless and useless in college football, for two major reasons: First, there is no parity like there is in the NFL. Sometimes one team is just a lot better at every skill position. No matter what the trends or historical factors say, the weaker team will definitely get their butt whipped by the dominant team! This is nothing like the NFL, where on any given Sunday anyone can beat anyone else. On any given Saturday, many lower-echelon college football teams have literally no chance to beat a top-ranked team!

Second, many top college players graduate every year. From year to year, college teams can be totally different teams with totally different personalities. So what Alabama does in certain situations this year has zero significance next year or the year after. So throw all the team-specific trends out completely—file them under "U" for useless. And for the most part, the historical trends aren't very useful either. Contrarian betting strategy is the only way to handicap winners in college football—with a few exceptions. Here they are.

The Early Season Coaching Disasters Theory

Coaches are even more important in the college ranks than in the pros because of the fact that the players are kids. These kids are still growing and learning. They are impressionable. A coach is their father figure. Learning a new game plan, studying a new playbook, learning new offensive and defensive schemes is much more challenging for young kids than it is for their NFL counterparts.

That same new-coaches theory that works so effectively in the NFL is doubly effective in college football. Look for any and every opportunity to go against a team with a new head coach on their first road game. Even a step better for college football is to look at the quarterback position as well. If a team has a new head coach *and* a new starting quarterback, then that first road game is sure to be a disaster. In this case, the team's success depends on a raw, inexperienced kid facing 60,000 screaming strangers in a hostile environment for the first time—with the added burden of a new coach and new offensive scheme. Good luck!

Bet against this situation with both fists. Obviously you can see that this has historical significance, no matter what team, coach, or quarterback is involved. This would be a difficult situation for anyone in the world! This is one of the few historical college-football trends I've found that consistently puts the odds in your favor.

The "Hasta la Vista, Baby" Theory

Those same impressionable kids are left in a state of shock and confusion when a famous and mighty head coach leaves for "greener pastures." They probably feel like children abandoned by their own fathers—

lost and helpless. The theory here is to wager against any college football team throughout the first season after their head coach resigns, retires, or leaves for a better contract somewhere else.

The catch in this case is that the coach needs to be a powerful and famous coach from a winning program. That kind of loss at the leadership position truly sucks the wind out of the young players. How do you replace a legend? You don't! That first year without the legendary head coach is almost always a transition year, an even season at best and possibly a losing one, but either way a big disappointment to the bettors and fans of the program. Of course, you might look extra hard at that first road game (see trend above) without the coaching legend on the sidelines.

Here's a commonsense situation that never changes, no matter the program, coach, or players. It is obviously a tough psychological spot for anyone to be in—another trend that puts the odds in your favor. Not by a large margin, but by just enough to grind the bookmaker down!

The Circle the Calendar Theory

Just like in pro football, revenge is a strong handicapping tool, and like in pro football, it has been overrated and bastardized by handicappers. Revenge is useful only in the right circumstances. But certain situations stick out like sore thumbs and make revenge a much bigger deal for the team that lost last year (or the last time they played). I look for only the worst loss of last season, something so humiliating and embarrassing that the losing team has circled it on his calendar and has been waiting all off-season for a chance at revenge.

But the game must stick out like a sore thumb: the single biggest loss margin of last year; a last-second loss to a bitter division rival that knocked a team out of a bowl game; the most points ever scored on that team's defense; the worst home loss of last year; the only time that team's offense was shut out in the last five years, etc. Isolate those "circle the calendar" games—losses that are sure to stick in a team's craw, losses they'll remember forever! Your job as a Contrarian bettor is, of course, to wager on the loser of last year's game in the rematch.

The only caveat here is to study each team's roster. If the college team that lost last year (and is looking for revenge this year) does not have the same head coach and starting quarterback returning, it's a no-bet. These situations veto the theory. Cross the game off your list. This is not pro football. The head coach and an experienced starting QB are everything in college ball. If those two key leaders aren't back from last year, there is no burning revenge within this team. If both are back, you have a solid high-percentage bet.

In each of the "memorable" situations above, you will have emotional intensity and the highest level of revenge on your side every time. In each of these cases, you have isolated *super* revenge games in which it's guaranteed that the loser has circled their calendars and been waiting for the rematch all year long.

The Perfection Doesn't Last Theory

This theory works the same as its pro-football counterpart above. Look for undefeated college football teams that start the season undefeated at 5-0, 6-0, or 7-0, to finally lose their first game, then wager against them in the very next game. Often they'll lose outright again—because they are in shock and mourning over their perfect season ending. But they'll almost always let down their intensity and lose versus the point spread. Remember that this team is coming back down to earth quickly, but public perception has not caught up with the reality. The public still sees them as a flawless and now almost-perfect team. So the point spread is guaranteed to be far too high in favor of the favorite. Once again, giving you, the dedicated Contrarian bettor, the high-percentage edge you need to grind out the bookie!

The "I Dragged My Girlfriend Down the Stairs by Her Hair" Theory

College sports (unfortunately) is full of thugs, young men who have no intention of getting a degree (unless it's in home economics or physical education) and who commit crimes while on campus waiting for their NFL career to start. Not a day seems to go by without another college player . . . or two or three, listed in the police blotter for committing disgraceful crimes against the public or their fellow students.

The crimes are many: drug dealing, drug possession, driving while under the influence of alcohol or drugs, shoplifting, theft, armed robbery, assault, rape, breaking and entering, even murder. And more than just being shocking to the university and its student body, they are shocking and upsetting to the team! I find that a criminal incident throws off the equilibrium, emotional intensity, and spirit of any college team. A star getting accused of a crime is like a knife to the heart of his teammates. It makes everyone associated with the athletic program feel dirty and guilty by association.

Those teams rarely perform up to their potential the very next game after the announcement. I therefore wager against any team whose star player commits a crime, flunks his courses, or gets kicked off the team for disciplinary reasons. Ditto for any coach who does or says something scandalous. Anything that causes negative headlines also causes team chemistry and psychology to be damaged or ruined (at least temporarily). Take advantage by wagering against that team in their very next game. It works year after year.

That's it as far as the college football trends and theories I use. The list is much smaller than for the NFL, but for good reason—winning at college football is all about Contrarian betting strategy. With so many games on the schedule each week, there are literally a dozen or more Contrarian betting opportunities a week—without even bothering to use any of the historical trends listed above.

The key is, as always, public perception. Just like the NFL, bet on the supposedly "bad teams" with no chance to win (but covering the point spread is a whole other story!), and against supposedly good teams with an "easy game" at hand. Take your polls, listen to talk radio, speak to your Cousin Vinny, and find out what all the experts think—and wager the opposite way. Nowhere does Contrarian betting strategy work more profitably than in college football (or college basketball). In college football, Contrarian betting strategy is historically accurate, year after year.

COLLEGE FOOTBALL BOWL TRENDS:

The Three's a Crowd Theory

Bet *against* any bowl team on a three-game-or-more winning streak (versus the point spread) heading into bowl season, and bet *on* teams with three or more consecutive losses (versus the point spread) heading into the bowls. This theory works like clockwork year after year.

This is a major portion of the foundation of my college bowl strategy. It guarantees that you'll be on underdogs about 80 percent of the time, and that's good, because dogs win bowl games. No surprise here—70 percent or more of the public (amateur bettors) will be betting on the powerful favorites on a long winning streak and against the "bad teams" on a long losing streak. So once again, this trend takes advantage of value.

The Gallup Poll Theory

No surprise here. This is just more Contrarian common sense. Poll, poll, and poll some more. It's easy to do during college bowl season. Start your own office pool and compile the results, or just ask a friend to give you the results of his or her office pool (or even better—host your own poll *and* get the results of others). Go the opposite way of all the most lopsided public picks. Only wager opposite the games that add up to 70 percent or more of the pool players on one side. This is another key piece of my bowl strategy.

The Best Offense Is Always a Good Defense Theory

Another big surprise, huh? Bet against the flashy, high-profile, high-octane offensive powerhouses—the best offense is *always* a great defense, especially in bowl season. As usual, the betting public is always on the flashy, high-profile teams, so the bonus is that you're getting value in the point spread, too!

The Home-Cooking Theory

No, this does not relate to the NFL home-underdog theory, but it does relate to the simple fact that bowl teams playing at home (in their home city or at their actual home stadium) do exceedingly well during bowl season. Having home-court advantage in the post-season is a huge advantage in the NFL playoffs—it's obviously no different in college football. This works for me year after year—another great historical angle at work.

The Bowl Blowout Theory

This is another simple but Contrarian betting trend. Here we are wagering on teams that lost their bowl game last year by twenty or more points. Why? Because you have a team that was humiliated and embarrassed in front of tens of thousands of their fans, all of whom flew long miles and spent big money to root for their team. Everyone's holiday season was ruined by the loss. Fans returned home with a bad taste in their mouth (and less money in their wallets). The players have had a year to think about it and are motivated to be sure their holidays are not ruined again this year.

The Big School Couldn't Care Less Theory

Here we wager on small, low-profile colleges playing against big-name football powerhouses in early bowl games (games before January 1). The theory here is that the high-profile schools (like USC, UCLA, Notre Dame, Michigan, Alabama, and Florida) are turned off by playing in an insignificant early bowl game versus a no-name opponent. The big school lacks motivation and is just going through the paces. The smaller school will be plenty motivated—their goal is to make a name for themselves by "scalping" a trophy school! The smaller school will in most cases be getting points. Once again, a perfect Contrarian betting opportunity.

The Perfection Doesn't Last Theory

Here we bet against any college bowl teams that go undefeated (or close to perfect) all season long and then lose their very last game to ruin a perfect or almost perfect season. Even better if that loss ruins that team's chance to play for the national championship. The team that just suffered that one bad loss will be in shock and mourning, and will lose interest and fail "to show up" (play with any emotional intensity) for their bowl game. Again, this situation almost guarantees that you'll be wagering on an underdog.

The Heisman/Schmeisman Theory

Bet against the team with the Heisman Trophy winner in bowl games. Everyone on the other team will be jealous, bitter, and gunning for him. The opposing team often plays the game of their lives and limits the Heisman winner to the worst single-game stats of his season. Once again, this theory almost guarantees that you'll be opposite the betting public—and getting points with a low-profile team with a chip on their shoulder. Great value.

The Chip on Their Shoulder Theory

Here we wager on any bowl team that has lost two or more bowl games in a row. Like the theory above that puts us on the side of teams that lost last year's bowl games by twenty points or more, here we have a team motivated to turn in a good performance lest the fans and alumni go home unhappy for a third year in a row. Any head coach that loses three bowl games in a row is probably in danger of losing his support from alumni, too. That's three holiday seasons where fans and alumni feel like Scrooge. Not a good thing for the team, but a good motivating factor for the smart Contrarian bettor.

The Big Dogs Eat on New Year's Day Theory

In our final bowl trend, we look to bet big underdogs (7 points or more, but especially double-digit dogs) on New Year's Day. New Year's Day (or any of the games beyond) features only the cream of the crop— the best teams in all of college football. These are teams that play only to win, and play with pride. You can be assured they'll play well as big underdogs. If they do not win outright, they will certainly have a good shot at covering the point spread. And that, my friends, fans, and readers, is why we play the game!

COLLEGE BASKETBALL

College basketball is without a doubt my most profitable and prosperous sport. It is also the fastest-growing betting sport in all of America. March Madness (see the specific March Madness Contrarian betting rules below) is now second in gambling dollars only to the NFL. More money is gambled in just the month of March on college basketball (conference tournaments, then the "Big Dance") than on any other sports event except the Super Bowl!

Once again, I'm not a fan of trends. Plain and simple, they don't work. Winning at college basketball is all about following the same Contrarian rules as in football above. Here are the key college hoops rules that have worked well for me and my clients over the past two decades. Once again, you'll find them all to be Contrarian in nature:

The Gallup Poll Theory

Just like in college football, in college basketball your job as the Contrarian gambler is to find out what the public is thinking. Taking daily polls is just not possible in college hoops—at least not during the regular season (March Madness is a whole different ballgame), but you can listen to sports talk radio, surf the net, monitor college-hoops chat rooms and blogs, watch all the TV sports shows, and read as many newspapers and sports magazines as you can get your hands on. Then, after compiling all those opinions, go the *opposite* way! Contrarian strategy works in every sport.

The Unranked Trap

An offshoot of the Home-Cooking Theory used so successfully in NFL, here we do not want to play home underdogs, but rather home *favorites*. Yes, Wayne Allyn Root does occasionally take favorites, but only in college basketball is it a regular part of my betting strategy. Here we simply keep track of the weekly top-twenty-five standings and wager on any *unranked* home team that comes up favored over a top-twenty-five-ranked opponent.

No, this is not betting underdogs. Yet it's still totally Contrarian in nature! This theory banks on a home team being angry and motivated—again with that proverbial chip on their shoulder—to knock off a high-profile, top-ranked opponent. The fact that the unranked team is favored is a sure sign that (A) they are very talented, and (B) the oddsmakers actually expect them to win. In most cases, they will! This theory has worked for me dozens of times a season for almost twenty years.

The Statement Game Theory

Just like with football above, look for "statement games" in college hoops, games where a team has won or lost by a million points—a complete utter rout; devastation; humiliation; season or historical lows or highs. Then look to wager on the opposite happening in the very next game.

Just like in football, college hoops teams that lose big often rebound to win big in their very next game. And you are getting value, because the team that lost in a humiliating fashion is often an underdog in their next game. The same goes for big wins. Wager against a team that just pulled off one of the biggest routs in school history.

The Circle the Calendar Theory

The same exact theory that works so well in football also works profitably in college hoops. Revenge is a strong handicapping tool in college basketball. But just like in the NFL, it has been overrated and bastardized by handicappers.

Certain situations stick out like sore thumbs and make revenge a much bigger deal for the team that lost last year (or the last time they played). I look for only the worst loss of last season (or, in the case of college hoops, the worst loss of *this* season, as teams play twice a year against conference rivals), something so humiliating and embarrassing that the losing team has circled it on his calendar and been waiting for weeks or months for a chance at redemption. But the game must stick out like a sore thumb—the single biggest loss margin of the season; a last-second loss to a bitter division rival that knocked a team out of the conference tournament; the most points ever scored on your team's defense; the worst home loss of last year, etc.

Just like in football, isolate those "circle the calendar" games—losses that are sure to stick in a team's craw, losses they'll remember forever! Your job as a Contrarian bettor is, of course, to wager on the loser of the last game in the rematch. In each of the "memorable" situations above, you will have emotional intensity and the highest level of revenge on your side every time. In each of these cases, you have isolated *super* revenge, games in which it's guaranteed that the loser has circled their calendars and has been waiting for the rematch all year long!

The College Teams Like to Get High Theory

No, I'm not talking about marijuana, although that might apply to most college players, too. What I am referring to here is the point spread. Look at all opening-morning lines in college hoops. Isolate one that sticks out like a sore thumb as way too high. I call that kind of a spread a "don't make sense" play. It looks ridiculous. It looks like the oddsmaker was high when he decided the point spread. It just doesn't make sense.

In almost every case, the favorite (who looked so ridiculously high) wins anyway! More proof that when you suspect someone is being played for a fool, it's usually you. Oddsmakers don't make big errors in judgment. If the line looks too high, it's probably because the professionals know something you don't! Wager with the house in situations like this. Put your money on the side that is favored by too much, and watch them win by a million!

The Perfection Doesn't Last Theory

This theory works the same as it does with its professional and college football counterparts. Look for undefeated college basketball teams that start the season perfect at 10-0 or higher (in college hoops the wins naturally pile up faster and higher) to finally lose their first game, then wager against them in the very next game. Often they'll lose outright again, because they are in shock and mourning over their perfect season ending. But they'll almost always let down their intensity and lose at least versus the still-inflated point spread.

Remember that this team is coming back down to earth quickly, but public perception has not caught up with the reality. The public still sees them as a flawless and now almost-perfect team. So the point spread is guaranteed to be far too high in favor of the favorite. Once again, giving you, the dedicated Contrarian bettor, the high-percentage edge you need to grind out the bookie.

The "I Dragged My Girlfriend Down the Stairs by Her Hair" Theory

An identical betting theory to its college football counterpart above. Scandal rocks college hoops early and often. Just like in football, it wreaks havoc with the psyches and emotions of a school and team. A star getting accused of a crime is like a knife to the heart of his teammates. It makes everyone associated with the athletic program feel dirty and guilty by association. Those teams rarely perform up to their potential the very next game after the announcement. I therefore wager against any team whose star player commits a crime, flunks his courses, or gets kicked off the team for disciplinary reasons. Ditto for any coach who does or says something scandalous. Anything that causes negative headlines also causes team chemistry and psychology to be damaged or ruined (at least temporarily). Take advantage by wagering against that college hoops team in their very next game. It works year after year, like clockwork.

Are you recognizing a pattern here? The Contrarian rules are virtually identical in football or basketball, college or pro. Same rules. Same situations. Same mind-set. Same winning (and profitable) results. But nothing wins in the Contrarian betting world like March Madness—my absolute favorite time of the year.

NCAA MARCH MADNESS COLLEGE BASKETBALL TOURNAMENT

As always, Contrarian rules, *rule!* I've won sixteen of the last eighteen years in March Madness—not a bad track record. The rules and theories I've used are almost identical to college football bowl games.

The Three's a Crowd Theory

Just as in the college football bowl games, bet *against* any NCAA tourney team on a three-game-or-more winning streak (versus the point spread) heading into March Madness, and bet *on* teams with three or more consecutive losses (versus the point spread) heading into the tourney (bowls in football). This theory works like clockwork year after year. It is the foundation of my March Madness strategy.

This approach guarantees that you'll be on underdogs about 80 percent of the time, and that's good because dogs win in the first two rounds of March Madness. As with college bowl games, 70 percent or more of the public (amateur bettors) will be betting on the powerful favorites on a long winning streak, and against the "bad teams" on a long losing streak. This trend takes advantage of value.

The Gallup Poll Theory

Poll, poll, and poll some more. It's easy to do during March Madness, when virtually every office in the good ol' USA is awash with March Madness office betting pools. Start your own office pool and compile the results, ask a friend to give you the results of his or her office pool, or, even better, host your own poll *and* get the results of others. Go the opposite way of all the most lopsided public picks. Only wager opposite the games that add up to 70 percent or more of the pool players on one side. This is the other foundation of my March Madness strategy.

The Best Offense Is ALWAYS
a Good Defense Theory

Against the flashy, high-profile, high-octane offensive powerhouses, the best offense is *always* a great defense—especially in March Madness. As usual, the betting public is always on the flashy, high-profile, high-scoring teams and the big-name players (also always high-scoring offensive stars), so the bonus is you're getting value in the point spread, too!

The Sports Illustrated Jinx Theory

For years we have all heard about the *SI* jinx—that anyone on the cover of *SI* suffered terrible results (a prolonged slump, a devastating loss) soon thereafter. I have said for years on many national TV talk shows that there is no jinx. This scenario is simply Contrarian philosophy at work. The player or team on the cover of *SI* now has a big, inflated ego, and worse, a giant bull's-eye on his chest. Every other player on every other team wants to destroy, embarrass, and humiliate the hero (or heroes) on the cover of *SI*.

The same holds true in March Madness for the high-profile major conference winners. These are the hero flyboys of the tournament, the guys with the leather jackets, mirror sunglasses, and glamorous blond girlfriends. The winners of the Big East, ACC, SEC, Pac 10, Big 10, and Big 12 all have huge egos and big red bull's-eyes on their chests. My advice: Bet against them throughout March Madness.

Whether they are upset or not does not matter. More important to bettors is that the favorites will not cover the heavy tariff their notoriety has forced upon them in the form of an inflated point spread. And the opposite holds true as well: Bet on the champions of the unheralded minor conferences like the WAC, Mountain West, and MAC. They are low-profile schools that have been playing and winning below the radar all season long. Their lack of exposure and smaller fan base is also built into the point spread. These teams represent value. Recognize the patterns again? Same theories, same strategies, same Contrarian thinking, just a different sport and time of the year.

The David versus Goliath Theory

This theory reflects all you just read about March Madness: Simply decide in every game who represents David and who represents Goliath. Your job is to wager on David in every matchup throughout March Madness. Bet on the teams that are on losing streaks heading into the Big Dance; bet against those on big winning streaks; bet against any team that reached the tournament with a big, high-profile win; bet on those who back in with a big, high-profile loss. Bet against the heroes of college hoops, the high-profile major conference champions, and top offensive players; bet on the low-profile minor conference champions; bet on the defensive teams with no heroes; bet against the glamorous high-scoring teams; bet on underdogs that the public ignores or gives little chance of winning; bet against the teams the public has fallen in love with. *March Madness is the ultimate Contrarian tournament.*

Those are the historical and Contrarian rules for major sports on which American gamblers love to bet: college and professional football, and college basketball. But we're not done yet. There's money to be made all year round. In the next chapter you'll find a twelve-month calendar that describes how to apply my winning betting strategies in every month of the year.

FOURTEEN

THE CONTRARIAN
BETTING CALENDAR

Winners Like Clockwork

January	Betting College Basketball Favorites
February	Betting College Basketball Underdogs— Contrarian Strategy
March	Betting March Madness, Contrarian Style
(My Favorite Month)	
April	Betting Baseball: Pitchers and Umpires
May	Betting the NBA Playoffs, Contrarian Style
June	Baseball Streaks and Tips
July	The Dog Days of Baseball
August	Pre-season Football: Psychology Is Profitable!
September	Betting College Football—Contrarian Strategy
October	Betting the NFL—Contrarian Strategy
November	Why Las Vegas Doesn't Want You to Bet College Basketball
December	My Contrarian Rules for College Football Bowl Games

Now that you understand my Contrarian Betting strategy and my Contrarian historical theories and trends, it's time to put it all together with my twelve-month calendar!

I want to thank my good friend Hollis Barnhart, the general manager of my company, GWIN, Inc. Hollis has provided my sports-handicapping investment advice to my private clients for almost fifteen years now. He knows my strategies, systems, and psychology better than anyone on this planet, with the possible exception of me. Hollis was the first person to point out that my strategies and tendencies form a pattern that repeats year after year, season after season, sport after sport.

One day Hollis said to me, "Wayne, I can time the months of the year based on your predictions. I know what's coming at the same time, year after year. If it's September, it must be your College Football Revenge Games. By October, your Contrarian strategies have kicked in. In December, it's your Contrarian bowl picks. March is time for Contrarian March Madness. Every April it's pitchers and umpires. There is a pattern to everything you do, and money to be made three hundred sixty-five days a year. You are a one-man sports-betting calendar!"

What I've done in this chapter is put it all together, so you can use this profitable advice every month of the year. This chapter points out a few of the crucial traits necessary for success, whether at sports gambling, business, or just plain life. Those traits are patience, discipline, organization, and an understanding of history (because history *always* repeats).

JANUARY—BETTING COLLEGE BASKETBALL FAVORITES

As previously stated, the King of Underdogs rarely sees an opportunity to bet favorites. However, that changes with college basketball during January.

Specific Proprietary Information
for the Month of January:

A. Favorites in college basketball win more often than any other sport because of

1. Strong home courts.

2. Huge packed crowds.

3. Unique arenas; fans close to the action.

4. Different hardwood floors.

5. Tight basketball rims.

6. Good coaching (makes a huge difference with only five young impressionable starters).

7. Experience (makes a big difference; teams with four or five returning starters have a huge advantage over younger, less experienced squads).

These are huge advantages for some home teams. As a professional handicapper, I pride myself on knowing which teams possess these huge advantages. Instead of slowing down as football winds down, January is often one of my most profitable months, and the only month that favorites play such a crucial role in my strategy.

B. Travel is another crucial factor in college basketball. College hoops squads play and travel twice a week. Small conference teams often travel to small towns and are forced to take the long bus rides from major airports to small towns by bus, leaving the long legs of 6-foot-8-inch bodies cramped and exhausted. The result is tired legs and a strong advantage (and betting edge) for home teams and favorites.

FEBRUARY—BETTING COLLEGE BASKETBALL UNDERDOGS— CONTRARIAN STRATEGY

This might be one of the greatest months to bet sports. February is conference-rivalry month. This is the second time around for these teams to meet each other. That situation also makes this "revenge season." Nothing is greater than the sweetness of revenge—in the right situation.

Here we have two teams having already played each other in the past month. We have a long-time history and rivalry between these two teams. I look for the situation where the weaker opponent is playing at home as an underdog, and I only play the teams who lost under special circumstances—the worst rout of the season, the worst defensive showing in years, etc. The rematch is now circled. The underdog is literally laying in wait to gain redemption and probably getting points.

What amazes me the most is that time and time again I hear and see the public ignoring this history. They don't even bother to look up the results of the previous game. I have had some of my biggest winning streaks during February betting on these conference-rivalry revenge underdogs. This is also the key month for my infamous unranked home teams favored over high-profile, top-twenty-five-ranked superteams. Two years ago I won seventeen straight games in February (one of my great all-time streaks) by doing my homework and looking for these perfect Contrarian betting opportunities. I found them by the bushel!

The betting public is on the opposite side of most of these conference rivalry dogs. Remember that the public got into a pattern of betting favorites in January—and winning—usually on the opposite side of my unranked favorites. So I am guaranteed to be getting value with both my February dogs (more points than I should be getting) and my favorites!

Why is revenge more effective in handicapping college hoops than football? In football, the sport that everybody loves to bet, revenge takes a different turn. If Iowa upsets Oklahoma during the season, it's not un-til a year later that we see this rematch. And 25 percent or more of the team has moved on due to graduation. They may not even have the same core of starters on the team.

Our basketball revenge is current—right now in the *same* season. We don't have to "wait until next year." We can profit immediately. And ad-ditionally, we have games six days a week instead of only once a week in college football, so this opportunity presents itself anywhere from four to eight times a week for the entire month. It's no wonder that February is one of my favorite Contrarian months of the year!

MARCH (MY FAVORITE MONTH)—BETTING MARCH MADNESS, CONTRARIAN STYLE

There are many Contrarian strategies, rules, trends, and handicapping situations that I use during March Madness. It's obvious why March is my favorite month: from conference tournaments thru March Madness, the betting opportunities just keep coming. In the last chapter, I ex-plained many of the key rules, and all of them are in play, from Three's a Crowd, Gallup Poll, and The Best Offense Is a Good Defense to The *Sports Illustrated* Jinx and David versus Goliath. These theories and trends work like magic year after year in March. Maybe that's why I've always felt like its Christmas all over again each March!

APRIL—BETTING BASEBALL: PITCHERS AND UMPIRES

If there were no point spread in football and the Super Bowl champion New England Patriots were playing the hapless Arizona Cardinals, who would you pick? What if the big, bad Philadelphia Eagles were playing the hapless Detroit Lions? Who would you take?

Well, that's what it's like to bet baseball. All you have to do is pick the winner. You never lose by a few runs. You never lose by the hook (a half point). There is no point spread to cover. Plus, you make extra money because of the generous odds offered to many underdogs. Everything is different in baseball than all the rules I've lectured you about in football and basketball. Throw all the Contrarian rules out the window.

Baseball is about streaks—winning and losing. It's about sweeps—gaining revenge for them in certain specific situations. It's about umpires and how they call the strike zone. It's about one-run losses and how teams respond to them. It's about pitchers—good ones win, no matter the odds. It's about how teams play on Astroturf versus grass, at night versus daytime. And believe it or not, it's even about parlays. Baseball is the one sport where I'll actually recommend underdog parlays that can turn a $200 risk into a $3,000 payoff. Six months of fun and profit starts in April! Another exciting and profitable month begins.

Trends and systems that I discourage in other sports work to perfection in baseball. Baseball is ever-changing. Winning depends on how you react to these changes in psychology and emotional intensity.

Early in the season, the cream often does not rise to the top. So underdogs are a good bet in April. Powerhouses like the New York Yankees or Atlanta Braves or Florida Marlins often start out slow. Injuries, cold or inclement weather, slow bats (pitchers are always ahead of hitters in early spring), and lack of motivation are all reasons why good teams start out slow.

Remember that even though it's early in the season, you're still forced to lay 2 to 1 or even higher odds on a good team—the same big odds as in the dog days of summer, when these powerhouses finally start to click and streak (and it's worth paying the large price for favorites). Amateurs don't understand the difference. To them, the Yankees are always worth

240 to 100 (a more than 2 to 1 favorite). To smart professionals, under-dogs are the only way to go early in the season.

Run production also matters early in the season. Because hitters are behind pitchers early, a team that scores a bunch of runs, especially one that sets records, has really accomplished something. Scoring twelve runs in July is ordinary. Scoring the same twelve runs on seventeen hits in April or May is exhausting. Teams that score a lot early in the season are good "go-against" opportunities the next day. I look for huge ef-forts—the most runs or hits scored all season (or better yet, in several seasons). Or back-to-back ten-plus run efforts. Then I bet against that high-scoring team the very next day. It's amazing how often they lose 1-0 or 2-1 after a high-scoring effort like that.

Umpires are important early in the season, at a time when we know little about the starting pitchers or how they will perform against each opponent. We monitor the umpires, their over and under totals, and the size of their strike zone. The strike zone may be the most consistent thing to measure in sports betting. Let me explain the theory of the home-plate umpire. These umpires are very consistent.

The reason we rarely hear pitchers complain about umpires is be-cause they are so consistent on calling balls and strikes. Each individual umpire has his own strike zone (you might call it his "comfort zone"). I don't care what major-league baseball wants the zone to be—each um-pire has his own. It's usually determined by the size of the umpire. If he is short and fat, then many times the strike zone is different than it would be for another umpire with a different build. Some umpires have tiny strike zones and therefore make you throw it exactly down the mid-dle, and some have very big strike zones, which help wilder pitchers or those who work on the corners of the plate.

This also really helps me profit on the "overs" and "unders." In base-ball, there are totals bets too—you can bet "over" or "under" a certain number of runs set by the oddsmaker. When the umpire has a wide strike zone, many times I choose to play the under. The batter is forced to swing at bad pitches. The pitcher can spot his pitches high and out-side, low and away, or inside. He can place the balls on all corners and get the called strike, where the batter is caught looking. If the batter does swing at a ball that is high and inside, he will rarely hit it very solidly. This combination of factors makes for a low total score all around, which is why it's a good indication that you should bet under.

However, when the umpires force you to throw the ball down the middle, a pitcher is in for a long day. The batter will simply sit back and wait for a pitch he can handle. I love to bet these umpires. Games with this kind of umpire behind the plate often soar over the total set by the oddsmaker. The bottom line is that the strike zone will remain a "per-sonalized" topic for each umpire. Understand the different personalities and habits of umpires and you can profit early in the season in baseball.

One other tip for April: We monitor how often each team uses their bullpen early in the season. It's early in the year, and cold at night. Teams will not overuse their relievers, as they would in the hot dog days of summer. Knowing how many pitches were thrown by the bullpen last night will determine what options a manager has in today's game. This gives us many high-percentage betting opportunities early in the season.

MAY—BETTING THE NBA PLAYOFFS, CONTRARIAN STYLE

If it seems like the NBA lasts all year long, that could be because it al-most does! The NBA begins in the fall, goes through the winter, then runs through the spring, and usually ends around the first week of sum-mer. I could never handicap or bet the NBA night after night for nine months, and there's no need to, because I win for virtually all of those months with college and pro football, and college basketball.

But there is a simple system that allows me to win big in the NBA playoffs. Not only can I enjoy the playoff games on TV, but I win over 60 percent of them year in and year out. Remember that NBA playoff teams are the best professional basketball teams in the world, playing night after night in what amounts to an elimination tournament. The emotional and physical toll is enormous. It is difficult to play two consecutive games at a peak performance. Teams that looked great last night often look completely different two days later. They manage to play a horrendous game, followed by the game of their lives. This is where I've successfully and profitably utilized a system called the NBA Playoff Bounce Back for almost twenty years. This bounce back hits above 60 percent for me consistently. There are several factors here to look for.

A. The team that shoots below 40 percent in a game will rebound to shoot well and get the win in their next game. I find these two teams often each reverse form and play a completely different game only twenty-four to forty-eight hours later. A little Contrarian psychology at work here!

B. The team that gets blown out in their last game (i.e., loses by 15 or more points) is embarrassed and motivated to rebound in the next game. The worse they lose, the bigger my wager in the next game. So losing by twenty or more is even better. Losing by thirty or more is best.

C. If neither of those two factors is present, just look for the outright loser of the last game to rebound or bounce back in the next game.

D. You also gain point-spread value in all these situations. You'll be against public perception (you're always on the team that lost or was crushed), so you'll be gaining an extra point or two in these games.

The NBA playoffs last throughout part of April, all of May, and on into June. Every day during this period is a Contrarian betting opportunity (or two). Use the bounce-back system and you'll always find yourself wagering on motivated teams looking for immediate revenge, you'll be getting value in the line, and you'll be playing against a team ready for an emotional letdown.

JUNE—BASEBALL STREAKS AND TIPS

By now we have enough baseball data to factor into our handicapping choices. We know how the teams are performing. We see home and away results, day versus night games, Astroturf versus grass, individual pitcher records versus each team, and most importantly, winning and losing streaks. Scoring trends are starting to help handicap the teams, not just the pitchers. We are seeing the number of runs scored over a series of games, and can make the prediction of performance based upon this and the pitcher. Many pitchers have a winning streak because of the team scoring runs for them.

I am now looking to play "bad teams" at home as underdogs, as well as "good teams" on the road giving small odds. There is tremendous value in the home dog in baseball, and I'll tell you why you have to pull the trigger on these plays: Teams that are at home simply try harder to win. One does not want to be embarrassed in front of their fans and family. They simply have something to prove.

The road favorite comes into the game a little overconfident or comes into the game totally discounting the underdog. April, May, and June are great months for home dogs. The hitters are ahead of the pitchers early in the year, and the pitchers rarely pitch a complete game. So teams rely on often-inadequate bullpens. It's very important to get off to a quick start by betting these home underdogs early.

On the other side of the equation are small road favorites. I like to take the best teams in baseball as small road favorites. Why? Value. At home these teams are unbettable 2 to 1 favorites (or higher). But the same team on the road is a pick 'em or small manageable favorite (−150 or less). That's value.

Another trend that takes place this time of the year is my three-peat. I define the most statistically significant point in a winning streak as games numbers four through six. After a team has won three games in a row, under the right circumstances (check opponent, pitching records, Astroturf versus grass, home versus away, and night record versus day), we bet on it to win games four, five, and six. And then stop.

Players really start paying attention to this streak after their team has won three games in a row, and that's the point at which they are playing with peak confidence, focus, and emotional intensity. And baseball, at it's simplest, is all about streaks. This also works the other way. It's time to go against teams that have lost three in a row, provided they are on the road and are favored. Not only will you be betting with this streak, but you will be betting on a home-dog team.

You'll win about 55 percent of these games, plus by getting them at the underdog price, you will quickly add to your bankroll. Even better in baseball is to look for teams that have won three or more in a row facing a team that has lost three in a row or more. This is an ideal play. You are betting on the perfect streak and against the worst possible slump, all at the same time!

Home stands are important for the players (a home stand is a grouping of games at home, usually lasting around ten days, usually containing three home series versus three different opponents). When I see a team lose their last home stand (lose more games than they win during that period at home), I am ready to pounce on them in their next home stand. They will be ready and focused. They will want to make it up to the fans. They will not want to disappoint the fans again. We might have to lay the number (playing favorites is called "laying the odds"), but it is well worth the risk.

Another tip to start observing is "the sweep." A sweep is when one team wins every game of a series versus their opponent. Betting on the home team in danger of being swept is not a profitable situation. Teams often lose three games in a row, and you'll find that you are laying a big price. Stay away from these games in most instances. The big odds you are forced to lay will build in a substantial loss for you.

On the other side of the sweep is, however, a powerful and profitable trend I call "sweep revenge." After a decent team is swept (a team with at least a .500 record), I bet them big in the first game of the next series they play against that same team that just swept them. It might be next week, next month, or three months from now, but the team that was unceremoniously swept (and humiliated) will never forget.

This is baseball's version of the Circle the Calendar Theory. That team will want revenge badly. Often they get it, but all I care about is that first game after the last sweep. That's where you have the big emotional and psychological edge. If they lose again, I come back even bigger on that same team in game number two. That's it, though. I never chase losers. There are exactly two opportunities to win—after that, stop.

I also love to make money on new pitchers making it to the "big show" (the major leagues). There is great value in "first-time starters." They usually don't get their first start until June, and the manager will make sure that this young, nervous kid gets every advantage in his first start. This start will usually be in the middle of a nice winning streak (so we know his team is hot), and usually against weaker competition. This rookie will almost certainly be an underdog or only a slight favorite, so I play him with confidence, knowing the manager wants him to have a fair shot at a win, to build up his confidence.

Finally, I bet with a pitcher that's pitching a recent rematch (one month or less) in which he pitched a good game but lost. He will bounce back against that opponent and get the win most of the time. Also, speaking of pitchers, we want to bet on a pitcher who had a win after a losing streak (two losses or more in a row). He's already had that bounce-back game and is now relaxed enough to win his second straight start.

June can be really exciting and profitable. Win here and it will carry through the entire baseball season. Stay disciplined and let baseball do its thing—*streak!*

JULY—THE DOG DAYS OF BASEBALL

Dog days here do not refer to underdogs but rather to the famous saying "the dog days of summer," which refers to a long, hot, humid, tiring month. Baseball is a long season. Players are tired by July. It's time for the all-star break. Injuries and heat are taking their toll. Streaks are more important than ever in this month. Teams that are on winning streaks now have momentum. Teams on losing streaks are physically tired and emotionally weak. They will continue losing. Keep betting the streaks, with special emphasis on three (or more) wins versus three (or more) losses.

Another baseball trend that has served me profitably each summer is the One Run Loss in the Last Game of a Series Trend. It's July, teams are tired and emotionally drained. Put yourself in their shoes. This is your fourth month of playing ball almost every day. Now you lose a game by one run, or in extra innings—a loss that defines tough. You're now depressed. And you have to fly to another city tonight, to play again tomorrow. Wow, how's that for exhausting? Bet against that team tomorrow, in their very next game after a one-run or extra-inning loss—but only if they play again on the road and on the very next day. You'll find five to ten plays a week for the rest of the summer with this psychological thriller!

AUGUST—PRE-SEASON FOOTBALL: PSYCHOLOGY IS PROFITABLE!

This August, think five. There are five reasons to play pre-season football—five reasons that will make August a profit center in your calendar year. Many amateur gamblers see these pre-season games as just meaningless exhibition games. The wise guys (smart money) in Las Vegas see these games as an opportunity to "stick it to the bookmaker." This is one of the few times all year when studying and understanding the coaches and players truly benefits the bettor. Remember, for me winning has more to do with public perception and value—where the money is going, and who the masses of amateur gamblers are betting on.

This is the only time in the entire football betting season that Las Vegas sportsbooks limit the amount of money that can be bet on each game. Think there might be a good reason? When it comes to gambling, nothing is ever easy, but if you want to wager on something the sportsbooks are afraid of, look at these pre-season games the same way a professional handicapper like myself does: as another opportunity to profit in your year-round sports gambling calendar! Here are five points to consider:

1. Who Is Trying and Who Is Lying?

The public does not know which key starters are playing, or for how long. Teams don't have to play all-out, and they never do in the first two pre-season games. Their goal is not to win but to get physically conditioned for the upcoming season, to learn the game plan and offensive/defensive schemes, and to try out new players (rookie draftees, new starters, and free agents). Understanding what the goals are for each team can result in big money for the smart professional.

2. New Coaches

New coaches like to start "a winning tradition" by applying discipline, positive attitude, and professional work habits, and perhaps most importantly, by putting their own personal stamp in place. Many veteran coaches couldn't care less about winning a pre-season game versus trying out the players and game plan they want to implement. What happens when a veteran coach meets a rookie coach in pre-season? There are many occasions where this situation occurs, because new coaches are being hired more frequently than ever (because old coaches are getting fired more quickly than ever), in the pressure cooker known as the NFL. Who is more interested in getting off to a good start? That's where the advice of a professional handicapper or gambler comes into play more than ever.

3. Season-ticket Sales

If season-ticket sales are down, going 0-4 in pre-season football will kill you, so sometimes a coach is instructed to leave the starters in the game long enough to insure a big win. Going 4-0 will create media buzz, raise hopes among the faithful, and sell tickets. Everybody from the fans and the beer vendors to the local media will get on the bandwagon and start buying tickets for the regular season if enough excitement builds during pre-season. Again, pre-season NFL is all about psychology.

4. Wrong Team Favorites

Oftentimes the oddsmaker will simply pick what looks like a "wrong team" as the favorite. There are dramatic new changes in the team "power ratings" every year—especially since the advent of free agency, which causes frequent wholesale changes in player personnel. The public is often unaware that Team A is no longer a powerhouse, or that Team B is no longer a patsy. The vast majority of the betting public thinks whatever happened last season applies to this season. This could not be more erroneous (or potentially disastrous for a bettor). But the odds-maker does not base his line on who is actually the better team. Rather, he bases his line on public perception—who the betting public *thinks* is the better team. Remember that the oddsmaker's main job is to get an even number of dollars bet on each side of the game, regardless of who's the better team. This creates interesting "line distortion situations" and great value in select pre-season games.

5. National Television Creates Opportunities for Profit

This is more pre-season psychology. What does it take to get a team's focus and intensity—emotional and physical—up for a meaningless pre-season game? Simple: a chance to shine on national TV! Only a select few pre-season games are broadcast nationally in August—usually by FOX, ESPN, or ABC's Monday Night Football. This is unlike the NFL regular season, where every game is on TV somewhere and any game is available to a national-TV audience on DIRECTV. Television in the pre-season is limited, and national TV is rare.

Players know this too. They want to shine in front of friends, family, fans, ex-teammates, and future Pro Bowl voters! National TV is, well, national TV! Who wouldn't or couldn't get up for a national-TV appearance? I go over the pre-season schedule each year in late July. I circle all the national-TV games. Then I study the teams playing in those high profile TV games, who they are playing the week before, and who they will play the week after. Those are fantastic opportunities to profit. The week before the big TV game, will a team care? Will a head coach care? Will star players care? How about the week after the big TV game? If the team won the big game in front of gushing announcers and an ador-ing national audience, will the star players give 100 percent again the week after, with no TV cameras turned on their every move? These TV games in pre-season create great opportunities for look-aheads and letdowns. It's only human nature and common sense. But for me, it's always been about dollars and cents!

So now I ask you: If pre-season is so hard to bet, why would Vegas sportsbooks limit your betting? Why wouldn't they encourage bettors to bet ever larger amounts? Because sportsbooks are vulnerable to the kind of professional thinking and smart money psychology described above. Start treating NFL pre-season like what it is—a chance to build your bankroll for the long and profitable football season ahead. Every dollar you earn this August is another valuable dollar you can use to beat the bookmaker come September, October, November, December, and January!

SEPTEMBER—BETTING COLLEGE FOOTBALL—CONTRARIAN STRATEGY

Ah, September—the grandest of months! Pro and college football—the loves of my life (and of most bettors')—have returned. But it's also a month to bet with caution. First, many gamblers rush into September with both fists bursting with dollars and their money burning holes in their pockets. *Big mistake!*

I can't even explain the number of gamblers I've met in my career who've lost so much, so quickly, that they either had to stop gambling here in the first month of the season, or worse, put themselves in such a deep hole that they never recovered. One I'd call death—sad and lonely, a season cut short before its time. The other is more like a coma—the bettor lingers on, suffering in pain, misery, and silence for the rest of the season. Both are conditions you don't want to experience.

Second, September is tricky for professionals like me because underdogs do not do well early in the season. Why? Because there are no emotional letdowns (or at least they are rare) in the first four weeks of foot-ball—not for young men playing a game they love with passion. By Oc-tober, November, and December, there will be lots of letdowns and upsets. But this early, no one is mentally or physically tired. So Contrar-ian strategy is not nearly as effective (especially in the NFL) this early.

Knowing this, I've also always felt that oddsmakers took advantage of the masses of public bettors by giving favorites a bit of a push early on. Yes, I've always felt that oddsmakers have a vested interest in letting the public win early on, to get them overconfident and hooked on gambling, to fool the bettors into thinking they have the edge over the bookmak-ers. Whether or not I'm right, favorites (and with them the public) seem to win much more often in the first month of football.

As a result, I make my money this month by playing mostly college football, and using theories that work remarkably well early in the sea-son such as Early Season Coaching Disasters, "Hasta La Vista, Baby," and Circle the Calendar. This last theory really works best in September. It is based on revenge from last season's worst loss, and teams have been waiting all off-season to collect! When the revenge game pops up early in the schedule, the pain of that humiliating loss is still fresh and bitter.

Later in the year, after playing half a dozen other bitter battles, the need for revenge for something that happened last year has faded. In NFL football, I bet against the rookie head coaches on the road in Sep-tember, and I look for rookie quarterbacks on young teams—and bet against them. They may be underdogs that I'll bet with frequency later in the season, but early on, these rookies are dead meat. So the King of Underdogs actually winds up on a few choice favorites in September. Enjoy it, because this will be the last time you'll see that!

OCTOBER—BETTING THE NFL— CONTRARIAN STRATEGY

Here, we begin the two big months that make up the heart of your annual football profits for the year. October and November spell *Contrarian!* This is where the naïve and unsuspecting public is led to the slaughter year after year. Bettors who have won consistently in September are literally crucified in the next eight weeks.

These next eight weeks are underdog heaven for sports bettors like me! This is where your Gallup Polling and Contrarian strategy kicks into high gear. Underdogs are wild—not just any underdogs, but the pathetic, unbettable, unthinkable, no-chance-of-winning underdogs, the kind of dogs that no normal person with a brain or any knowledge of football would even consider betting on.

But thank God, you are no longer "normal." Thanks to this book, you no longer follow the masses of "normal people" or listen to the advice of experts. You are now a Contrarian, and you're profitably traveling the road less traveled! Of course, these pathetic, unbettable dogs not only cover throughout October and November, they win outright with frightening regularity!

Over the next two months, you will poll, and poll, and poll some more—then bet *opposite* everything and everyone you've heard. Bring a big leather bag—you'll need it to carry all your winnings to the bank. And don't forget to thank the masses of asses coming out of the bank with sad faces, as you're going in to deposit your winnings. Their losses (on games that looked too good to be true) made your phenomenal success possible! During the next two months, follow the Contrarian rules of Chapters 9 and 12 to the T, and I'll see you at the bank!

NOVEMBER—WHY LAS VEGAS DOESN'T WANT YOU TO BET COLLEGE BASKETBALL

1. They Can't Adjust the Lines Fast Enough.

The reason Las Vegas sportsbooks allow you to play $100,000 on an NFL game but limit the same person to just $3,000 on college basketball is because the football lines come out on Sunday night for the following week, and oddsmakers have all week long, approximately six days until game day, to adjust the line. In basketball, the point spread comes out the morning of the game, and there's not a lot of movement on it until late afternoon. Suddenly, at that time, there's such a frenzy of action, the sportsbooks have no time to make the proper point-spread adjustment.

2. More on Line Adjustment

College basketball teams play two and sometimes three games during the same week. The Las Vegas oddsmakers cannot make the necessary adjustments on the point spreads on a game-by-game basis. Sometimes three or four games are played until those adjustments are made during a one- to two-week period. As astute bettors, the wise guys (smart money from professional gamblers and handicappers) recognize the lack of adjustment and jump on those games with regularity until the oddsmaker catches up with proper line adjustment.

3. New Player

A college basketball team that graduates three starters from the previous year's team represents a 60 percent change in the starting lineup, so a team that is good one year might not be nearly as good the next year. There are some coaches who have players ready to seamlessly come off the bench and replace those graduates, without missing a beat. And there are teams in which the coach's philosophy is to recruit talented JC (junior college) players and really don't miss a beat. Then there's that third group: coaches whose cupboards are bare. They are in for a rocky road, but none worse than November and December (especially with a new starting point guard—the quarterback of the offense in hoops). Another note on these players: Losing 60 percent of its starters to graduation might not necessarily be a bad thing for some teams, because those starters might not have been very good in the first place.

4. New Coach

In this day and age, coaches are always getting fired and replaced. In fact, nowadays nobody would keep around a coach like John Wooden, who didn't win a championship until his fifteenth year coaching at UCLA! Do you think the UCLA alumni of today would stand for that?! No way! There are lots of new coaches in college basketball. When a new coach is hired, he inherits a disgruntled team in disarray, and very likely will choose to insert a new system, a new style, and new philosophies. It takes awhile for the team to gel and play to the new system.

5. Small Schools

There are many schools that every bettor has heard of because they are either very good in basketball, or high-profile in football. But in basketball, there are many small schools that are huge within the college-basketball system, that are almost invisible to the betting public. Teams such as Ball State, Butler, Gonzaga (the Zags are not so invisible anymore, but they're still not UCONN, Syracuse, or Duke), Pepperdine, George Mason, and Northern Iowa are teams that not many bettors know well—or trust with their hard-earned money. That makes them "value plays," especially early in the season.

6. Board Teams

Las Vegas oddsmakers use about eighty-five "board teams" (teams who are listed on the board at sportsbooks and are therefore bettable) that they research and know all about in college football. However, in college basketball the board increases to about 200 teams. There are almost too many college basketball teams playing for the oddsmakers to keep track of. However, as a gambler, I don't have to bet every game. I just pick and choose the ones that I've researched and done my homework on. Because gamblers are not required to bet every game or every night and have the luxury of picking and choosing their spots, I usually look to November and early December for some profitable early-season college hoop opportunities. Unfortunately, the oddsmakers and bookmakers understand this only too well. The result is bets are limited.

In football I can bet anything I want (up to $100,000 per game), but in basketball in November, because of the plethora of teams, the difficulty in being able to adjust the lines under severe time limitations, and other factors discussed above, every Las Vegas sportsbook either limits action or makes it very uncomfortable for you to bet any large amounts on college basketball.

There are two good reasons not to worry about the limits: First, anytime you're winning, don't complain. Second, because you're winning so much betting on college and pro football in November, your early-season college hoop plays become an afterthought. Now isn't that a nice problem to have?

DECEMBER—MY CONTRARIAN RULES FOR COLLEGE FOOTBALL BOWL GAMES

That brings us to the final month of our calendar—and what a way to end with a big bang! Bowls are as Contrarian as you get (only March Madness has such a Contrarian bent), and that being the case, a winning bowl season has added up to a very merry Christmas, and a magnificent New Year for me for most of the past two decades!

To create your own winning holiday tradition, just refer back to last chapter's Contrarian rules for bowl season, putting to use such proven theories as Three's a Crowd, the Gallup Poll, the Best Offense Is Always a Good Defense, Late Season Home-Cooking, Bowl Blowouts, Big Schools Couldn't Care Less, Perfection Doesn't Last, Heisman/Schmeisman, the Chip on Their Shoulder, and Big Dogs Eat on New Year's Day during those two magical weeks between mid-December and the New Year, and watch your New Year brighten magically with Christmas cheer, goodwill to man, and holiday gold!

PART THREE

RISKING IT ALL AND WINNING

∎

FIFTEEN

CONTRARIAN POKER

No book on gambling could possibly leave out the topic of poker. Because of the success of *World Poker Tour* on the Travel Channel, poker mania is sweeping the world. Five to six million viewers tune into *World Poker Tour* every Wednesday night on Travel. Amazing. Even grandmothers and housewives are now playing poker online!

So is there a strategy to winning at poker? I know I sound like a broken record, but winning at poker is *also* about utilizing Contrarian strategy. The average amateur poker player thinks it's a game of luck. As usual, they are dead wrong. Poker is a game of *skill*, not luck. And it is not for amateurs. As with all other forms of gambling, those who do not study and understand the game and the odds are just flushing their money down the toilet.

I interviewed many top professional poker players and champions to gain a sense of why they win. The answers I got were both interesting and (so what else is new?) Contrarian. What was most interesting is how much in common these champions of poker have with sports gambling champions. Here is their winning strategy in a nutshell:

- **Just like any other form of gambling, the key to poker success is grinding out a profit.**

The best poker players bet *small* twenty hands in a row, stay patient, see an opening (their cards getting hot), then instantly shift into overdrive (bet *big*). The typical amateurs (otherwise known as "losers") are too impatient. They start out betting way too big *before* they've even gotten the lay of the land, before they've seen a hot streak develop. And of course (didn't you see this one coming?) they go bust (run out of money) early in the game—right before the hot streak they were waiting for develops.

That's the story of all gamblers—sports, casino, stocks, no matter. They consistently blow their money on low-percentage wagers they have no reason or right to be betting at all. That causes them to go bust. Then they complain that they have no luck. Or that it's impossible to win in gambling: "The odds are stacked against you," they say.

Well, sure the odds are against you—when you're an *idiot*, when you're betting big when you should be betting small, when you have no patience, when you don't understand the odds of the game you're playing, when you're talking and showing off and staring at breasts between poker hands (there's *that* problem again) when you should be closely watching and memorizing every move your poker opponents are making. The typical amateur makes every mistake in the book.

But the really sad part is that I'm not just talking about his or her first few attempts to play poker. I'm talking forever. Dummies never learn from their mistakes or failures. They never improve. They keep losing. So it goes in poker (just like sports gambling, casino gambling, and stocks). Winning is all about grinding out a profit.

- **Just like any other form of gambling, the key to poker success
is knowledge. Study the game. Know the odds.**

Most poker players don't have a clue when they should call, when they should raise, when they should drop out. They don't know the odds or percentages of each and every hand they are holding. When the pros play poker, they *know* (based on the cards they are holding) *their exact odds of winning.* Therefore they are able to calculate whether the risk is worth it or not (staying in, calling, raising, bluffing, etc.). Nothing they do is haphazard or by coincidence. There is a strategy and an understanding.

Poker is like a criminal trial. The oldest lawyers' rule in the book is to never ask a question if you don't already know the answer. (Best example: Marcia Clark and Chris Darden asking O.J. Simpson to try on the murder gloves, when they didn't know if the gloves would fit or not.)

In poker, your first rule is never to make a move without knowing the percentages and the psychology. You should be able to predict accurately what each opponent's response will be to your move. If you can't, you shouldn't be playing. That reminds me of that funny observation I've mentioned before: It is said that the key to winning at poker is to look around the table to see who the sucker is. If you can't figure out who it is, it's *you!*

- **Just like any other form of gambling, the key to poker success
is having a game plan.**

Most NFL head coaches decide long before the game exactly what the first fifteen to twenty plays will be. They've already outlined most, if not all, of the plays of the first quarter, and they will stick to their plan. That makes things simple. It's easy to focus when you already know exactly what you're doing. You've done it in practice exactly the same way. And you've already visualized it in your mind exactly the same way. Now all you have to do is execute.

Additionally, the point of all this detailed preplanning is to test your opponent, to see how he reacts to each move you make. Based on that response, now you draw up a new game plan to capitalize on his weaknesses. Most poker players (99 percent) have no game plan. They bet on a whim, or worse, because they are bored. These players are not focused on the strategy. They just want to have fun, or they like action (they are addicted to gambling), or it's just a social occasion for them. They engage in social conversation . . . they talk and talk . . . they drink and drink . . . they play sloppy.

The best poker players (the winners) take it seriously. They are not there to have fun. They are only there with one thing in mind—*winning money*. Like an NFL head coach, these poker pros have already pre-planned their first twenty poker plays. They have practiced each play in their heads (visualization). They know exactly how they want the game to proceed. They will play the first twenty hands the following way: AA—KK—AK—QQ. Their only goals are:

1. Find *big* hands to play.
2. Test their opponents and use that information later to intimidate or bluff them.
3. Show no tendencies or weaknesses to their opponents that can be used against *them*.

Those are the only three things that matter early in a poker tournament. You can lose a tournament early, but you can *never* win a tournament in the first few hours. Everything they do early is setting them up for the win later. Everything for these pros is about planning and discipline.

• **The key to poker success is to stay focused at all times.**

A winning poker player controls his actions and is almost always the only one at the table with discipline and a game plan. He is mentally prepared and focused from the second he sits down until the moment he leaves the table. This isn't fun—it's *serious* business. (Although it is fun to make money playing poker.) Unlike the other players who will engage in conversation when they are out of the hand, a pro will study the other players. They all have certain "tells." A pro is busy learning those traits or signals (weaknesses) that give away an opponent's hand or strategy. Amateurs think this is a social event. A pro is there to win! If you want friends, buy a dog. If you want to make money at poker, stay focused on the game at hand.

- **Once the action gets serious, so does a winning poker player.**

During the first third of a poker tourney, the pro is watching and learning (and setting himself up for victory later). But during the middle, he (or she) changes strategy and gets *aggressive*. A pro knows that winning is all about the hand you're dealt. So the definition of aggressive is to either fold or raise on almost every hand. The pros tell me they rarely "call" from this point on. Their hand is either good enough to raise, or they shouldn't be playing in the first place.

Amateurs, on the other hand, are constantly playing hands that they have no right to be playing! If you don't know the odds of your particular combination winning, you shouldn't be playing. So knowledge is your foundation. And aggressive is the way to capitalize on your knowledge. If you know what you're doing, know the odds you're facing, then it's a calculated, high-percentage risk (sound familiar?).

To top it off, not only is a winning poker player the aggressor later in a tournament, but now he has the added advantage of confusion. After all, earlier in the tournament he was anything but aggressive. He was downright meek. So the other players are now confused. His style has radically changed. He's now an uncaged animal instead of a domesticated pussycat! That alone is enough to unnerve and intimidate everyone else at his table.

- **The finale.**

Once a professional has made it to the "final table" (the place where the winner is determined), winning the championship is all about paying attention to chip counts. First yours, and second those of everyone else. The pros tell me that at this stage, counting chips is the difference between life and death.

Yet most amateurs are too nervous or oblivious (or ignorant about the game they are playing) to pay any attention to chip counts. They're too busy staring at their hand. Or fantasizing about how they'll spend the winnings. Or frozen like a deer caught in headlights. But it's always *bankroll* that matters. The Golden Rule applies here: He with the gold rules! The number-one rule at that final table is to know who the chip leaders are and to *stay away* from them! Don't challenge them: They'll eat you alive. They have more chips, so they can outlast you.

The number-two rule is *never* to give up (and in the end of the book, we'll see how great men like Winston Churchill, Abe Lincoln, and Walt Disney never did, and where it got them). Even if you're down to one last chip, you are alive. For that reason, it is crucial to always hold on to one last chip. Never bet it all. Go "all in," but minus *one chip*. The pros tell me that players have won entire tournaments with only one chip left. Or that one chip could keep you alive long enough to move from sixth to third, thereby collecting a whole lot more money! All because of that "Lone Ranger chip" and your "never say die" attitude.

Rule number three is to be aggressive. Once you're at the final table, a few good hands (a little lady luck) are your best chance to win it all. So don't be cautious when you get dealt a good hand—go "all in" aggressively. As usual, skill may get you close to victory, but only risk can put you over the top. Yes, you'll need a little luck from this point forward (without a good hand, you'll have nothing to risk on). But skill, discipline, focus, patience, courage, a solid game plan, and a Contrarian attitude will determine the difference most of the time. Those attributes alone will give you an edge over 99 percent of your poker opponents— an edge that works for any other form of gambling, too.

SIXTEEN

THE ZEN OF POKER

"People give you their money. In four years I made
more money than most people make in a lifetime."

—JOHNNY MOSS, THREE-TIME WORLD

SERIES OF POKER WINNER

During the 2005 World Series of Poker, I was asked to host a
television show and interview several of the biggest stars of
the poker world. My good friend poker professional Hollis "Harvard"
Barnhart was going to be playing in one of the events that day. I picked
him up and we headed to the Rio (a Harrah's Entertainment property;
the Rio hosts the World Series of Poker). As we pulled in front of the
place, a valet told us that valet parking was full because of the crowds
and media from around the world attending the tournament. I didn't
want to drive my Hummer around the many lots to look for a place to
park, and a $100 bill magically found me an open spot in valet parking.
It still amazes me how a $100 bill can get so much done in Vegas (and
in many other places, too).

When we walked inside the Rio, we were greeted with a sign, "Welcome to the 2005 World Series of Poker," with an arrow directing us to the venue. Our trek through the casino took us past people playing craps, blackjack, and roulette. Gorgeous cocktail waitresses in revealing outfits were serving drinks. Another sign with an arrow directed us down a long hallway. Walking along, we could hear comments like, "I can't believe I got knocked out with ace-king suited," and, "Some guy at my table went all-in with seven-nine off-suit." The hallway was filled with people who had been playing, watching, or reporting (media) or who were headed to do so. If I wasn't sure how many poker sites existed on the Internet before this WSOP visit, I now knew there were *a lot*, as everyone seemed to have a shirt or a hat featuring the name of a poker dot-com.

As we neared the venue, the buzz became unnerving. A steady stream of humanity was headed in the same direction as we were. We passed the registration area, where people were lined up to buy their way into one event or another.

Along a hallway, vendors were selling all kinds of items. Need poker tables? Got 'em. New shirts or hats? Got 'em. Lucky charms for the tables? Got 'em. Books or DVDs to learn how to play better poker? Got 'em, by the hundreds! Every booth had a sexy female in a skimpy outfit to entice the males to buy. From my viewpoint it was certainly working—millions of dollars were being spent *without* a hand of poker being played!

We then turned into the poker room. It took my breath away to see the size of this cathedral for poker. More than two hundred tables, the only sound the endless clicking of poker chips. One event was in full swing in one section, a satellite tournament in another, and cash games were being played virtually everywhere else. For the cash games, the Rio had had to build a special area to hold the money. Deposit boxes the size of Brinks trucks were filled with money, and a plethora of angry-looking armed guards made sure no one got any creative ideas. Spectators lined the aisles to view the tables, and with a mob scene like this, passing through the poker room was time-consuming and difficult.

ESPN had set up a special area for the poker table it was going to feature during broadcasts. Bleachers surrounded the table, and the lights against the backdrop created a dramatic effect. The scene was overwhelming; it made even the nonplaying spectators feel like entering an event. Testosterone was in the air. Poker had obviously hit the big time (and the mainstream). But enough about the thrill, excitement, and hysteria attached to big poker events like the World Series of Poker or the World Poker Tour. Now it's time to educate you on how to capitalize, win, and most important, *profit!*

THREE TYPES OF PLAYERS

There are three types of players at most poker tables, whether you're playing in a local poker room or at big-time events like the WSOP: Beginners, Dead Money, and Real Players. It's hard to believe there are Beginners at an event as prestigious and expensive as the WSOP, and they are rare, but they do show up. They may start out as Beginners, but after their first big tournament, they are quickly promoted to the next level, Dead Money. This is a wonderful development for the Real Players (but deadly for the Beginners). In an event as big as the WSOP, out of 20,000 contestants who play during the five intense weeks, as many as 18,000 can be classified as Dead Money. These 18,000 don't have a prayer of winning (anything). Yet they continue to show up with their cash because—in their minds—ninety-nine percent of the time, the hand that beat them was not their fault. Proof positive that rationalization is the key to happiness! Poker players call this kind of unfair hand from the gambling gods a "bad beat." What a concept. At any other time, in any other event or competition, the amateurs and dreamers would exit forever, convinced of the superiority of the competition—but not poker players. Not our Dead Money boys and girls. They just pony up more cash for the next event and swear to play "a little more solid." They envision playing only the premium hands, those 220-to-1 ace-ace "pocket rockets." *The next time*, they say, they'll be able to last longer and knock out one of their poker heroes. Unfortunately (or fortunately for Real Players), it's *always* "next time."

One reason for the abundance of Dead Money players in the poker world is that only in this sport do average Joes get the rare opportunity to move "from the stands to the playing field." Only in poker do accountants from Pacoima have the opportunity to rub elbows with celebrities they watch regularly on ESPN or Travel Channel or Fox Sports or Spike TV (on my show *King of Vegas*). Only in poker do unknown amateurs have a chance to knock out the Babe Ruths of poker, big stars like Doyle Brunson, Johnny Chan, Daniel Negreanu, Mike "The Mouth" Matusow, David Williams, or one of the famous Phils: Ivey, Gordon, or Helmuth. They not only get to play with the legends of the game, they get to sit next to them and match wits with them as equals (at least until they go bust and must exit stage right). But wait—it gets even better! Professional poker is the only sport in which you can watch the World Series one year . . . *and have a chance at* winning *it next year*! I can't even imagine getting the opportunity to play football alongside Joe Namath or Joe Montana or Roger Staubach in their prime, let alone having a legitimate chance to *beat* them. I would have paid thousands to be able to tell my friends of such an experience. And of course, I would have also been Dead Money. This Cinderella dream, this one-in-a-million long shot, is what turns ordinary poker players into Dead Money (and causes millions of dollars to change hands).

Ironically, the Real Players (as dominant as they are) aren't necessarily a sure thing when going up against amateurs at big tournaments. That's because the Dead Money amateurs are not at these tournaments to win. They are there to bag a trophy—to knock off a Real Player—so they can brag to their friends back home in Iowa. They arrive fearless, full of excitement, and armed with cash. It's not long before fear and reality take over, and they leave both the excitement and the cash on the green felt. The Real Players are truly masters at their craft. These pros are so good that on any given day, the Dead Money player may win (at best) one out of twenty times in a cash game. The pros have a huge edge *before they even sit down!* And one big thing that separates the Real Money pros from the Dead Money players is "pot odds." The pros know how to calculate odds. Knowing and understanding the odds is what separates the men from the boys.

During the main event at the WSOP, the number-one problem for the professionals is the number of players they must outlast to reach the final table. Some 6,500 players paid the $10,000 entry fee at the 2005 series. That created "land mines" throughout the seven-day main event. Imagine walking through a big rice paddy. In the paddy, buried under the water, are 6,500 land mines. And you have to maneuver around every one of those land mines for seven consecutive days, without getting blown to bits. It's not an easy task for anyone, pros or average Joes. The main difference between Dead Money and Real Players (other than understanding those all-important pot odds) is that Real Players avoid confrontations—unless they have "the nuts" (a *great* hand). I rarely see pros throw their chips into the pot on a draw (a good but *not* great hand that just doesn't give them a superior advantage). But time after time, low-ranked amateurs will call a bet on the "if-come" and put their money in the pot on a draw. The pro will recognize, seize, and exploit this opportunity. But smart players have to appreciate Dead Money players; they've driven up the TV ratings, popularity, and prize money of poker. That prize money (more than $100 million dollars for the entire tournament, making WSOP the richest sporting event ever), amazingly, made *everybody* at the World Series main-event final table an instant millionaire!

STARTING HANDS

When it comes to starting hands, the key to success is exactly as in real estate: *location, location, location*. Not all hands are created equal. I remember the first ring game I saw: A player had 3-3 in late position. That hand warranted a call. But later, when I was in the small blind and the button raised, I called and learned that they were two different hands. That 3-3 in the small blind was considerably worse than 3-3 on the button. The main reason was the location of the button—which allowed me to act (and bet) last. If I'm on the button and 3-3 in the small blind is first to act after the flop, I have the advantage, because 3-3 cannot withstand a preflop raise. As I have learned the hard way, a poker hand's value depends on the player's position. When playing starting hands, you have to know that the button is the most important and *valuable* location on the table. The player sitting on the button has the right to act last, and thus has the huge advantage of seeing how all the others play their hands, *before* he has to act. He gets to put a read (or "tell") on the other players. He gets to decide whether to call, fold, or raise. He gets to make the last decision—always a big advantage in the gambling (or business) world!

My poker-pro friend Hollis told me a story that he heard thirty years ago from a world champion and one of the most colorful characters in the poker world, Amarillo Slim. Asked about his favorite starting hand, Slim told Hollis it was a jack-10 suited. The reason he liked this starting hand so much is that a player can make five different straights with these two cards. The possibilities are A-10, K-9, Q-8, J-7, and 10-6. This is how Slim would play the hand—three different ways to play the same starting hand, all based on *location*. When he was "under the gun" (in the seat next to the big blind, or early position), Slim would fold. But, with the same J-10 in middle position, he would call, or match the bet already on the table. In late position, that same J-10 would warrant raising the pot, simply because of his position on the button. In this superior late position, the poker pro wants to raise the pot to control the table and to be aggressive. Being aggressive is key to winning big-time in poker, but only when weighed against location at the table. Your position determines if you'll fold, call, or raise aggressively. That's three different actions with the same two cards. The crucial characteristic about starting hands is, therefore, position. A good player will decide to make one hand playable in one position on the poker table, and totally unplayable from another position. You can also bust out the players who hold an ace or those who make two pair with A-Q, K-Q, and A-J after the flop. It's all about location—lying in the weeds waiting to bust someone out.

Let me clue you in on starting hands. Below I've listed the Top 16 starting hands in descending order of value, from best (1) to worst of the best (16). I've heard many "bad beat" stories, and what they all have in common is poor strategy, because most of the time, the hands that the Dead Money amateurs lost with were not any of those on the list below. Which means these players did *not* start out with the best hand. Which means they should not have still been in the hand in the first place; they could have avoided a bad beat and a large loss of bankroll. Those weren't bad beats at all; they were in fact "dumb beats." That's why average-Joe amateurs are called Dead Money. Often they are dead *before* the game even starts, because they just don't understand the rules or the strategy of the game they are playing.

Here are your best starting hands:

(1) A-A   (2) K-K   (3) Q-Q   (4) A-K   (5) J-J
(6) T-T (10-10)   (7) A-Q   (8) 9-9   (9) K-Q   (10) A-J
(11) K-J   (12) A-T   (13) Q-J   (14) K-T   (15) A-9   (16) 8-8

I've laughed hysterically listening to players say, "But my cards were suited." That is no reason to play a hand, under most circumstances. If your two starting cards are suited, you must ask yourself: "Would I play the same two cards if they weren't suited?" If you are dealt a 4-5 unsuited, would you play the same 4-5 because they are both diamonds? The correct answer is "Maybe." I would play those cards only if I was in late position on the button. *It's all about location, location, and more location!*

WATCH THEIR HANDS

Hollis "Harvard" Barnhart (I'll explain the "Harvard" part later—more good poker psychology) was standing on the rail with me at a WSOP $2,500 event. He had just been knocked out with A-Q suited (as if suited mattered). As for this bad-beat story, here's what happened to Harvard: First position limped in. Hollis simply called, as he was in middle position. The button called, and the small blind folded. The flop came, Q-7-2, a perfect flop if ever there was one. The big blind checked, and the player in first position bet out the minimum. Hollis thought long and hard, and decided the best way to play this hand was to isolate the player in first position; so Hollis went all-in, betting everything he had. The button and the big blind both folded, and the man in first position called the all-in bet. ESPN cameras were summoned over for filming. Hollis looked like an angry, shocked deer caught in the headlights when the player in first position turned over "pocket rockets," two aces. This superior hand gets dealt once every 220 hands on average. Hollis's pair of queens was basically worthless. He had a five-percent chance to get one of the two remaining queens he needed. It didn't happen. Like many winners in poker and life, Hollis is always aggressive—sometimes too aggressive. I'd rather be overly aggressive than timid, fearful, or intimidated. Aggressive wins much of the time, in gambling, business, and life. Hollis's only comment was that he couldn't believe that a Real Player would ever slow-play aces. It was a stupid strategy. So Dead Money ended up knocking out a Real Player.

This gave Hollis and me a chance to "railbird" some poker pros for the TV interviews I had to do later that day. We went over to a table with Mike Sexton, host of the popular World Poker Tour. I wanted to see how he played, and Hollis wanted to teach me more about reading players, watching their "tells." He pointed out something about "watching their hands." He is very studious at the table, always a hundred percent focused, always watching; even as a mere spectator, he has the same intensity he has as a player. We observed one player paying more attention to the cocktail waitress than to the players. Another player was girl-watching. A third was daydreaming, clearly paying no attention to the game. Which led me to ask Hollis, "Do you watch their eyes?" Hollis said, "No, you should watch their hands." As soon as a player completes a raise, start watching his hands: does he still go for his chips or does he look at his hole cards again and stop touching his chips—indicating he is weak. I started watching the players' hands before the flop to see whether they were holding their cards cocked, which would suggest they were ready to "muck" them. I've seen players looking to muck their hand, but they continue to play because of preflop weakness (shown by "limpers"). One player had his hand cocked, ready to fold, but he played anyway. Hollis pointed this out to me and put him on a very weak hand—he judged him a player with no confidence, trying to steal the pot later after the flop. If you see a player like that, raise him—he's almost always bluffing.

Watch the players to your left if you are close to the cut-off position, and if they have their hands cocked to muck, then observe the player on the button. Maybe he also is indicating that he plans on mucking his cards, by flashing his cocked wrist. This is a great chance to raise with a marginal hand. His folding makes you the button. Your hand can now control the betting and the check-raise. This is a great position to be in— that magical and valuable location that allows you to act last. And you obtained ownership of that valuable position simply by observing the players to your left and the tells they provided free of charge.

READING THE PLAYERS

In business, much as in sports or gambling, you are forever reading the strengths and weaknesses of your competition. This aspect of poker is what draws me to the game. One good part of my résumé is my uncanny ability to read people. In business negotiations, I am always drawing on this unique skill. I've sat in meetings and known almost to the dollar how much the rival CEO sitting across the table was willing to pay. In other words, I could call his bluff. I apply that same skill to the green felt.

There are four poker players to typecast. Though occasionally they might seem to change gears, they really will not change. They always draw on their instincts when playing. It's part of their innate being. This is another thing that separates the Dead Money amateurs from the top poker pros: the ability to read players and really change gears in the middle of a tournament.

First are loose passive players. I think of them as "the Will Rogers of poker"—they never met any two cards they didn't like, and they will play any two cards. They are calling stations. They don't do much raising, but they want to see every flop—and they're willing to pay for it. They drive all great players crazy. If you ever hear about a 7-9 off-suit taking out pocket queens, most likely it came from one of these loose players. And if you really want to add misery to your life, try bluffing them. It won't happen. You can't get them out of the hand. They will play it to the river. And they will kill you on the river when that third miracle flush card falls into play. One of the tells of loose passives is that they will call. I love playing against these types, but I have to be very patient.

The next types to observe (instead of the cocktail waitresses) are the loose aggressive players—I call them "the Maniacs." The main difference between loose aggressives and loose passives is that the aggressives play most hands before the flop and get the most enjoyment in raising every

pot with any ace or any two-suited cards. And look out when they are
holding two picture cards in their starting hand; now you are destined to
see a raise and raise big and reraise even bigger. Aggressives just love to
gamble. They love the action. Their tell is that they play too many hands.
Make a mental note of that at the table. Their personality trait is to run
too many bluffs by trying to be the bully. They're difficult to read and
they will be fearless, but they cancel that good aggressive trait by being
loose and impatient. These players rarely make the final table. I am very,
very patient with these types, too.

Now let's shift gears and talk about "The Rock." This player in this
third category is solid (like a rock) and very conservative. There are
many retirees in this group. If you see an old person sitting at your
table, his shirt buttoned up to his neck, he's likely in this group. Rocks
play only premium starting hands. They play only two big cards. They
are easy to bluff because they don't like to call raises. I think they are the
easiest players to read and compete against. And their number-one tell?
They rarely bluff—so look out and *get out of the way* when they raise!

My friend Hollis "Harvard" Barnhart told me of the one time he laid
down pocket kings. If you've never done so, I can certainly understand why.
It is almost impossible to lay them down into the muck. You just cannot get
away from a hand this big, unless of course you know how to read players.
Harvard was playing in a tournament, and a twenty-minute break had just
ended. During the first hand after the break, he was dealt pocket kings. He
was sitting in early position and made a raise three times the big blind.
Three competitors folded, and then an eighty-year-old with a flannel shirt
buttoned up to his neck came over the top and went all-in. Everybody
folded to Harvard. He studied and thought. He knew the following:

1. This man was a rock.
2. The man had played only one hand the past hour.
3. He was old, and that shirt buttoned to the top was staring at Hollis.

4. The old man had raised a raiser. (Always beware of this.)

5. The man would not play like a rock till now and then suddenly come out firing right after a break.

Hollis could not put the man on A-K or Q-Q; the odds were that the man had been dealt pocket rockets. Hollis tossed his K-K into the muck, and the old man exposed his hole cards: sure enough, two aces.

I call the fourth group "Real Players" (just like the third basic type discussed earlier). These are your most solid players. They are tight, they play only great cards, and they are aggressive (because they play only great cards). They tend to control the table, but more important, they control the hand they're playing. Real Players are masters of the check-raise, and they use it effectively. They know how to let others do the betting for them, know when to let others lead or when to do the betting themselves. They will raise effectively to get a free card. They are usually all about math (the numbers, the odds). And while the other players are wondering, they are calculating the pot odds. And every second the Real Player's mind is working like a calculator, he is also watching you. He will try to engage you in conversation. He will see how you handled your chips and how you placed them in the pot. He will read your body language. He is fearless. He is a pro's pro. He is the real deal. If you see 3-4-5 players calculating the pot and observing other players, if you notice mannerisms suggesting a superior type, get out of the game! And if you're observing around the table, watching all the players and their mannerisms and tells, and after two rounds you still don't know who the sucker is . . . *it's you!*

WHEN TO FOLD

Folding—what a concept! People love to see the flop. But then they are self-induced to play a marginal hand they never should have been playing in the first place. Learn when to fold—it's that plain and simple. And do not beat yourself up when you fold the suited 9-5 and the flop is three suited cards giving you a flush. This is not a game for what-ifs. Do not put your-self in a mental frenzy when the flop reveals a 6-7-8 giving you a straight. Just go to the next hand and count up all the times you folded and nothing hit on the flop. My good friend Harvard is all about either folding or raising. So here we'll turn our attention to folding. Let's ask, "When do I fold?"

1. Dump any hand that will not make you money. Forget about being or playing "on a draw." Playing on a draw is for our Dead Money friends. Waiting for the flush draw is for complete idiots or amateurs.

2. Do not play cards because they were suited. I love to see players do this, as it makes them losers in most hands, and it is a huge tell for me. I now *know for sure* they are weak players. Fold these hands. You should ask yourself: "Would I play these cards whether they were suited or not?" And for you math majors: In the game of per-centages, add only three percent to suited cards, as opposed to the same two cards that are not suited.

3. As a rule, I play about twenty-five percent of my starting hands and fold the rest. If you find yourself playing more than that, tighten up your starting card requirements immediately.

4. Be especially careful after a bad beat. Do not try to get your chips back by going full-tilt. Calm down and fold those marginal hands. Show some patience. You should play no differently after a bad beat from how you played after any other kind of hand. Just as in sports gambling, never try to regain your losses in one fell swoop. Going for broke almost always leaves you *broke*. The only way to win is to grind it out, winning a little at a time.

5. I bet you didn't know this sound and simple advice that can help anybody. Harvard taught me that fifty percent of pocket pairs will *not* improve after the flop. So you'd better like those pocket cards before you go all-in with them. Dump those 2-2's and 3-3's after the flop, or before if you are in early position.

6. Play aggressively, or do not play. Either fold or raise in most positions. If your hand is not good enough to raise, you should not be playing. This is not to say that you can't play the button with a weak-ace. But of course, as you know, the button is all about location, and that alone changes the rules!

7. Don't be afraid to fold the small blind. And you don't have to protect the big blind. After a call from the blind, you still have to act first in horrible position. There is no advantage to playing from this position with bad cards, so just fold!

RAISING BEFORE THE FLOP

Harvard and I rushed out of the live interviews I had just completed with some of the most famous names in the poker world—Doyle Brunson, David Williams, Mike "The Mouth" Matusow, Jennifer Harmon, among others. Some of them were interesting, and some didn't have a clue how to animate an interview. Maybe that's why they can sit for hours at the table totally expressionless, seemingly void of all thoughts, barely appearing to be alive. They wear the same face whether they are holding A-A or 4-5 off-suit. If that's what it takes to be at the top of the poker world, then count me out! I love to play. My way of playing at the table is one of passion and fascination; I love the challenge of putting a read on a person.

I've given you advice on being in a pot before the flop from three positions. You must make this second nature at the table. Location is position. Are you in early, middle, or late position? Are you one of the blinds? Are you sitting in late position with a 3-3, willing to raise from that position and realizing that same 3-3 would be folded from early position? You must always, *always* play proper starting hands, and always be aware of your position—unless you have a boatload of money you're mad at and want to generously give away.

There are only four things you can do after you look at your two starting cards:

1. Check.
2. Call.
3. Fold.
4. RAISE.

Raise whenever you can. Harvard plays at least one tournament a month in which he will *not* call a single bet. This is his way of "playing the correct way," a method he uses to remain at the top of his game. Let's analyze this style of play. You have two choices, fold or raise. This forces each hand to be played correctly. You will be forced to fold bad hands, play premium hands, and play aggressively by having to raise all starting hands. Harvard won a tournament recently and *never* called one bet the entire six hours. Every hand he played was either folded or raised. Why should you raise before the flop? Identifying the reasons may make you a better player, aggressive and solid.

1. To obtain valuable information. You will have no idea of the strength of your opponent's hand if you check. So raise, three to four times the large blind. This is how you can gain information on the other players. The odds are three to one that a raiser does not have a pair. If he has two big cards, then your pair is the favorite in most hands. But if he calls or reraises, you've gained a world of information about his hand.

2. To obtain a free card. Everyone has heard the expression "Let's check to the raiser." This allows you, the raiser, a chance to bet or take a free card if you missed the flop. And if you really want to slow-play your hand, this allows for that. Many times I have raised preflop, and all checked to me after the flop. My three choices then: (a) I can bet if I hit my hand; (b) I can start a bluff; or (c) I can

check . . . and they *still* don't know whether I checked because I am slow-playing a big hand or whether I missed my cards. This is how solid players control the hands they are playing.

3. To protect your starting hand. The only way to protect your hand is by raising. And I am talking about a starting hand of J-J or Q-Q. You must take down the pot at this moment. No exceptions! These jacks or queens cannot go up against any ace or king. And what else are one or two limpers going to be sitting with in their starting hands? Certainly not 8-6 off-suit. So any ace or king that flops beats your big hand. Force these players to lay down their hand— *before the flop.*

4. If you have ace-ace. Once you have the best starting hand in poker, you *must* force everybody to pay to see the flop. There's no free lunch. Do not slow-play aces. Yes, on occasion it works, but it's the rare time you let in limpers and one of them gets "dumb lucky" and hits his card on the river. You'll generally make this amateur mistake once in your life, so if you haven't had the feeling of getting your A-A cracked by slow-playing, get it over with and out of the way and *never* do it again.

5. If you want to eliminate other players and isolate one-on-one with a weak player. Let's say you are holding A-K or a pair of tens. You want to get rid of as many players as possible so that with fewer players your hand has a better chance of winning. Raise to force players out. Ace-king is worthless after the flop if it doesn't hit. If an ace or a king does not flop, your hand is usually dead.

6. To set up a bluff or semibluff. This allows for a situation where you can take down the pot later, even if you don't hit the flop. Harvard is a master of this. At times I could swear he had K-K because of his mannerisms and his raise. And then I saw that he was setting up a bluff; he followed his preflop raise and raised after the flop, and he had others convinced that he had a big hand. The bottom line: You

must be aggressive. This game is *not* for the meek or weak. This is a game for real men or women to become Real Players.

PLAYING YOUR OPPONENT'S PREFLOP RAISE

We were on the rail at the WSOP, and Harvard asked me, "When do you call your opponent's preflop raise?" That's the reverse of what I described above. I thought for a moment; there were several factors involved. Let's look at some of the things I considered:

1. Who made the raise? Is he a Rock, one of those old men with a buttoned-up shirt? Is he a Maniac? Has he been drinking? You need to put a read on your opponents.
2. How many other players have called the raise, and which players might have their starting cards in their hand, cocked and ready to toss into the muck?
3. What are the pot odds? While calculating this, be mindful and wary of good players calling from early position.
4. Will someone else be coming over the top? If your hand cannot withstand another raise, then fold. If you notice other players handling their chips or reaching for their stacks, figure out how many players are left to call this raise behind you.

Harvard was impressed with my list, but he wanted to put my Ivy League degree to a test, so he pulled out this question: "If you hold A-K and you put your opponent on A-Q, what are your odds?" I came back with, "I'm a four-to-one favorite after the flop if we both missed our hands." Another question when analyzing hands: "Am I on a draw like

A-K, or do I have a premium hand like Q-Q?" And I have to put the raiser on a hand. I cannot consider just my cards. I must think about *his* cards; I have to put him on a possible hand or ask myself what he could be holding. That's what separates the bad players from their money.

RAISING THE POT

I love to observe good players. The difference between great players and bad players is that great players know *when* to raise. All great players are aggressive, *period*. They put pressure on their opponents to make tough decisions. Aggressive players raise with all pairs and most face cards, depending on their position. Some will even raise with ace-anything. Hollis says not to do that. There are hands that you put money into the pot with, an ace-6 for example. The flop is A-8-4. You still haven't established good-enough cards to take down the pot; even after you've gotten the ace on the flop, you don't have a winner because of your kicker. So why get involved in the first place? The exception is if you are simply calling from the button preflop.

Another type of hand to raise with is the "suited connector." Down to the 5-6 suited, you have a chance to bust somebody with the right flop. And a 6-high straight will always bust a straight from the person who called the preflop hand with A-5. As the 2-3-4 make you a 6-high straight, it makes your opponent a 5-high straight. He will never put you on this hand. That's why it's so valuable. Suited connectors will not stand a reraise from an opponent who comes over the top.

I've noticed three types of raises:

First, the "pot sweetener." This is by far the worst type; in fact, I don't even classify this as a raise. It is very ineffective, as it seldom puts pressure on an opponent to make a tough decision. There is one exception that Harvard taught me concerning this type of raise, though, which involves playing heads-up (one-on-one with only one opponent). When you are on the button, use this type of raise. Why?

1. By raising on the button heads-up, you usually will force your opponent to fold. If he calls, that will set up your next bet after the flop.
2. This will also force a called raise to have to bet or check after the flop. If your opponent does not hit his hand, he will usually check. Your time to take down the pot is right in front of you. All you have to do is bet, and most of the time he will muck his cards.
3. Most great players play this style of aggressive poker, so it goes without saying that if your opponent is *not* raising on the button, chances are he is not a very good player. Another Dead Money player for your trophy case!

The second type of raise, a normal raise, is set at three to four times the big blind. To be less obvious to the competition, it is advisable that you consistently raise this amount, so Real Players can't get a read on you.

The granddaddy of all the raises—drumroll, please—is the all-in raise. I was walking through the Bellagio one day when I heard some tourist ask where he could play all-in. He didn't even know the game was called Texas hold 'em. This was an instant tip-off—a Dead Money player! The all-in raise is intriguing. Most players use it with a bluff or a semibluff. Let's face it, if you have the nuts (a great hand, remember), would you ever go all-in after the river card is dealt? Of course not. Use it sparingly, especially early in a tournament. It is used preflop to take down the pot. The biggest mistake I've observed with an all-in bet was with ace-king preflop. Many people think this hand is the nuts, and they put all their chips into the pot. Odds are 110 to 1 of being dealt A-K, so I guess that gets players excited. The odds you flop an ace and a king are four percent. The odds that you flop either an ace or a king for one pair are forty percent. And that does not guarantee that you have a winner. Hollis plays A-K as if he will win about thirty percent of the time. Ask yourself: Should you put in a hundred percent of your money with only a thirty-percent chance of winning? It depends on your position and the number of players in the pot.

Good players don't need to go all-in. They are comfortable outthinking and outplaying others and using the tournament clock to their advantage. And they are not in favor of risking all their tournament chips by going all-in. The only exception is a good player who is short-stacked. Consider betting the size of the pot instead of going all-in. Leave the all-in bets to the weak players looking for big plays and big bluffs. For the last twenty-one years at the WSOP, the opening-day chip leader has *never* won the tournament. So raise the pot . . . over and over. Be aggressive and play solid, and by all means do not be a calling station. Either fold those bad or marginal hands or raise the pot. Save the dramatic all-in move for only the most perfect and opportune moments.

BLUFFING: WHEN *NOT* TO BLUFF

There is nothing more exciting than coming over the top with a stone-cold bluff. And doing it all along with a straight face. Without telling anybody—except once in a while. Rarely show your cards. I make it a point to show a bluffed hand only *once* during a tournament. I keep my bluffs to myself and let others wonder. I love to bluff, but my friend Harvard is always reminding me about when *not* to bluff. He feels that most players think a bluff requires two things: first, bad cards and a willingness to make a play at the pot; second, wanting to put all your chips in the pot to force your opponents to lay down their hands. But Harvard has pointed out some rules to follow. Let's look at his wisdom before we talk about when to bluff:

1. You cannot take a chance on bluffing when an ace hits on the flop, unless you want to indicate that you have an ace. Generally you'll find that someone called a preflop hand and limped in only because he was holding a weak-ace. The odds are fifteen percent that before the flop no one else is holding an ace if you aren't. For this reason alone, do *not* bluff after an ace hits on the flop. An ace will be dealt seven out of eight hands in a ten-handed game.

2. So many players love to play the Holy Grail (jack-10 suited) that you must be very careful when a J-10 hits on the flop. Do *not* bluff when you see these two cards. Someone will be holding a J-10, or someone will limp in with a K-Q or an A-Q and will be on a draw to make a big hand with that J-10 flop.

3. Do not bluff when there are multiple callers preflop. Someone will call your bluff, and you do not want to put all your chips in on a bluff and then have someone sitting with a big hand call you.

4. Never, never, *never* bluff when someone has raised preflop. Do not try to bluff the raiser. He will call you—and often with a big hand!

Harvard has said repeatedly that you cannot bluff for a living. A bluff is a tool. Don't wear out your tool. You just can't get some people to lay down their cards on a bluff, so you will get called occasionally with a bad grin on your face, holding 6-9 suited. If you can't remember about "when not to bluff," just keep this in mind: You *cannot* bluff in a limit game.

BLUFFING: WHEN TO BLUFF

This brings me to my favorite part of the game—bluffing. I love to bluff. I love to play aggressively. I love check-raising with nothing. I don't do any of this recklessly, but only after I've put a read on my opponent. There's nothing more exciting than coming over the top and watching everyone surrender to my 6-9. What a rush! It's a very big part of the game. Let's face it; you can't wait for the nuts, the perfect hand, every time. You'll be dealt A-A only once every 220 hands. You can't afford to lose all your blinds while waiting for that monster starting hand. You must add to your chip count—so you bluff. Let's talk about when to bluff:

1. I get the best pot odds when there's a big pot and I'm going heads-up (one-on-one with only one opponent). I won't win all of the race-offs, but the ones I do win, as my opponent folds, make up for the rare loss in the long run.

2. I love to bluff against very good players. They are smart enough to give you credit for a good hand. They will ask themselves, "What does he have?" They think through the entire process and will lay down a hand *if* they put you on a big hand. Bad players, like our Dead Money friends, are not good enough to put you on a hand, and will therefore call your bluff, so be careful of those weaker opponents and stick to bluffing against very good players.

3. The higher the stakes, the easier it is to bluff. In a small-limit game, it is nearly impossible to bluff effectively.

4. When I raise preflop but miss everything on the flop *and* there is nothing strong on the board, I continue to bet as if I'd made my hand and bluff.

5. When I have A-K and miss the flop, I continue to bet if I sense that the table respects my play. If the others think I'm a solid player, they will fold. If I play like a Maniac, they will call. I'll take this shot against one to two players only.

6. I love faking a rush. After I've won a hand or two, or three out of the last four pots, I will continue my rush and make a play at the pot with a bluff. It looks like I'm on a hot streak, so it's perfect to keep everyone guessing (and intimidated)!

7. When I want to represent a big flop, and if I have nothing and an A-A-9 flops, for example, I will make a small bet, so that it looks as if

I'm trying to suck everyone into a call. If someone calls or raises, I can easily release the hand. But it's amazing how many hands I actually win in this situation, as good players outthink themselves and usually fold.

BLUFFING: ON THE RIVER

Bluffing on the river has its own set of rules and standards. Follow these and, as my good friend Harvard assures me, you will pick up many chips and find yourself at the final table. Here are "The River Rules." Bluff on the river:

1. If you can steal the pot with one bet. Make sure it is a very big pot.
2. If the hand is such that every player checked on any given round. It's worth taking a shot at the pot if everyone signals weakness.
3. If the river card produced no possible straight or flush draws.
4. If you raised the pot preflop and no aces or face cards have hit the table.
5. If you want to represent that you have something that matches the board.
6. If you're heads-up against an opponent you've been beating.
7. When you're going heads-up (again, one-on-one with only one opponent).

Remember that bluffing is a great tool. But I caution you to reread often this section on when to bluff and when not to bluff. This will keep you in tournaments. I remember an amazing WSOP tournament I was sweating with Harvard. After five hours he had the most chips at his table, and the biggest hand he started with was a pair of sixes, which he promptly folded after the flop produced nothing. Bluffing was a major part of his strategy that night. You should make it a big part of yours, too.

SITTING PRETTY

My Favorite Tell

Tells can be verbal or nonverbal. Watch the TV poker stars and examine some of their antics. They verbally assault their opponents, trying
to engage them in a battle of words. Their goal is simple: to gain information. This is not always a show. For many players, this is a science. And
if one player stays tight-lipped, the others study his face. Does it crack?
Is it rigid? They look at nonverbal mannerisms. Is he sitting stiffly, or is
he relaxed? Many experts believe that in poker, looking strong means
you're holding a weak hand, while looking weak and relaxed means
you're holding a very big hand. But it's actually the opposite. When I see
someone trying to intimidate me into calling by acting as if he has the
nuts, I choose to call—and usually watch him muck his hand as I gather
up all his chips!

Try this tip every time you are making a big move on the pot by bluffing. It's my experience that when my opponent bluffs, he immediately
puts his elbows on the table and leans toward me as if trying to intimidate me. In contrast, when he has a big hand he leans back in his chair
and looks very relaxed, even puts his hands behind his head. A tell involves a physical action. So let's do this physical action in reverse: When
you bluff, put your chips into the pot and then sit back and look at
everything around you *except* your opponent. Look relaxed. He will
muck his hand more times than you think. Do not talk. Just sit there and
feel the pressure you have thrown his way. Keep it this simple.

Remember to think and act Contrarian (where have you heard that
one before?). In the Contrarian world of poker, weak means strong . . .
and strong means weak. When somebody is acting impatient, he probably has a strong hand. I see this all the time. When someone goes from
slouching to sitting straight up, look out—he's holding a big hand. If

somebody is having a conversation at the table and then goes into a quiet lock-down mode, he has a big hand that he wants to pay special attention to. A player who covers his mouth is usually weak, so go after him aggressively. And finally, when a player throws in his chips and makes a big deal about it, or tosses them at you forcefully, reraise him; he's bluffing. There are many such tells in poker—so pay attention to the table while you're playing. You have only one job: to pay attention to your opponents. After all, they're holding *your* money.

A Great Story of Poker Lore

So you can have a strong "table image" as you relate a story that makes you look like a poker expert, let me tell you where the poker phrase "He has the nuts" originated. In the days of pioneers, covered wagons, and the Wild West, poker was a popular game. Many pioneer players didn't have cash, as everything they owned was tied up in their wagon and team of horses. Some players would risk everything—not all that surprising, since the cross-country trip itself was usually a life-and-death risk. The pioneers who settled the West were true gamblers. A wagon train would often stop for the evening on the edge of a town, the men gathering in the town saloon, the women staying back to tend to the children. The men might get into a poker game with the locals, and during such a game, if the traveling man had what he thought was a winning hand, he would go to his wagon and remove the metal nuts, then bring them to the saloon and put them on the poker table—showing everyone that he was betting his wagon, horses—all his belongings—on that one hand. Many of these pioneers never left town, after losing everything they owned in a poker game. The moral of the story: Be very careful when you think you have "the nuts." And if you want respect at the poker table, tell this story the next time you're in a game; your opponents will peg you as a student of poker history. That might win you a few hands down the line from players who think you're a lot smarter than you are!

The Best Poker Story Ever!

This story is courtesy of my friend Barney Vinson, a gambling author who served as expert consultant on *King of Vegas*. This really happened, to a poker dealer in Gardenia, California. Nine people were playing $30–$60 hold 'em, with one player so drunk he could barely sit upright. The dealer dealt two cards facedown to each player. The first player raised, the second player raised, then the drunk raised. Three players folded, the others called. Here comes the flop: three garbage cards, but two of them are hearts. The first player raised, the second player raised, the drunk raised. Three players folded. The first two remaining called. The dealer flopped another heart. The first player raised, the second player raised, the drunk raised. The first two called. The dealer flopped the last card, a five of clubs. The first player checked, the second player checked, the drunk bet the maximum. The first two players folded. The drunk won the pot. There was $3,000 in the middle of the table, and the dealer shoved it all to the drunk. "Cards, please," the dealer asked the players, so he could shuffle and start a new game. "Cards?" the drunk slurred. "Hell, I don't have any cards." It seems the dealer, who was seated next to the drunk, accidentally picked up his cards when the first three players folded.

As bedlam broke out at the table, the manager hurried over. "Did everybody else fold?" he asked. When told that the other players had folded, he ruled that the pot indeed belonged to the drunk. So there you have it—the best poker story *ever!* The drunk won $3,000 at poker—*without any cards!* The moral of the story: If you're a good-enough bluffer, you don't even need cards to win the pot.

Walking the Dog

Every morning at around six, I walk the dog. At least one professional gambler in Vegas is up daily at the crack of dawn! But every night my friend Harvard "walks the dog," while playing in a Vegas poker tournament. My dog is a German shepherd. Harvard doesn't even have a dog, but he plays like a pit bull on certain hands. Let me explain. "Walking the dog" means you let others do the betting for you. You lay a trap, then pounce on your opponent with everything you have. There are some basic rules in laying down this trap:

1. Get into these hands cheaply. You cannot stand a preflop raise, and you do *not* want to put out a raise, either.
2. The hands you want to look for are low pairs—twos, threes, fours, fives. You can also play small suited connectors like 5-6 hearts or 7-8 clubs.
3. Look for a monster flop. When you get the right flop, *check!* Slow-play this hand. Continue to check and call. Let others do your betting. Do not tip off your hand by betting first or raising, until after the river card is dealt. And then check-raise.

Let me describe a hand Harvard had in the WSOP last year. He was in the big blind and looked down to see a pair of threes. There were four limpers. And Harvard just called. The flop produced a A-K-3. Harvard checked. The man in middle position checked, and the next player followed with another check. The button bet the amount of the pot. The button was holding A-K. Harvard called, and the other two players folded. The turn card showed an 8. Harvard checked the turn, and the button put in another large bet. Harvard simply called. A 6 fell on the river, and Harvard checked. The button put in another bet, and Harvard came over the top with a check-raise and took what was left of the button's chips. Had Harvard started betting after his set fell on the flop, he would not have made the maximum number of chips.

The same applies if you are lucky enough to flop a big hand like a full house or quads. Check the flop, check the turn, and even check the river if you think the other players at your table will do the betting for you.

Harvard

I promised that I'd explain where Hollis "Harvard" Barnhart got his nickname. He was raised in Las Vegas and attended UNLV on a golf scholarship—although he should have been awarded a poker scholarship. Never in his life has he even been *near* Harvard, but he did take Harvard Business School executive classes. But he understands that poker is not so much a game of skill as a game of psychology and intimidation. One day soon after returning from his Harvard Business School executive course, he sat down at a poker table in a major Vegas tournament wearing a souvenir from his business school experience, a Harvard baseball cap. *Hollis won the tournament*—his first big win. Throughout the competition, he noticed that other players had acted oddly toward him. They seemed intimidated, passive, weak, fearful. They folded at the first sign of a raise by this mysterious fellow from Harvard. Hollis realized the psychological effect that his choice of cap had created. His fellow players would not have looked twice at a player with a UNLV cap. But the name Harvard strikes fear into millions of average Americans. It psychs them out. It brings up feelings of inferiority—"How can I compete with a genius from Harvard?" It makes them second-guess their math skills—"Well, I've got an A-Q . . . but if that brainiac from Harvard is raising, he must know something I don't. I'll fold." Hollis has worn the hat ever since, and thus the nickname "Harvard." That name has struck fear in the hearts of many Vegas poker players.

The story of the drunk poker player proves that if you have the balls, you don't even need cards. Hollis's story proves that you don't need a Harvard degree to become a winner in life—you only need the hat! My friend is living proof that winning big, like profiting big at poker, is much less about luck, and much more about balls, aggressive play, bluffing, reading tells, and psychology.

Now you should truly understand what I call "The Zen of Poker." And it's time for me to say good-bye and go walk my dog. Yes, my *real* dog, Maverick!

"One day my whole family was playing cards, even my two-year-old granddaughter. I said, 'Well, that's really great. I didn't think she'd learn to play poker this fast.' My daughter said, 'She's not as smart as she looks. She's lost four hands in a row.'"

—POKER PLAYER JACK "TREETOP" STRAUS

GLOSSARY OF COMMON

GAMBLING TERMS

Action: A wager or bet.

All-in: To run out of chips when betting or calling, or to push all of your money or chips into the poker pot.

ATS: Acronym for "against the spread," as in "this team is a 75 percent winner against the spread."

Bad beat: When a heavily favored poker hand loses to a big underdog.

Bases: Gambler's slang for baseball. When a bettor bets baseball, he or she is said to be "betting the bases."

Bet: Any risking of money or other assets based on the outcome of a sporting event or casino game of chance. Also called a wager or gamble. Note: This author thinks of an investment on a Wall Street stock as a bet too!

Betting exchange: A form of gambling available on the Internet that allows individuals to bet with each other, on any event, at any odds the individuals agree upon.

Bettor: A person making a bet. Also called a gambler or wagerer; in England a bettor is called a "punter."

Blind (big and small): A predetermined bet required to get the action started in a game of poker. A small blind is half of the big blind.

Board: A list of bets available on an electronic display at a sportsbook, as in "How many games are on the board today?" Another word for "the board" would be a sports schedule. Schedule books are printed by many casinos, sportsbooks and offshore sportsbooks for their clients (the bettors).

Bookmaker: A person who accepts bets on sporting events, either legally or illegally. An illegal bookmaker is often called a "bookie." A legal bookmaker in Las Vegas is called a sportsbook. There are now also over 1,000 Internet sportsbooks, often called offshore sportsbooks.

Button: A disk that indicates which player is the dealer in a game of poker.

Call: Betting a sum equal to the amount of money put in the pot during the most recent poker bet or raise.

Calling station: A very passive poker player who seldom raises the pot or folds. He just calls every bet.

Chalk: Another word for the favorite, as in "The public is betting the chalk again."

Check: A bet of zero dollars in a game of poker.

Check raise: First you check, then a player behind you bets, then you raise him, in poker.

Contrarian: A bettor who is always against the public or the masses of amateur bettors. A Contrarian always takes a different path—it is usually the road less traveled (opposite of the crowds of losers who all think alike).

Cover: To beat the spread, as in "Dallas was a 5-point favorite and won the game by 10 points. Therefore they covered."

Cracked: When a large hand gets beat in poker ("I got my kings cracked").

Dime: Gambler's slang for a bet to win $1,000, as in "I bet a dime on the Dallas Cowboys. If they cover the spread, I win $1,000."

Dollar: Gambler's slang for a bet to win $100, as in "I bet a dollar on the Dallas Cowboys. If they cover the spread, I win $100." Also called a buck.

Early/middle/late position: In a table game of nine poker players, the first three players are in "early" position, the next three are in "middle" position, and the last three up to the button are in "late" position.

Edge: Gambler's slang for having an advantage. Every gambler is looking for the edge over the bookmaker. An edge would be a high-percentage bet (it has a high percentage of winning).

Exotic bet: Long-shot bets such as parlays, teasers, reverses, and prop bets. These bets offer big payouts but little chance of winning.

Favorite: The team that is considered most likely to win by the professional oddsmakers or sportsbooks. A team can be an favorite either based on a point spread (this team is favored to win by 5 points) or the moneyline (this team is a 3 to 1 favorite).

Flop: The top three community cards, which the poker dealer distributes face up.

Formula: A system for selecting winners using factors most likely to affect the outcome of a game. Also sometimes called a trend, angle, or system for winning handicapping.

Free card: In poker, when you get to see "the turn" or "river card" without calling or making a bet.

Futures bets: Bets made with sportsbooks that are decided by an outcome that is far into the future—i.e., betting in August on the Dallas Cowboys to win the Super Bowl in January, six months later. Or betting, before the season begins, that the Oakland Raiders will win more or less than nine games this football season.

Handicapper: A professional analyst who predicts the outcome of sporting events based on numerous factors including history, trends, the pointspread, injuries, weather, or even the popularity of the teams. Also called a tout, prognosticator, or sports-gambling expert.

Handle: The total amount wagered on a sporting event or in a casino game.

Heads-up: A contested pot of just two poker players.

Hook: Gambler's slang for a half point—as in "I'm betting Dallas minus 5 and a hook." This means –5½ points. At most sportsbooks you can "buy the hook," meaning you would pay higher odds to buy an extra half point off the point spread.

Hoops: Gambler's slang for basketball. When a bettor bets basketball, he or she is said to be "betting hoops." An alternate phrase is "betting the baskets."

House: Gambler's slang for the casino, sportsbook, or bookmaker, whoever is taking the bets. The "house edge" is the advantage the house has over all bettors.

If-come: In poker, betting or calling in the hopes that you'll draw to a straight or flush, when you need one more perfect card to make your hand.

Limit: The money cutoff point for betting on a game, as in "This bettor's limit is $1,000 per game."

Long shot: Bets with a slim chance of winning but therefore offering a large payout.

Middle: Gambler's slang for having multiple bets on the same game, where it is possible to win both bets if the outcome falls right in the middle of your bets, as in "I bet Dallas minus 5 points, but found a middle with the Redskins plus 3 points. If the game lands on exactly 4 points, I'd win both my bets." That's a middle.

MLB: Major League Baseball.

Moneyline: A straight money bet on the outcome of the game with no point spread involved. Instead of points, oddsmakers set only odds (i.e., 2 to 1, 3 to 1, 7 to 1, etc.).

Muck: The pile of folded cards that sits in front of the poker dealer.

NBA: National Basketball Association.

NCAA: National Collegiate Athletic Association—college football or college basketball.

NFL: National Football League.

Nickel: Gambler's slang for a bet to win $500, as in "I bet a nickel on the Dallas Cowboys. If they cover the spread, I win $500."

The nuts: In poker, the best hand of the community cards on the board.

Odds: The probability that a bet is more or less likely to win or lose. Odds are set by professional oddsmakers who work for casinos.

Off-suit: In poker, two starting cards of different suits.

Offshore sportsbooks: A sportsbook located off the shores of the United States or online (or both). American sports bettors, poker players, or casino gamblers can make a bet by dialing the toll-free numbers of these sportsbooks, or by surfing online to their web sites. Bettors then wire money and open up accounts. The biggest and most respected offshore sportsbooks are SBGGlobal.com and BetOnSports.com. They each accept billions of dollars per year in handle.

Opening line: The very first line (or point spread) posted on any sporting event by sportsbooks or oddsmakers.

Pari-mutuel: A betting system in which the odds are set by the bettors. The bookmaker (or "the track" in horse racing) takes a fixed percentage off the top and distributes the remainder to winning ticket holders.

Parlay: A bet involving two or more events, as in "I'm making a two-team parlay bet." The payoff is larger than making two separate bets, but the catch is that every team in the parlay must win or the bettor loses the entire bet.

Percentage: A method of calculating a team's performance in terms of the number of times it has won, or calculating a handicapper's winning percentage. A team or handicapper who wins five out of ten games has a 50 percent winning percentage. A team or handicapper who wins six out of ten has a 60 percent winning percentage.

Pick: A bet or selection recommended by a professional sports handicapper.

Pick 'em: A bet where there are zero points given on either team in a bet, as in "Dallas is a pick 'em over the New York Giants." In this case, it is an even game with no points involved.

Pocket: The two starting cards dealt to each player in a game of poker.

Pocket rocket: In poker, two starting cards that are both aces.

Point spread: The range of points given by a favorite, or taken by an underdog, in any given sports event. This point spread is set by a sportsbook or professional odds-maker. With a point spread in place, bets are now placed by gamblers at 11 to 10 odds on any side—i.e., no matter which side a gambler chooses to wager on, he or she must risk $110 for every $100 bet. The point spread is also called the line or the spread.

Prop bet: An exotic menu of bets offered by oddsmakers on high-profile games like the Super Bowl—for example the sportsbook might offer a prop bet on which team will score first, which team will fumble first, or which quarterback will throw an interception first.

Public bet: A bet on which the masses of asses, or the majority of amateur sports bettors, are all in agreement. Another name for the public is "a square," as in "All the squares are on the favorite again."

Push: A tie. If a game finishes exactly on the point spread (i.e., Dallas –5 wins by exactly 5), the wager is a tie and all monies are refunded. There are no winners or losers in a push.

Quads: Any four of a kind in a poker hand.

River: The final community card, which the poker dealer distributes face up.

Road dog: A team playing on the road (away from their home stadium), considered the underdog in a game, as determined by the sportsbook or oddsmaker.

Road favorite: A team playing on the road (away from their home stadium), considered the favorite in a game, as determined by the sportsbook or oddsmaker.

Sharp: The opposite of a "square." While a square is an amateur bettor, a sharp is a sophisticated professional gambler. Another word for sharp is "smart money" or "wise guy."

Sportsbook: The place where sports gamblers make their wagers. Most Nevada casinos have a sportsbook. There are also offshore sportsbooks based in Costa Rica and Caribbean islands that take bets from American gamblers. They have taken a tremendous amount of business away from Nevada sportsbooks and illegal bookmakers across the USA. Why? Because any sports bettor sitting in his bedroom or living room or office can pick up a phone or click online to make a bet—with little or no regulation or hassle. It's convenient and easy. Popular offshore sportsbooks such as SBG Global.com or BetonSports.com take in several billion dollars per year in wagers! There are also offshore casino and poker web sites like GoldenPalace.com that take in billions of dollars in wagers per year from American citizens.

Straight bet: A wager that picks an outright winner of a sporting event and is not affected by the point spread. Winning "straight-up" means the team won the game outright, with no point spread involved. Another name for a straight bet is a moneyline bet. There are no point spreads in a moneyline bet, only odds determining the payout.

Sucker bet: A bet that looks easy or has a big payoff but in reality has almost no chance of winning. The bettor is at a huge disadvantage. Amateurs make "sucker bets."

Suited connector: In a game of poker, two starting cards that are of the same suit and numerically connected, such as the 8 and 9 of hearts.

Take down the pot: In poker, betting enough money to get everyone else to fold.

Teaser: A special bet where the oddsmaker "teases" you with extra points. These bets often look too desirable to pass up, e.g., Dallas is a 6-point favorite over Washington. But in a 6-point teaser Dallas becomes an even money bet. By adding 6 extra points to your side, Dallas suddenly is pick 'em or even. If they win by even 1 point in this case, you win your teaser bet. You can "tease" the other side too, e.g., Washington gets +12 instead of +6 points. In this way, you have doubled your points. But teasers don't involve only one game. You must bet two or more to get those extra points. Therein lies the catch. Both teams just rarely seem to win as easily as the bettor expects with those extra points. The reality is, if it looks too good to be true, it usually is! Buyer (or in this case, bettor) beware.

Tell: A clue or hint (usually physical) that an opponent inadvertently gives about his poker hand.

Tilt/full tilt: A poker player who gets upset over a loss (often after a bad beat) and plays poorly and recklessly.

Totals: A different (but common) kind of bet that involves picking not the winner of the sporting event but instead the total number of points scored. Bettors can pick either "over" or "under" a total set by professional oddsmakers. Betting on the over or under is called "betting totals."

Trends: In sports, a pattern of winning or losing by teams or groups of teams over the course of a season or historically.

Trips: Any three of a kind in a poker hand.

Underdog: The team that is considered least likely to win by the professional oddsmakers or sportsbooks. A team can be an underdog either based on a point spread ("This dog is getting 5 points") or the moneyline ("This team is a 3 to 1 underdog").

Under the gun: The player to the left of the big blind, who must act first in a poker hand.

Vigorish: A charge or commission on each losing bet extracted by the bookmaker. Also called "the vig."

Wager: A bet on the chances of something, someone, or some team winning or losing. The payoff is money or some negotiable asset. Also called a gamble or bet. The person who makes the bet is called a bettor, gambler, or wagerer.

Weak-ace: When one of your starting cards in poker is an ace, but the other starting card is very small. An A-6, for example, would be described as a "weak-ace."

Wise guys: Term for smart professional gamblers. Also called "smart money."

CONCLUSION

THE JOY OF RISK

Be One of the World's
Greatest Gamblers

"Far better to dare mighty things, to win glorious triumphs, even
though checkered by failure, than to take rank with those poor
spirits who neither enjoy much nor suffer much, because they
live in the gray twilight that knows not victory nor defeat."

THEODORE ROOSEVELT

In conclusion, I'd like to take a look at great risk-takers in business, battle, politics, sports, and entertainment. With proven examples of Contrarian risk-taking in all walks of life, I will show you one last time how
others have fared beyond their dreams, just by embracing the philosophies taught in this book. These superstars are the real Riverboat Gamblers! Will you be the next person I write about? Readers, start your
engines! Start dreaming, risking, and achieving!

GEORGE WASHINGTON, GENERAL OF THE CONTINENTAL ARMY, 1776

Suppose you were in charge of the Continental Army in December 1776. You started out as an army of 20,000 in New York, fought a battle with the British, suffered a humiliating defeat, and had to retreat. Every battle fought since then has been lost in full retreat. Your army has been decimated—literally and psychologically.

You finally find yourself on the New Jersey side of the natural border between Pennsylvania and New Jersey—the Delaware River. Your army must cross the river to avoid the advancing British, some 20,000 strong. But you have no boats. To cross the river, you commandeer boats from an unwilling boat owner—another critic who shouts, "You've got no chance! Give up now! I'll see you all hang!" Ahhh, the critics. The masses. They're everywhere—especially when you *least* need them!

Ten miles away across the river in the New Jersey town of Trenton is a garrison of 1,200 Hessians. These are the most feared mercenary soldiers fighting in the war—and they're on the British side! The Brits have already instilled fear in the minds of the Continental Army by mercilessly defeating the Continentals at Brooklyn, then moving the betting line by signing the big-time warriors, the Hessians.

You are down to 10 percent of the force of 20,000 you started with—less than 2,000 soldiers. You have no money to buy supplies, shelter, or clothing. Your funds from Congress to pay your soldiers run out December 31. Nobody believes in you—the critics, the experts, and the masses are all calling for your head. Even the Continental Congress has assumed you can no longer defend their capital, Philadelphia. They leave Philadelphia and head for Baltimore. What do you do?

Just what *did* General George Washington do in December 1776? Did he follow the masses and quit? Did he yield to his critics—his own generals who felt the cause was lost? Did he listen to the "expert," General Horatio Gates, who said this army was no army, that the soldiers were not soldiers, and that Washington himself was *not* a General? Sounds familiar to me—a bit like people telling me I couldn't make it as a broadcast journalist, or as a professional handicapper, or as an entrepreneur and CEO of a public company.

Well, we all know how the American Revolution turned out, because George Washington was one of the great leaders and risk-takers of history. Hell no, Washington never listened to the critics or naysayers—he was a Contrarian! He rolled up his sleeves and gambled that one last time! He gambled that tenth time, when anyone else would have quit after losing nine times. He gambled that tenth time because he knew he was an underdog, because he knew the British were overconfident. He gambled one more time because quitting wasn't an option.

He just didn't gamble stupid. Although he was risking everything—they either were going to win or die trying—he wasn't going to do it blindly. First, he put an audacious plan together: *attack the Hessians!* Then he got rid of his worst critic: the "expert," General Gates. The plan couldn't survive with anyone trying to make it fail.

He put the odds in his favor. He figured that the Hessians' strength—their disciplined approach to battle—was actually going to be their weakness. He would attack them before they could assemble into their orderly formations. Also, he rightfully reasoned that on Christmas Eve, they would be celebrating and drinking—so much so that the following day they would be too hungover to awaken and form any order anyway. Washington was setting up the perfect underdog situation. I'll bet you didn't realize that America was founded by a professional handicapper—that George Washington was the very first King of Underdogs!

Washington also knew his men. Although the army had been battered and beaten and their numbers had dwindled, he knew that what army he had left were the ones who would fight—the faithful ones who hadn't given up yet. He knew his underdog team was hungry and ready for a win.

On Christmas Eve 1776, the remains of the Continental Army crossed the Delaware River. The plan was that they would be across the river, assembled, and attacking the Hessians by daylight. But the crossing took longer than estimated, and the attack didn't form up and take place at Trenton until 8:00 a.m.—a full two hours late. What was the result?

The entire Hessian garrison of 1,200 were defeated and surrendered without a single Continental Army casualty! Furthermore, they captured much-needed supplies—twelve cannons, four wagons of munitions, and seven tons of food and clothing.

Did Washington sit back and gloat on his one victory and call it a day? *No!* He ordered his tired, victorious army back across the river to avoid the British mounting any kind of counterattack on Trenton. He wasn't about to sit back and consider his one victory a victory for the entire war. That one daring risk changed the momentum of the American Revolution—and made believers out of the critics. Washington was never maligned again. The British never recovered. We owe our great country to one of the greatest gambles in history.

OPRAH WINFREY

One of the most famous women in the world built her career on a foundation of failure and rejection. After losing her first job as a television anchorwoman (her boss called her "too emotional"), Oprah Winfrey switched gears and became an actress and talk-show host. Her first syndicated show, *People Are Talking*, made it to only thirteen cities before it was pulled off the air. But she learned from her failures and risked again. Her next talk-show effort was anything but a failure. By 1996, *The Oprah Winfrey Show* had grossed almost $200 million! Oprah herself earned over $70 million for the second year in a row! Just the threat of her retirement in 1997 sent syndication giant King World's stock tumbling!

Oprah is a role model. She is one of the most popular women in the world, and she is a billionaire, too. She changes people's lives and inspires viewers with her positive attitude toward life. But the only reason she is able to empower millions of others is because she stayed confident and committed in the face of failure and rejection. She didn't give up—rather, she was willing to keep risking. When you believe in yourself, it's easy to see things others don't. It's easy to have confidence when others are running scared. It's easy to be a risk-taker. The payoff is golden.

PRESIDENT BILL CLINTON

I must confess that I'm a Republican. I was no fan of the politics of Bill Clinton. But I am a fan of what the boy from Hope, Arkansas, achieved against all odds. Bill Clinton, perhaps more than any politician ever, is a Riverboat Gambler. He grew up in poverty, with no father and a single mother who spent much of her time enjoying alcohol and gambling at racetracks and casinos.

Yet tough beginnings did not stop Bill Clinton from thinking big and risking big. From the day a young Bill Clinton met President John F. Kennedy, he planned on becoming president of the United States. Then he took the risks necessary to pull it off! This bold risk-taker thought nothing of coming back from a failed run for Congress to run for governor of Arkansas (he won). Or from coming back from a reelection loss as governor of Arkansas to run again (he won). Or to rebound from damaging allegations of infidelity, pot smoking, draft dodging, and business fraud (Whitewater) on the presidential campaign trail in 1992. No candidate in presidential history had ever survived serious allegations like this.

It was a foregone conclusion that Clinton would drop out of the race.

Not one political expert could even imagine Clinton had any other option. What kind of a reckless risk-taker would ignore all those charges and roll the dice? Only a gambler like Bill Clinton. He suffered a tough defeat in New Hampshire, but Clinton didn't call it a defeat. He called his second-place finish "a huge victory" and called himself the Comeback Kid. Now that defines chutzpah! Clinton was off and running. Americans love a gambler. When the smoke cleared, Bill Clinton was president of the United States. Only a true Riverboat Gambler from Little Rock could have survived.

But Clinton's biggest defeat didn't come on the campaign trail. That defeat was at the 1988 Democratic National Convention. As an obscure young governor from a tiny state, Clinton gave the nominating speech for presidential candidate Michael Dukakis. This was Bill Clinton's big chance to make a name for himself on a national stage. It would instead serve as his most humiliating failure. Clinton's speech was so boring and long-winded that he was literally booed and cat-called off the podium. Clinton had to stop speaking twice to ask the audience for respect. The only applause came when he said, "In conclusion . . ." Political commentators wrote Bill Clinton's political obituary that night. Johnny Carson called him a "windbag" and "a cure for insomnia." *The Washington Post* headline referred to his performance as "The Numb and the Restless." And NBC political commentator John Chancellor said, "It's a sad night, because a young man lost his political career tonight."

Who in their right mind would put himself back on the national stage only a few short years later? Who would be willing to show his face at that same Democratic convention, in front of the same delegates that booed him off the stage? Who would have the chutzpah to say to them, "I deserve your nomination for president" after that performance? Only a daring risk-taker. Only a true gambler.

Bill Clinton became president of the United States only four years after that humiliating personal disaster. Bill Clinton understands the importance of risk. Fail a thousand times—no matter. But keep going, keep risking, and succeed only once—you've changed your life, and perhaps even the world!

FREDERICK SMITH OF FEDERAL EXPRESS

Ever think about launching a nationwide delivery system that required airplanes, trucks, landing rights in twenty-one cities, a massive hub, and delivery systems in all twenty-one cities? Maybe a comment Fred Smith made sums it up: "I wasn't afraid. I had been to Vietnam."

The first part of Federal Express was launched as a term-paper concept while Smith was an undergraduate at Yale in 1966. His paper talked about the computer industry coming of age, which he felt would create a new priority for companies that relied on computers. Once their computers went down, the company was in the dark—they were essentially out of business. So, Smith reasoned, some sort of delivery system for the computer parts would be needed. A delivery system that was nationwide and could deliver quickly. He got a C on the paper.

Fred Smith graduated from Yale and went on to serve in Vietnam in the Marines. He was a platoon leader, then a pilot. He returned to the United States in 1971 and saw that his idea about computers had borne fruit: Computers were everywhere. So were their service calls and the need to have parts shipped quickly anywhere in the country. At twenty-seven years old, Frederick Smith was about to take a risk—starting a business. A very big business.

At one point, he faced bankruptcy with that fledgling business. But Fred Smith is a gambler. He took the last $25,000 he had to Las Vegas and gambled everything. He won $100,000—the exact amount he needed to save his company. Now that's a real gambler!

Thirty-three years later, this high-risk, high-profile C-grade concept paper had grown to over $20 billion, over 200,000 employees, delivering to over 200 countries. You may know it as FedEx. Not too bad! To what does he attribute his success, besides not being afraid of risk? "Companies [experts] that don't recognize that their business is going to be commoditized [become masses] if they don't take risks [have some chutzpah]—some of which are going to work [when you're on a roll] and some of which aren't [you don't always win]—are going to get punched up by the marketplace [lose to people like me]."

STEVE JOBS OF APPLE

Ever heard of the "Lisa"? Of course everyone has heard of Apple's Macintosh computers, but few know that Apple's first computer was a complete failure. The Lisa almost bankrupted Steve Jobs's company, but that didn't stop Jobs from risking again with the Mac.

From the ashes of that terrible defeat rose the Apple II—one of the world's first great personal computers. A few years later, things turned sour again. Apple was in financial trouble. Steve Jobs was forced out of the company he had founded. Ridiculed by the press and called a has-been, he started all over again (Riverboat Gamblers *always* do). The next decade was full of constant anguish and disappointment for Jobs. His new creation, the NeXT Corporation, lost over $100 million, laid off half its workforce, and came close to extinction when its new personal computers were a bust.

Another of Jobs's investments, Pixar, also piled up huge losses, but after the release of a little film called *Toy Story* in December 1996, Jobs achieved sweet revenge. Pixar went public and within hours Jobs's stock was worth nearly $1.5 billion. Few entrepreneurs have ever hit it big *twice* in a lifetime.

Next, Jobs confounded the experts by taking the helm of Apple all over again. On the verge of extinction, suffering from massive losses and bad press, the odds against Jobs and Apple looked insurmountable. But Jobs is a Contrarian. He turned Apple around and made their computers hip all over again. Once again, he proved the critics wrong and risked his way to the top for the third time: Steve Jobs wins "the triple crown" of success!

GREG NORMAN

Few of the failures cited above compare to golfer Greg Norman's failures. Norman has failed in front of worldwide audiences with regularity. He lost an unheard of seven majors on the last hole (including four majors in a playoff). He finished second at more golf tournaments than any player of his era. The man known as the "Great White Shark" made a habit of fading down the late stretch at golf tournaments. His failure at the 1996 Masters to hold a six-stroke lead on the final day was the most crushing and humiliating collapse in the history of golf.

Yet Norman never once ran away and hid from the press or the world. He reveled in his successes. Failures, no matter how spectacular or devastating, never stopped him from putting it all on the line again. He came back after each collapse to risk again. This bravado earned Norman the respect and adulation of fans across the globe—and made him wealthy beyond imagination.

This "perennial bridesmaid" is now estimated to be worth several hundred million dollars. His collection of spectacular mansions all over the world, exotic autos (including seven Ferraris), private jets, helicopters, and incredible yachts is legendary. So is the $70 million dollar deal he signed with Cobra Golf. And the $15 million dollars a year he makes in other endorsements! How does a golfer known for losing and "choking" gain all that wealth and fame? By risking and winning, that's how!

Yes, Norman lost a lot. But that's because he never settled for the easy shots. He went for broke. And with the spectacular losses also came spectacular wins, including two British Opens and seventy-four tournaments worldwide (making him one of the winningest golfers of all time).

During the 1980s and 90s Norman spent an incredible 331 weeks as the number one golfer in the world! I guess it's "lucky" he was willing to go back out there after each defeat and risk his reputation and sanity again. In the end, daring risk-takers are rewarded for their courage. It is their great successes that are remembered and rewarded above all else. That one *yes*. Greg Norman proves that the key to success is being a daring gambler.

CHARLES SCHWAB

Few of my successful failures endured more adversity than Charles Schwab—yes, that Schwab—the billionaire Wall Street discount broker! Growing up, it was Schwab's intelligence that was discounted. He could barely read or write. In college, friends had to take notes for him because he couldn't listen to a lecture and then write down what he had heard. Schwab flunked French once and basic English twice! His difficulties continued in the business world when his mutual fund collapsed in 1969, leaving him over a hundred thousand dollars in debt.

By 1975, however, he had come up with the idea of discounting brokerage fees for stock transactions. By 1983, his company, Charles Schwab Co., was traded publicly on the stock exchange and was valued at $425 million. Today, Charles Schwab's holdings are worth over $1 billion! It wasn't until a few years ago that Schwab found out the source of all his early problems—he had dyslexia!

WALT DISNEY

Few daring dreamers and business risk-takers can hold a candle to Walt Disney. Disney was fired from his first job as an illustrator at an advertising agency and told that he could not draw! So what does a risk-taker do when he gets fired? He starts his own business, of course!

Disney's first film failed, along with his first animation company, because his distributor ran out of money. A second film flopped because Disney himself ran out of money during production. His first big cartoon character, Oswald the Rabbit, was stolen away from him by his own distributor. Other Disney creations—Mickey Mouse, Bambi, Fantasia, and Pinocchio—were rejected hundreds of times. MGM told Disney that Mickey Mouse would terrify women and children.

Snow White was his first big movie, but it was so expensive that Hollywood "insiders" called it "Disney's folly." *Pinocchio* was another miserable failure in it's first release—losing over $1 million in 1940.

All this failure, rejection, and humiliation caused Walt Disney to collapse under the strain of a nervous breakdown. After thirty years in show business, Disney was broke and heavily in debt. Yet Walt Disney never once gave up. He kept risking on new ideas, new cartoon characters, new films. He kept rereleasing his movies (most of which bombed the first time around) until he eventually succeeded. These movies became hits the second or third time around—the second or third roll of the dice. Walt Disney was a Riverboat Gambler.

The company Disney founded is today the second biggest media conglomerate in the world, with over $27 billion in revenues and 112,000 employees. Disney owns ABC and ESPN. And Walt's ultimate dreams (which were laughed at by critics), Disneyland and Walt Disney World, are the most successful theme parks ever. Thank God for big dreamers and daring risk-takers!

DR. NORMAN VINCENT PEALE, BILLY GRAHAM, AND THE REVEREND ROBERT H. SCHULLER

Even religion demands great risk-takers. Did you know that Dr. Norman Vincent Peale had his manuscript for *The Power of Positive Thinking* rejected by every publisher in New York? The king of positive thinking himself threw the manuscript in the garbage. His wife fished it out and resubmitted it to publishers without Norman's knowledge. Today, that book is the second best-selling nonfiction book of all time (behind only the Bible). It was almost lost to a garbage can! Lucky Dr. Peale's wife was a gambler.

Then there's the legendary Billy Graham. Other preachers of the Gospel went to "normal" and "comfortable" places, with receptive and enthusiastic audiences. Not Billy Graham. He was a bold risk-taker, some would say a Riverboat Gambler. Rev. Graham preached in places like Communist Russia, China, and to religious leaders in the most difficult place on earth—New York City.

Critics laughed when Graham decided to preach in New York in 1957. Yet despite vicious critiques and attacks by his fellow ministers, who thought he'd gone mad, Graham preached to packed houses at New York's Madison Square Garden. Over sixteen weeks in New York (supposedly the worst place in America to preach evangelism) over 2 million New Yorkers attended Graham's sermons. More importantly, that bold risk put Graham "on the map." Almost 100 million TV viewers watched at least one of Graham's sermons in New York!

In 1991 Graham announced he'd preach in New York's Central Park. Again critics scoffed. Yet over a quarter of a million people showed up—the largest crowd to ever hear Billy Graham preach in North America. Gambles paid off big-time for Rev. Graham!

He was also a huge gambler when it came to television. No preacher had ever appeared on popular mainstream talk and entertainment shows before Billy Graham decided to take the gamble. Graham was savagely criticized. He was accused by critics of setting his religion back 100 years. One leading minister called Rev. Graham's work "not of God." Yet by appearing on *The Steve Allen Show, The Jack Paar Show, The Tonight Show with Johnny Carson, Good Morning America,* NBC's *Today,* even *Laugh-In,* Rev. Graham broke new ground and touched the lives of millions by introducing his brand of religion to many that would never enter a church. A brilliant marketer. A daring risk-taker. And through those risks, Billy Graham became the most influential man of God of our times—a confidant to nine United States presidents.

Finally, I come to the Reverend Robert H. Schuller. His career started steeped in controversy and risk. Schuller became the first Christian minister to preach in a drive-in movie theatre! "Only in kooky California," the critics scoffed. "Heresy" and "undignified" the traditionalists screamed.

But the bold risk paid off big-time! By the 1980s Schuller had become the most popular preacher in America. He was able to build the world-famous, all-glass, architectural wonder, the Crystal Cathedral, in Garden Grove, California. Today over one million Christians a year visit the Crystal Cathedral. And more people watch Rev. Schuller on television than any religious leader ever on his syndicated *Hour of Power,* which airs on more than 200 stations worldwide and attracts 30 million weekly viewers.

Rev. Schuller is the author of more than thirty books, including six *New York Times* best-sellers. And it all started with the biggest (and craziest) risk in the history of Christianity: preaching God in a drive-in movie theatre in Southern California. Yes, even men of God like Norman Vincent Peale, Billy Graham, and Robert H. Schuller are Riverboat Gamblers. I'll bet you never imagined you'd buy a book on gambling and find stories on three of the greatest Christian preachers of all time. I told you I was a Contrarian!

PRESIDENT RONALD REAGAN

Now we're down to the final three—my personal all-time favorite risk-takers. Let's start with the late Ronald Reagan, former president of the United States.

Peter Robinson had an incredible job at the youthful age of thirty—White House speechwriter! He wrote speeches that the most powerful person in the world would present to the people: United States President Ronald Reagan. The speeches he wrote were always subject to scrutiny, not just by the president but by all the cabinet members and presidential advisers.

Speechwriters are so critical to conveying the message of the president to the masses, the experts, and the critics. And they are no less subject to constant second-guessing and armchair quarterbacking than you are when you risk doing something unconventional. Yet without these great speeches, without the risk of saying something unique (or contrarian), we have no memories, no impression, and no convictions about what the presidency means—not only historically but for our future.

Some speeches are more challenging than others because of their subject material, or their audience. One such speech faced Peter Robinson. His president had to deliver a speech in Berlin. There was a lot of turmoil surrounding Ronald Reagan. He was not popular in Europe, accused of inciting possible nuclear war by confronting the "Evil Empire."

Doing some homework preparation for the speech, Peter was told by the local "experts" not to inject anything regarding the Berlin Wall into the speech. He had been told that the people of West Berlin had heard it many times before and it was old and worn out. But Peter wasn't sure about this, so he decided to talk to some Berliners himself.

What he found out amazed him and was the opposite (Contrarian!) of what the "experts" had told him: Berliners were *not* used to the wall being there, and were *quite tired of the wall itself*, not the rhetoric about the wall. Peter Robinson decided to take a risk. He wrote a phrase into the speech for his president that addressed the Berlin Wall directly.

For three weeks the speech was reviewed and debated by White House aides, the cabinet, and the president's inner circle. Whereas the president had circled the phrase regarding the Wall because he *liked* it, everyone else circled it in red because *they wanted it removed*. The pressure was hot and heavy to remove the line from the speech. The so-called "experts" called it too confrontational. Too provocative. Too risky.

After all the negativity, the challenges by the experts, and the certainty of inciting the masses and critics, the president stuck with what Peter Robinson believed in—that the risk to do the right thing instead of the popular thing was worth it. To this day, the most famous words ever spoken by President Ronald Reagan are "Mr. Gorbachev, tear down this wall!"

The critics and naysayers didn't want that line in Reagan's speech. After President Reagan recited the line, those same critics and naysayers called that line a "naïve joke" and a "utopian dream." But to the world's amazement, only two years later, that wall was torn down! The Soviet Union itself soon came tumbling down—just as President Reagan had predicted. One man had single-handedly toppled Communism! Today over one billion people are free that were not free before Ronald Reagan became president. One Contrarian risk-taker changed the lives and the freedom of over one billion people.

Ronald Reagan took a calculated risk—and it changed the world. Almost single-handedly, Ronald Reagan had gambled to end the Cold War and the threat of nuclear annihilation. I'll never forget the critics and naysayers at the beginning of his presidency calling Reagan a "cowboy." They may not have realized it, but they were paying him a compliment.

Cowboys are Contrarians. They are gamblers. Reagan gambled again and again during his presidency. When he entered office, America was at its lowest point in history. Our economy was a shambles. Inflation, un-employment, and interest rates were all soaring. Our prestige in the world was crumbling. Our military strength was mocked. Our citizens were being held hostage in Iran. America's morale was at an all-time low.

Many "experts" said that the United States was no longer a world power. These same experts said our best days were behind us and that the president was no longer capable of making a difference. Some called for a reduced role for the presidency. President Jimmy Carter told Americans we should get used to living with less. He wanted us to *settle*. His way of confronting the Soviet Union was to punish our athletes and boycott the 1980 Olympics held in Moscow. Not too risky at all. Sound familiar?

Then a risk-taking cowboy took office. He told Americans that our best days were still ahead of us. He boldly called the Soviets the "Evil Empire," and vowed to win the arms race. He promised to restore American military supremacy. He vowed to cut welfare rolls and the size of government dramatically. He promised to cut taxes and red tape dramatically to unleash the American economy from the shackles of government, to end the social welfare state.

Against all odds and the frantic screams of critics who predicted starving mothers and children in the streets, vast increases in homelessness, and disaster for America, Ronald Reagan took every one of those risks. He boldly rolled the dice with the biggest tax cuts in history, right in the middle of a devastating recession.

And America magically responded with the greatest economic expansion the world had ever seen. More jobs, more entrepreneurs, more new businesses, more revenues were created than at any time in history. The stock market rose to unimagined heights. Inflation, unemployment, and interest rates all sank to new lows. This economic expansion unleashed by Reagan (which by the way primarily benefited entrepreneurs—risk-takers) led to twenty-five years of unprecedented growth that is still working today. And it led to the bankruptcy of the Soviet Union.

I'm putting the finishing touches on this book during the week of Ronald Reagan's funeral—a week in which America witnessed the most amazing outpouring of love, respect, and sorrow for a leader ever, not just in the United States but in capitals all over the world. More world leaders and dignitaries showed up for former President Reagan's funeral than for any funeral in world history. Hundreds of thousands of Americans lined the streets for one last chance to wave good-bye to President Reagan. They waited in line for hours to see his flag-draped casket in both California and Washington, D.C.

The news media presented virtually twenty-four-hour coverage for a week. New polls showed Americans believed that Ronald Reagan was one of the finest United States presidents ever, and one of the two best of the twentieth century (along with FDR). Again and again news commentators said, that what made Reagan so beloved is that he was the most *unconventional* president ever. He broke all the rules. He didn't care what the experts thought. He believed nothing was impossible. President Reagan's obituary in *USA Today* was headlined with the words "An Unconventional Politician." Ronald Reagan was a true Contrarian, a risk-taker extraordinaire, and a rule-breaker—the very definition of an American cowboy.

ABRAHAM LINCOLN

But even Ronald Reagan's willingness to gamble pales in comparison to another great American president. He was born dirt poor. Not only did his family live in a log cabin—they lost the log cabin! His first attempt at business failed. He decided to try his hand at politics. His first run for local office was failure. But he was a risk-taker. So he ran again—and lost again. He ran yet again—and lost again.

He gave up on local office. This time he ran for Congress and lost. Then he ran for the Senate—and lost. He ran for Senate a second time—and lost again. He now chose to run for vice president of the United States—no surprise, he lost once again! After all that risking and failing, there was no political office left for him to run for but president. So he risked onward and upward. This time he won.

That's how Abraham Lincoln became president of the United States! Fortunately for the United States he did, for he was the right person, at the right place, at the right time in history. A man of conviction, Lincoln thought it was morally wrong to hold people in slavery. He also saw the big picture—that the states belonged to a union and as a whole would be much better and stronger united. Lincoln saw that the states' rights issue pushed by the Southern states would only cause chaos and create a medieval dark ages in North America.

Not willing to shy away from the difficult task at hand, he engaged in the bloodiest conflict in American history to preserve the Union and free the slaves. He was Contrarian not just because of the fact that he believed that slavery was wrong; he was Contrarian because he actually was *willing to do something* about it, even if that something was unpopular—fighting a war that killed over 600,000 young men.

Further exacerbating the situation was the fact that the Civil War went very badly for the North in the beginning. Battle after battle had been lost by the North, and one Northern army commander after another had been dismissed. What were they doing wrong? They were timid. The generals leading the Northern armies were unwilling to take risks. They were facing one of the great military risk-takers of all time, Confederate General Robert E. Lee.

Lee commanded a much smaller force, poorly equipped, lacking the necessary food, gear, guns, artillery, ammo—in many cases, even lacking shoes. Yet because Lee was a Contrarian thinker and a daring risk-taker, the Confederates won battle after battle against the North's generals unwilling to play such a high-stakes poker game.

Finally, Lincoln appointed a very unpopular general, one who was labeled as "a worthless drunk." But this Contrarian general, Ulysses S. Grant, was willing to risk big—just like Lee. Those risks turned the tide of the Civil War toward the North. Lincoln said of Grant, "Finally I have someone who isn't afraid to fight!" Grant went on to break the back of Lee and his army, and to end the war. Thank God for the United States of America that Lincoln knew a fellow Contrarian when he saw one. Thank God Lincoln was one of the great Riverboat Gamblers in history!

WINSTON CHURCHILL

But my favorite single individual risk-taker in world history has to be Winston Churchill. Never has there been a bigger or more confident Riverboat Gambler, and his gambles were played in the big leagues: they saved Britain, Europe, and the Allied cause from Nazi domination.

Churchill was a man unafraid of failure or humiliation. He first ran for Parliament (the British version of Congress) in 1899—and lost. Later as the head of Britain's navy he was blamed for the worst loss in British naval history. Many men and ships were lost. He resigned in disgrace.

Yet by 1922 he was risking it all again with another run for Parliament— which he lost again. By 1924, he was running and losing again. Are you getting the opinion Sir Winston didn't mind risking? By 1925, the original "Comeback Kid" was back again, named to a major cabinet post overseeing the British economy. His policies led to disaster—massive unemployment, a nationwide strike, and a world economic crisis. In 1929 his political party lost again, knocking him out of office for what all critics assumed would be the last time. He spent the next ten years out of politics and even wrote his memoirs, thinking his career was over.

True risk-takers are always ready to put it all on the line when history comes calling. Churchill watched from the sidelines and predicted Hitler's rise to prominence. He was a huge critic of appeasement and correctly predicted that Hitler was a threat to all of Europe unless stopped with force. In response, he was written off by critics as a has-been and a warmonger. When he was proven correct, the British people demanded he take power as prime minister during Britain's darkest hour.

His record of wartime leadership and inspiration may never be equaled in world history. It was Churchill's magnificent oratory, and his passionate belief that Britain must never give in to Hitler, that inspired the British people and Allied forces to keep fighting. This Riverboat Gambler at one point decided to bomb France's naval vessels, killing thousands of French sailors (Britain's ally) rather than let French battle-ships fall into Nazi hands. The decision was controversial and risky, but it saved many British lives.

Churchill was recognized the world over for his courage and leader-ship: he was knighted, won the Nobel Prize, was voted "Greatest Living Englishman," and was declared an "honorary American" by the United States Congress.

What was his reward for all those honors? The British electorate threw him out of office in 1945! But the great gambler wasn't done just yet. By 1951, Sir Winston was back again, winning yet another election as the oldest Prime Minister in British history (at age seventy-seven). I count Winston Churchill as the greatest leader, statesman, and historical figure of the twentieth century. And one of the most Contrarian risk-takers ever.

By now I'm sure you realize that many (if not *most*) of the famous superachievers in history were valiant risk-takers. They had to be willing to be Contrarian, to choose to challenge the masses, the critics, and the experts. They had to be willing to risk failure and humiliation. Now it's your turn.

"Go after your dreams with such passion, such spirit, such op-timism, such tenacity, such determination, such intensity, such commitment, such unbridled energy that you'll either succeed or explode!"

WAYNE ALLYN ROOT

A FEW PARTING WORDS

This doesn't have to be an ending. It can be a beginning. I'd love to hear from you! Please e-mail me or write with your comments. For contact information, visit my website at www.WinningEDGE.com, or e-mail me directly at wayne@winningEDGE.com.

WHERE TO GET MORE INFORMATION ON WAYNE ALLYN ROOT'S HANDICAPPING SERVICES

If you would like more information about services or exclusive private client services, please visit my website, www.WinningEDGE.com.

AN IMPORTANT CLOSING MESSAGE

I ask that all readers of this book bet with their heads, *not* over them. For those who have ever experienced problems or addictions due to gambling, *please* contact Arnie Wexler of the Compulsive Gambling Foundation of New Jersey. For contact information, visit www.aswexler.com.